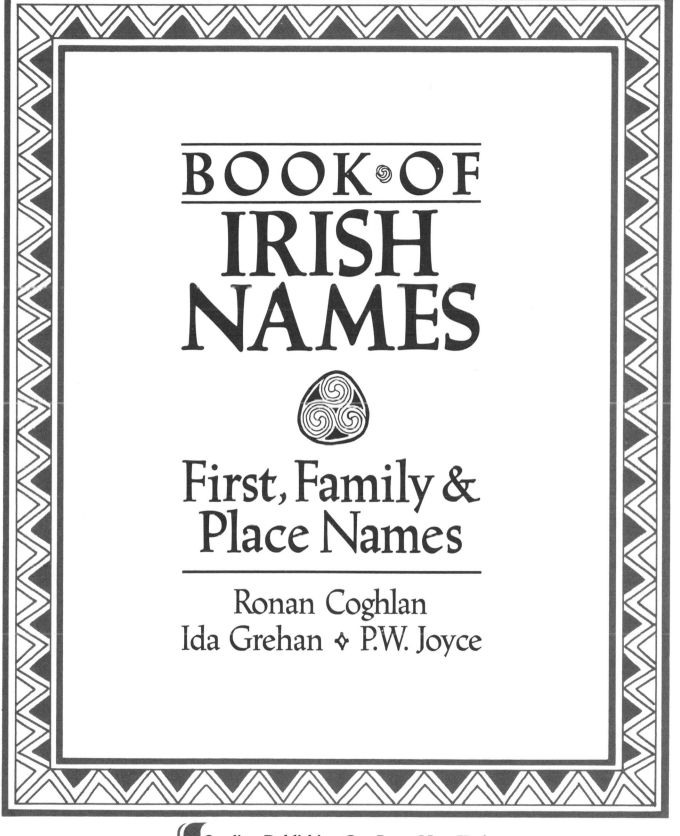

BOOK·OF
IRISH
NAMES

First, Family & Place Names

Ronan Coghlan
Ida Grehan ⬦ P.W. Joyce

Sterling Publishing Co., Inc.   New York

Library of Congress Cataloging-in-Publication Data

Coghlan, Ronan.
  The book of Irish names : first, family & place names / by Ronan
Coghlan, Ida Grehan & P.W. Joyce.
     p. cm.
  Includes index.
  ISBN 0-8069-6944-X
  1. Names, Irish. 2. Names—Ireland. 3. Names, Personal—Irish.
4. Names, Personal—Ireland. 5. Names, Geographical—Irish.
6. Names, Geographical—Ireland. I. Grehan, Ida. II. Joyce, P. W.
(Patrick Weston), 1827–1914. III. Title.
DA979.C64   1989
929.4′0899162—dc20   89-32660
                                                              CIP

Contents

See Pronunciation Guide on page 128.

BOOK I

IRISH FIRST NAMES

by Ronan Coghlan

Acknowledgments

I would like to extend my thanks to a number of people who have helped me with the preparation of this work: to my sisters, Lin and Valerie, who provided help in compiling the statistics and in preparing the typescript; to Leslie Dunkling for pointing out a number of errors in the work; and to Eileen Ryan of St Andrews, Scotland, who provided me with details of some unusual Irish feminine names. The principal institutions in which research for this work was carried out were the Library of Trinity College, Dublin, and the National Library of Ireland, Dublin.

Introduction

Since the publication in 1923 of Father Patrick Woulfe's *Irish Names for Children,* no work on Irish first names has appeared in print. When Woulfe wrote the Irish, especially in the country districts, were exceedingly conservative in their choice of names. Woulfe hoped to broaden the selection of names in use. To do this he included a number of older Irish names, as well as names generally in use at the time.

His work was undoubtedly influential. Ireland had attained independence in 1921 and a spirit of nationalism was rampant. People began seeking out old Gaelic names to give their children, and they found Woulfe's work a handy quarry. Since his time Irish naming patterns have changed so considerably that a new work on the subject is again needed.

The greatest changes have taken place in recent years. Even after Woulfe's work had appeared, names such as *John, William, Mary* and *Annie* were still the commonest names in Irish households. However, these names are now rapidly falling from favour, giving way to a host of newcomers, many of them exotic.

I have had to use certain criteria for selecting names to include in this book. I have included all names which originated in the Irish language and whose derivations I was able to trace. I have also included a number of names which sprang from the fertile imaginations of Irish writers. Names in this category include *Vanessa* and *Gloria,* which are widespread today.

The original language of the Celts, in prehistoric times, split into two branches, the Goidelic and the Brythonic. Irish, Scottish Gaelic and Manx belong to the former; Welsh, Cornish and Breton to the latter. The Irish language is sometimes called Gaelic, but this can lead to confusion with the Scottish Gaelic. (The word Gaelic, incidentally, is pronounced *Gaylik* in Ireland, *Gallik* in Scotland and the languages are mutually intelligible.) Irish is also sometimes wrongly called Erse – a word looked on with distaste by the Irish themselves.

Irish was the principal language of the country until the mid-nineteenth century. When people wanted to 'translate' their names into English, they frequently used an English name that bore some resemblance – often phonetic – to their own, for example, *Jeremiah* and *Cornelius* were used as equivalents of *Dermot* and *Connor.* In this way non-Irish names like *Daniel, Denis* and *Hugh* came to be established in Ireland.

Reference is made in the text to 'Hiberno-English': this is a term employed by linguists to describe the species of English spoken in Ireland today. It is supplanting the older 'Anglo-Irish'.

Where appropriate, I have given the Irish translation of the English name, usually after it. The Irish form often differs from the English, and sometimes it is the version given at the registration of the child's birth.

In each article I have given the derivation and history of the name, with particular reference to its usage in Ireland. Derivations cannot always be regarded as certain, especially as some names are so old that their roots are almost impossible to uncover. Take, for example, the name *Adam.* The standard authority on English Christian names, Withycombe, says this is a Hebrew name, meaning 'red'; yet there is evidence that the name means 'man'; and it may not even be Hebrew at all, but Akkadian, meaning 'creature'.

Does a book like this help anyone other than parents? I believe it does. Naming patterns change and continue, forming a history. I hope, for instance, that this book will assist the writer looking for unusual or historical names. I remember once being irritated to find, in Cecilia Holland's novel *The Kings in Winter,* set in the time of Brian Boru, characters named *Sean* and *Liam.* Irish names, yes – but you would not have found them in Ireland in the eleventh century.

In early times the names used in Ireland reflected the heroic spirit of the age – names such as *Murrough,* 'sea warrior', *Cathal,* 'battle mighty' and *Niall,* 'champion'. Many of these names have been revived in the twentieth century. Later, the Christians would choose the name of a saint for their offspring and prefix to it *mael* or *gille,* meaning 'servant' – a pattern which is still continued today amongst Roman Catholics in Ireland, although nowadays the prefix is seldom found. The Vikings brought with them Norse names such as *Olaf,* which spread widely in its Gaelic form *Amhlaoibh.* The Normans, who invaded Ireland in 1169, introduced a host of new names, e.g. *Edward, Gerald, William, Pierce.*

It is my hope that this book will fill a gap and provide a comprehensive dictionary of the names found in Ireland; and even that it may help to revive some of the rarer names that it contains.

Irish First Names

A

Aaron [*Árón*] (m) This name comes from the Bible. It was borne by the brother of Moses in the Old Testament, and it is possibly of Egyptian origin. The meaning 'high mountain' has been suggested. It is sometimes used in Ireland today.

Abigail [*Abaigeal*] (f) 'father rejoiced'. A name which, in Ireland, was used to anglicise the native name, *Gobinet*.

Abraham [*Ábraham*] (m) Hebrew, 'father of a multitude'. The name has occasionally been used in Ireland, e.g. by Abraham ('Bram') Stoker, author of *Dracula* (1897). *Abracham* is another Gaelic form.

Abram (m) Hebrew, 'high father'. This was the name originally borne by Abraham in the Old Testament. It was used in the *Clibborn* family of Moate Castle, Co. Westmeath.

Achaius (m) A form of *Eochaidh*, mainly used in Scotland.

Adam [*Ádhamh*] (m) A name of uncertain meaning. 'Red earth' and 'ruddy' have been suggested, but it possibly signifies 'man'. Adam has been quite a popular name in Ireland, where is appears to have been in use from early times. The Hebrews themselves do not seem to have bestowed the name, and its use as a Christian name probably started with the early Irish and Scottish Christians.

Adamnan [*Adhamhnan*] (m) 'little Adam'. The name of an important Irish saint (*c.* 624-704), the biographer of St Columba and an acquaintance of the Venerable Bede. He is the first known writer to speak of a monster in Loch Ness. Many variants of the name, e.g. *Awnan, Odanodan, O(u)nan, Junan* are given under separate headings.

Adrian [*Aidrian*] (m) Latin, 'of the Adriatic'. In its original form, *Hadrianus,* this was the name of a well-known Roman emperor. The name seems quite popular in Ireland today.

Aeneas [*Aenéas*] (m) Greek, 'worthy of praise'. The name of a character in Homer's *Iliad* who became the hero of Virgil's *Aeneid.* It has been used in Ireland to anglicise the native name *Aengus,* 'one vigour'.

Aengus [*Aonghus*] (m) 'one vigour'. This early name, still found in Ireland, was once often used. Aengus of the Birds was the love god of the pagan Irish. St Aengus the Culdee was a well-known bearer of the name. Another form probably occurs in Arthurian romance, borne by King *Anguish* of Ireland. *Aeneas* was used as a substitute name. The Scottish form of Aengus, *Angus,* is also found in Ireland. The variants *Oengus, Hungus, Ungus* and *Enos* are also found.

Afric (f) Variant of *Africa.*

Africa [*Aifric*] (f) 'pleasant'. This name has no connection with the continent of Africa. Its associations are with both Ireland and the Isle of Man, where its use is recorded in the eleventh and twelfth centuries. The daughter of the Manx monarch, Godred, bore the name. Another king of Man, Olaus the Swarthy, married Africa, daughter of Fergus of Galway. *Afric* is a variant.

Agatha [*Agata*] (f) Greek, 'good'. The name of a third-century Sicilian martyr.

Aghy (m) A form of *Eochaidh.*

Agnes [*Aignéis*] (f) Greek, 'pure'. This name was brought to Ireland by the English. It is sometimes equated with *Una,* perhaps because it was thought to derive from the Latin *agnus,* 'lamb', the Irish for lamb being *uan.* The name *Ina* (Irish *Aghna*) may be a native form of Agnes.

Aichlinn (m) There was a harper named Aichlinn competing in the Harpers' Meeting which was held in Belfast in 1792. It is perhaps a form of *Echlin.*

Aidan [*Aodhan*] (m) 'little fire'. St Aidan (died 651), a monk at Iona who became bishop of Lindisfarne, is perhaps the most famous bearer of this name. It was quite common in Ireland in the eighth and ninth centuries and it is still used today. *Mogue* is a variant. It has even been employed as a feminine name, but *Edana* is the more usual feminine form.

Aideen (f) Variant of *Etain.*

Aileen (f) Variant of *Eileen.*

Ailill (m) 'sprite'. It was a common name in early times. Ailill Molt was an early Irish king.

Áine (f) 'joy'; 'praise'; also 'fasting'. Áine was said to be the queen of the South Munster fairies, living at Knockany (Irish *Cnoc Áine* – Áine's hill'). The name is still used in Ireland. It has tended to become confused with *Anne.* There have been various attempts to anglicise it as *Anna, Hannah* and, perhaps, *Anastasia.*

Ainmire (m) 'great lord'. A name which occurs quite frequently in Irish history. It was borne by St Ainmire, a monk of Co. Donegal, and by Ainmire, king of Tara (died *c.* 569).

Alan [*Ailín*] (m) Woulfe regards this as an early Irish name, perhaps connected with *ail,* 'noble', but the name is by no means confined to Ireland. It may have been the name of a Celtic deity, the brother of Bran; compare also the Welsh *Alawn,* 'harmony'. Its use in England and Scotland can be traced to Alan Fergeant, Count of Brittany, who came to England with the Conqueror. In English lore, Alan-a-Dale is associated with Robin Hood. Alan is frequently encountered in Ireland today. *Allan* and *Allen* are variants. Allen was used by the novelist Rider Haggard for his hero, Allen Quartermain.

Alana (f) Also spelt *Alannah.* This is not the feminine of *Alan* – though in Scotland it is often treated as such – but it comes from the Irish *a leanbh,* 'O child'. It is not a common name.

Alastrina [*Alastríona*] (f) A feminine of *Alistair.* In Irish *Alastríona* translates *Alexandra* and *Alexandrina.*

Albany (m) The Irish name *Fionn* (English *Finn)* came from *find,* 'white' or 'fair'. This was anglicised as *Albany,* from Latin *albus,* 'white'.

Albert (m) Germanic, 'noble bright'. In Ireland this name has been used as an anglicisation of *Ailbe* (English *Alby).* It appears to be little used today.

Alby [*Ailbe*] (m) The name of an Irish saint. It has sometimes been anglicised as *Albert. Ailbhe* is a variant in Irish; *Elli* and *Elly* are variants in English.

Alexander [*Alastar*] (m) Greek, 'helper of man'. A popular name in the Hellenic world: it was the name of Alexander the Great, king of Macedonia, and it was also another name given to the Trojan prince, Paris. A number of early saints were called Alexander. The name spread widely, becoming *Alexandre* in French, *Alessandro* in Italian and *Alejandro* in Spanish. It seems to have been brought to Scotland by Queen Margaret (*c.* 1046-93), who was raised in Hungary, and who gave the name to one of her sons. The English brought it to Ireland, where it throve amongst the settlers of the Middle Ages. *Alastar* became the normal Gaelic form; *Alsander, Alastrann* and *Alastrom* were also used.

Alfred [*Ailfrid*] (m) Anglo-Saxon, 'elf counsel'. This name was imported into Ireland by the English. It is established, but not common.

Alice [*Ailís*] (f) Old French *Aliz,* coming ultimately from Germanic *Adelaide,* 'noble sort'. The name was introduced into Ireland by the English. A medieval Irish example is Alice Kettler, who figured in a witchcraft trial. It is perhaps, but by no means certainly, the origin of an Irish name *Aylce.* Lewis Carroll's *Alice's Adventures in Wonderland* (1865) greatly increased the popularity of the name. See also *Alicia, Alison.*

Alicia [*Ailíse*] (f) A latinised form of Alice, occasionally used in Ireland.

Alison [*Allsún*] (f) A diminutive of *Alice,* in use at least from the thirteenth century, when it was recorded in France. It has occasionally been employed in Ireland.

Alistair (m) An anglicised form of *Alastar,* the Gaelic for *Alexander.*

Alma (f) 'all good'. An early Irish name; but its modern usage can be traced to diverse origins – it is the feminine of Latin *almus,* 'loving' or 'good' and, as such, it is applied to the Blessed Virgin. St Alma, the mother of St Tudwal, may derive her name from this source. Alma, as used by Spenser in *The Faerie Queene* (1590/6), comes from the Italian meaning 'soul', though Spenser may have heard the Irish name during his stay in Ireland. In later times, Alma was used in England after the Battle of Alma (1854) in the Crimean War. The name of the River Alma, where the battle was fought, may have been Celtic in origin.

Alma became popular in the United States in the 1920s and was exported from there to Britain. In this instance it probably came from the Latin, as in *alma mater,* a title originally applied to classical goddesses and later to academic institutions.

Alma occurs as a masculine name in Irish legend: Alma One-Tooth was the name of a son of Nemed. Alma is also a masculine name in the Book of Mormon.

Aloysius [*Alaois*] (m) Like *Ludovicus,* a Latin form of *Louis,* borne of St Aloysius Gonzaga (died 1591; canonised 1726). In everyday life he was known by the Italian form *Luigi.* Aloysius was introduced into Ireland in commemoration of him, and it was used to translate *Lughaidh.* Its Gaelic forms are *Alaois, Alabhaois.*

Alphonsus [*Alfonsus*] (m) Germanic, 'noble ready'. This name was introduced into Ireland to commemorate St Alphonsus Liguori (1696-1787; canonised 1839). It has sometimes been used to anglicise *Anlon.*

Alvy (f) Variant of *Elva.*

Amalgith [*Amalgaid*] (m) According to the Welsh chronicler, Nennius, Amalgith was a man whose seven sons were baptised by St Patrick. It is said that their descendants, the Uí Amalgaid, gave their name to Tirawley (*Tir*

Amalgaid). The surname *Macaulay* is connected with them. As a result of Norse influence, *Amhlaoibh* came to replace this name.

Amanda (f) This name, apparently a literary invention, is now quite widespread in Ireland. It comes from Latin and means 'worthy of love'. It is first recorded in Cibber's play *Love's Last Shift* (1694). *Mandy* is a pet form.

Ambrose [*Ambrós*] (m) Greek, 'immortal'. The name of a saintly bishop of Milan (*c.* 340-97). In Ireland it was used to anglicise the native name, *Anmchadh.*

Anastasia [*Anstás*] (f) Greek, 'risen once more'. This name occurs in England in the thirteenth century. It spread from there to Ireland. It is still used from time to time in Ireland but it appears to be sharply declining in popularity. The pet form is *Stasia* (Irish, *Steise).*

André (m) The French form of *Andrew* which has sometimes been used in Ireland in modern times.

Andrea (f) A feminine form of *Andrew,* increasingly popular in Ireland in modern times.

Andrew [*Aindréas*] (m) Greek, 'manly'. The name of one of the twelve Apostles. It was probably introduced into Ireland after the Norman Invasion of 1169. The Irish forms are *Aindreas* and *Aindrias* (forms which show an affinity with the original Greek *Andreas),* and *Aindriu,* which comes from the Norman French *Andreu* (modern French *André).* Andrew is a popular name in Ireland today. *Andy* and *Drew* are pet forms of this name.

Aneas (m) This unusual name was borne by one Aneas McDonnell (1783-1858), a native of Westport, Co. Mayo. It is presumably a form of *Aeneas* or *Aengus.*

Angela [*Aingeal*] (f) Latin *Angela,* feminine of *angelus,* 'angel', from Greek *angelos,* 'messenger', corresponding to Hebrew *malak.* Angela is quite a popular name in modern Ireland. *Angie* is used as a pet form. The masculine form is *Angelo;* compare the Arabic feminine name *Melek,* 'angel'.

Angus (m) This is the Scottish form of the Irish name *Aengus;* but it is used in Ireland too. The Scots, who have a habit of coining feminine equivalents to masculine names, have produced the female *Angusina.*

Anita (f) The Spanish diminutive of *Anne* which is used in Ireland.

Anlon [*Anluan*] (m) 'great champion'. Woulfe informs us that this name was confined to a few families, notably the *O'Briens.* See also *Alphonsus.*

Anmcha [*Anmchadh*] (m) 'courageous'. This name was confined to the *O'Madden* family.

Anna (f) A form of *Anne* found in many European languages, including Irish. It was employed in Ireland to anglicise the native name *Áine.* The Irish actress, Anna Manahan, is a contemporary example of this name.

Annabel [*Annábla*] (f) The Irish *Annábla* translates *Annabel, Annabella* and *Arabella* – names of obscure origin associated with Scotland, and introduced into Ireland in the twelfth century after the Norman Invasion.

Annabella (f) See *Annabel.*

Anne [*Anna*] (f) Hebrew, 'He has favoured me'. St Anne is the traditional name of the mother of the Blessed Virgin. Anna, great-granddaughter of a Byzantine emperor, brought the name to Western Europe by her marriage to Henry I, king of France. Anne is very popular in Ireland today. It has been used to some extent to anglicise the native

name *Áine*. *Nancy* is a pet form. See also *Anna* and *Annie*.
Annette (f) The French diminutive of *Anne*.
Annie (f) Originally this was a pet form of *Anne* but it is now used as a separate name. In Ireland it was employed to anglicise the native name *Ethna* (Irish *Eithne)*.
Ant(h)ony [*Antaine*] (m) A Roman sept name of unknown derivation. There are various Irish forms: *Antaine, Antoine, Anntoin* and *Antoin*. Anthony was sometimes used to anglicise *Uaithne* and *Hewney*. It has only become popular in Ireland in modern times.
Aodh (m) 'fire'. Once a popular Irish name which was anglicised as *Hugh*. It was latinised as *Aedus, Aidus* – the name of a number of saints. It gave rise to the surname *MacAodha,* variously translated as *Magee* or *MacHugh* in Ireland, and *Mackay* in Scotland. Aodh (or Hugh) O'Neill and Oadh Rua (Red Hugh) O'Donnell were two famous Irish rebels who raised an insurrection in the reign of Elizabeth I. The name was also borne by six kings of Tara. The variant *Ea* occurs, and *Y* has been recorded.
Aodhfin [*Aodhfionn*] (m) 'white fire'. An early name.
Archibald (m) Germanic, 'simple bold'. A name which was used in Ulster and Scotland to anglicise *Giolla Easpaig*. *Archie* is a pet form.
Ardal [*Ardál*] (m) 'high valour'. An old historic name, which finally gave way to anglicisation as *Arnold*. See also *Artegal, Arthgallo*.
Arnold (m) Germanic, 'eagle power'. A name used in Ireland to anglicise *Ardal*.
Art (m) 'stone' or 'bear'. In England Art is a pet form of *Arthur,* but in Ireland it constitutes a separate name, though it was at times anglicised Arthur. Art McMurrough, the medieval king of Leinster, who bore arms valiantly against the forces of King John, is named Arthur by Froissart. Arthur Griffin (1872-1922), the Nationalist leader, translated his name into Irish as Art.
Artegal (m) A form of *Ardal* used in Spenser's *Faerie Queene* (1590/6).
Arthgallo (m) A form of Ardal which occurs in Geoffrey of Monmouth's *Historia Regum Brittaniae* (1139).
Arthur [*Artúr*] (m) A name of doubtful derivation, perhaps Celtic in origin, or perhaps a Roman sept name, borne by the legendary king of the Britons. The first historical record of the name occurs in the writings of St Adamnan (*c.* 624-704), who mentions an Irishman bearing the name. The name is used in Ireland today. In Irish legend there was an *Artúr,* son of Nemed, who may have been an early Arthur. See also *Atty*.
Ashling [*Aisling*] (f) 'dream', 'vision', 'daydream'. A name originally used in the regions of Derry and Omeath, which is now more widespread. It has sometimes been anglicised as *Esther,* the true Irish form of which is *Eistir*. Today the name is found as *Ashling, Aislinn* and *Aisling*. *Isleen* is a variant.
Asthore (f) Irish *a stoir,* 'loved one'. A name of Irish derivation listed by Loughead, though it does not seem to be used in Ireland itself.
Attracta [*Athracht*] (f) The name of a Co. Sligo saint. Its use now seems to be declining.
Atty [*Ataigh*] (m) Perhaps a form of *Eochaidh* or possibly a derivative of *ard,* 'high'. This name has been anglicised as *Arthur*.
Audrey (f) Anglo-Saxon, 'noble strength'. An early name revived in England in the present century. Quite widespread in England, it has reached Ireland where it is now fairly well established.
Augusteen (f) An Irish femminine form of *Augustine*.
Augustine [*Agaistin*] (m) Latin 'venerable'. The name of two famous saints, Augustine of Hippo (354-430), author of the *Confessions* and *The City of God,* and Augustine of Canterbury (died *c.* 613). The name has been used quite frequently in Ireland. A feminine *Augusteen* is also found. See also *Austin*.
Auliffe [*Amhlaoibh*] (m) An Irish form of Norse *Olaf,* 'ancestor relics'. Introduced originally by the Norsemen, it was used to replace a native name *Amalgith*. It was sometimes anglicised *Humphrey:* Humphrey O'Sullivan, who kept a diary in Irish, translated his first name as *Amhlaoibh*. There is a church dedicated to St Olaf in Waterford, formerly a Norse city.
Aurnia (f) A variant or equivalent of *Orla,* borne by Aurnia (died 1306), daughter of Donal Og MacCarthy Mor, and wife of Turlogh More O'Brien.
Austin [*Oistin*] (m) A form of *Augustine* which came to be used in England, and presumably spread from there to Ireland.
Avril (f) A name of recent origin, coming from French, *Avril*. 'April'. It is increasingly popular in modern Ireland.
Awnan (m) A form of *Adamnan* found at Skreen.
Aylce [*Ailis*] (f) It is not certain whether this name is a variant of *Alice* or a native name; if the latter, it may derive from *ail,* 'noble'.

B

Baethan [*Baothán*] (m) 'little foolish one'. An early name.
Balthasar [*Patifarsa*] (m) Akkadian, 'Bel protect the king'. A name applied by tradition to one of the Magi. It was used in Ireland in the *Nugent* family. Presumably this is the name of Baltazard André Aylmer, Chevalier de St Louis, an Irishman who became a captain in the French Army in 1770. The Gaelic form comes from the Leabhar Breac, a medieval compilation.
Banan (m) Derivative of *ban,* 'white'. Shakespeare's Banquo in *Macbeth* is another derivative of this word.
Banba (f) A name applied to Ireland; it is also the name of an early Irish goddess identified with the country.
Banbhan (m) A diminutive of *banbh,* 'piglet'. An early name.
Barbara [*Bairbre*] (f) Greek, 'strange'. A name used in Ireland both in its own right and to anglicise a native name, *Gormley*.
Barclay (m) A name used as an anglicisation of *Partholon*.
Barnaby [*Barnaib*] (m) An English form of *Barnabas,* meaning uncertain. Barnaby was used in the Castlekevin branch of the *O'Toole* family in the sixteenth and seventeenth centuries. The name has also been used to anglicise *Brian*. The Irish form, *Barnaib,* is taken from the *Martyrology of Gorman*.
Barran (f) 'little top'. The name of an Irish saint.
Barry [*Bearach*] (m) 'spearlike'. St Barry was a disciple of St Kevin and later a missionary in Scotland. Barry is used both as an independent name and as a pet form of *Finbar,* in which case the Irish form is *Barra*. *Bercan* is a diminutive. It is popular today outside Ireland where it may sometimes

Aoifa = Efa

come from Welsh *ap Harry*, 'son of Harry'.

Bartholomew (m) Hebrew, 'son of Talmai', rendered in Irish as *Pathalón*, and *Bairtliméad*. *Parthalón* (English *Partholon*) is a native name. It is the name of a legendary early settler in Ireland.

Bartley [*Beartlaí*] (m) A variant of *Bartholomew*.

Basil (m) Greek, 'royal'. This name is used in Ireland to anglicise *Brazil*.

Bec [*Beag*] (m) 'small'. The name, or perhaps the nickname, of an early Irish saint known as 'the Prophet'.

Becan [*Beacán*] (m) 'little one'. St Becan founded a monastery in Westmeath in the sixth century.

Beheen [*Baothín*] (m) A diminutive of *baoth*, 'fool'.

Behellagh (m) A variant of *Beolagh*.

Beircheart (m) From Anglo-Saxon, 'bright army'. This name has been variously anglicised as *Benjamin* and *Bernard*.

Benedict (m) Latin, 'blessed'. A name used in Ireland to translate a native name, *Maolbheannachta*, 'hoper for blessing'.

Benen [*Beineon*] (m) An Irish form of the Latin name *Benignus*, 'kind'. *Beanon*, *Beinean* and *Binean* are variants in Irish.

Benjamin (m) Hebrew, 'southerner'. This name is used in Ireland, in Cork, Kerry and Limerick, to anglicise *Beircheart*, itself a name of Anglo-Saxon origin.

Beolagh [*Baothghalach*] (m) 'foolish, valorous'. A name variously rendered in English as *Behellagh*, *Beolagh*, *Boetius* and *Bowes;* and used amongst the *MacEgans*, *O'Dalys*, etc.

Berc(n)an [*Bearchan*] (m) A diminutive of *Barry*. St Bercan is associated with Eigg in Scotland. *Bergin* is a variant.

Berghetta (f) This is the name of the heroine of *Maurice and Berghetta* (1819), anonymously written by William Parnell, Knight of the Shire for Wicklow. The name, which seems to be the author's invention, is perhaps intended to be a form of *Bridget*.

Bergin (m) Variant of *Bercan*.

Berkley (m) This name is used as an anglicisation of *Partholon*.

Bernadette (f) A feminine diminutive of *Bernard*, used in memory of St Bernadette (1844-79), the visionary at Lourdes. It is a popular name in Ireland, but at present it is declining.

Bernard [*Bearnard*] (m) Germanic, 'bear stern'. Bernard is used in Ireland to anglicise *Brian* and *Beircheart* (the latter is itself originally Anglo-Saxon). It persists to this day, but it is growing less popular. *Bernadette* and *Berneen* are feminine forms.

Berneen (f) An Irish diminutive feminine form of *Bernard*. It has the characteristic Irish diminutive suffix -een, representing Gaelic -in.

Betha [*Beatha*] (f) 'life'. A Celtic name, latinised as *Begga*. *Bahee* is a Manx name of similar meaning.

Bidelia (f) A variant of *Bridget*, supposed to be somewhat genteel, and rarely, if ever, used nowadays. It was probably formed by adding the suffix -elia to *Biddy*, a pet form of Bridget.

Bidina (f) Variant of *Bridget*.

Blanche [*Blinne*] (f) French feminine of *blanc*, 'white'. The Irish translation, *Blinne*, is a corruption of *Moninne*, a native Irish name. Neither form is frequently found.

Blathmac (m) 'flower son'. The name of a king of Tara who ruled in the first half of the seventh century.

Boetius (m) A name used to anglicise *Beolagh* and *Buagh*.

Bowes (m) A name used to anglicise *Beolagh*.

Boynton (m) A name associated with the Irish River Boyne, where a famous battle of the Jacobite War took place of 1st July 1690.

Bran (m) 'raven'. The name of a Celtic deity, known on both sides of the Irish Sea. His adventures are chronicled in the early Irish literary work, *The Voyage of Bran Son of Febal*. In the *Mabinogion*, a collection of medieval Welsh tales, he appears as *Bendigeidfran* ('blest Bran'), a giant. Bran was also the name of a dog belonging to the legendary hero, Finn MacCool. Woulfe notes the use of the name in the *O'Brien* family. See also *Brandan*.

Brandan (m) Perhaps a derivative of *bran*, 'raven'. St Brandan (c. 484-577) was an Irish preacher and abbot.

Branduff [*Brandubh*] (m) 'black raven'. This was the name of a medieval king of Leinster.

Brasil (m) Variant of *Brazil*.

Brazil [*Breasal*] (m) 'strife'. St Brazil (died 801) was a monk of Iona. *Brasil* and *Bresal* are variant forms of this name.

Breeda (f) Variant of *Bridget*.

Brenda (f) In Ireland this is thought of as a feminine form of *Brendan*, but the two names are in fact unconnected. Brenda has its origin in the Shetland Islands, and may mean 'sword'.

Brendan [*Breandan*] (m) 'prince'. A name used in Ireland from early times. St Brendan of Birr (died 571) was called the Chief Prophet of Ireland. St Brendan the Navigator, an Irish saint of the sixth century, made a legendary voyage of which two Latin accounts existed. It has been suggested that he may have journeyed as far as America. His name is often incorrectly rendered *Brandan*, perhaps because of Mount Brandon in Co. Kerry (which was named after him), and possibly because of the Kerry surname *Brandon* (Irish *Mac Breandain*, 'son of Brendan') borne by a branch of the *Fitzmaurice* family. The name is frequently found in Ireland today. It is also used in Britain, and it is very popular in Australia.

Bresal (m) Variant of *Brazil*.

Brian (m) The first part of this name is Celtic and signifies 'hill'. Brian has always been popular in Ireland. It was the name of the most famous of Irish high kings, Brian Boru (reigned 1002-14), the victor of the decisive Battle of Clontarf which put paid to any Norse hopes for the conquest of Ireland. Brian was also the name of the Co. Clare poet, Brian Merriman (c. 1757-1808), whose extraordinary work, *Cúirt an Mheadhoin Oidhche* is an early advocation of the emancipation of women. A more recent Irish writer was Brian O'Nolan (1911-66) who wrote under the pseudonyms Flann O'Brien and Myles na Gopaleen.

The name was also known in medieval Brittany, and it was introduced into England from there. The surnames derived from it include *Brian*, *Brien*, *Bryan*, *O'Brien* and *O'Byrne*. *Bernard* and *Barnaby* were used to anglicise it. The name remains widespread in Ireland. It has been revived in England, and is quite common in the United States and Canada. It is found in Italy as *Briano*. *Bryan*, *Brion* and *Bryant* are variants.

Briana (f) A feminine form of *Brian*.

Bride (f) Variant of *Bridget*.

Bridget [*Bríd*] (f) 'high one'. The name of a celebrated Irish saint (*c.*452-523). The English form comes from the Old Irish *Brigit* (hence the modern English form *Brigid*), through Latin *Brigitta* and Old French *Brigette* (modern French *Brigitte*). Bridget was not used in Ireland until the seventeenth century, probably due to reverence for the saint. *Clog Bride,* St Bridget's Bell, said to have been the property of the saint, was exhibited on both sides of the Irish Sea until Henry V put a stop to this practice. The head of St Bridget was supposed to be in Lisbon which resulted in the use of the name in Portugal.

The suggestion that the etymology is the early Irish, *breosaighead*, 'fire arrow' is without foundation. In fact the name is linked with Brigantes, a tribe who inhabited what is now the north of England in early times. There is also a Teutonic name *Bridget* meaning 'mountain protection', borne by a Swedish saint. This name has no relation to the Irish one. *Bre(e)da, Bride* (from which comes the English word *bridewell)*, *Bidelia* and *Bidina* are all variants. *Biddy* is a pet form used by Dickens in *Great Expectations* (1860/1).

Brona (f) A derivative of *brón*, 'sorrow', which is occasionally used in modern times.

Brone [*Brón*] (m) 'sorrow'. St Brone was an Irish monk and bishop.

Bryan (m) Variant of *Brian.*

Buagh [*Buach*] (m) 'conqueror'. A name related etymologically to *Boudicca* or *Boadicaea* (died AD 62), queen of the Iceni and leader of a celebrated uprising of the Britons against the Romans in AD 61. *Boetius* and *Victor* have been used to anglicise it.

C

Cadhla (m) 'handsome'. A name used in the Middle Ages. It was borne by the archbishop of Tuam who in 1539 acted as the representative of Rory O'Conor, the last high king of Ireland. In his case it was latinised as *Catholicus,* 'universal'.

Caffar [*Catabharr*] (m) 'helmet'. A name used by the O'Donnells, a family which ruled Tyrconnel, in Co. Donegal, up to the seventeenth century.

Cahal (m) An anglicised spelling of *Cathal.*

Cahir [*Cathaoir*] (m) 'warrior'. A name which was once popular in Leinster. *Cathair* was a variant found in a number of families. The name is still used in Ireland today.

Cain [*Cáin*] (m) Hebrew, 'smith'. This name was used to anglicise *Cian*, though why the name of such an unedifying Biblical character should have been chosen is something of a mystery. The use of this name is not confined to Ireland. Dunkling notes that he has traced six bearers of it.

Cairbre (m) 'strong man'. In legend, Cairbre was the first of the Milesians to settle in Ulster. Another legendary Cairbre was said to have defeated the Fianna at the Battle of Gabhra.

Callaghan [*Ceallachán*] (m) A diminutive of *ceallach,* 'strife'. This is normally thought of as a surname though it is also used as a first name. The surname denotes descent from King Callaghan of Munster who ruled in the tenth century. St Callaghan was a monk at Clontibret.

Callough (m) Variant of *Calvagh.*

Calvagh [*Calbhach*] (m) 'bald', cf. Latin *calvinus*. This name, once widespread, is now rare or obsolete. In Irish it was sometimes *An Calbhach*, 'the bald'. *Callough* is a

variant. *Charles* was used to anglicise it.

Canice [*Coinneach*] (m) 'comely'. The name of a saint (*c.* 515-599) who founded a monastery at Aghaboe and who gave his name to the city of Kilkenny, in Irish *Cill Coinneach,* 'Canice's church'. The name is in use today. *Kenny* is a variant. *Kenneth* was formerly used to translate it.

Carl (m) A form of *Charles* which occurs in several North European languages, e.g. German. It is used from time to time in Ireland. Travel, films and literature may all have contributed to its use there. *Karl*, an alternative spelling, is also found.

Carla (f) A feminine form of *Carl*, occasionally used in Ireland.

Carleen (f) An Irish feminine form of *Charles.*

Carmel (f) Hebrew, 'the garden'. A name used in Ireland in honour of Our Lady of Mount Carmel, in the Holy Land. According to legend, the Blessed Virgin was often in the vicinity of this mountain. The Spanish form, *Carmen,* was made well known to opera lovers by Bizet.

Carol (f) A feminine form of *Charles* which is increasingly popular in Ireland.

Caroline (f) A feminine form of *Charles* which is gaining popularity in Ireland.

Carrick [*Carraig*] (m) 'rock'. A name which is found in America and is of Irish derivation; but it is not employed in Ireland itself.

Carroll [*Cearbhall*] (m) 'champion warrior'. A name sometimes anglicised *Charles*, which becomes *Carolus* in Latin. Cearbhall O'Dalaigh (1911-78) was a former President of the Irish Republic.

Carthage [*Carthach*] (m) 'loving'. St Carthage (died 637) was a bishop in Westmeath.

Carthy (m) Variant of *Carthage.*

Cashel [*Caiseal*] (m) An Irish placename meaning 'bulwark', the seat of an archdiocese in Tipperary, and the ancient capital of Munster.

Cashlin [*Caislín*] (m) 'little castle'. A name of Irish derivation, but it does not seem to be used in Ireland itself.

Cathal (m) 'battle mighty'. This was once a common name, and it is still sometimes employed nowadays. Cathal Crobhdhearg, 'Red Hand' (died 1224), was king of Connacht. Modern use of Cathal has been stimulated by the patriot Cathal Brugha (1874-1922), who was killed in the Irish Civil War. *Cathal* is a spelling variant. *Charles* was used as an anglicisation. The Scottish surname *Cadell* is probably derived from Cathal.

Catherine (f) A spelling variant of *Katherine.*

Cathleen (f) A spelling variant of *Kathleen.*

Catriona [*Caitríona*] (f) A Gaelic form of *Katherine,* used by Robert Louis Stevenson in his novel of the same name (1893). The name is at present popular in Ireland.

Cavan (m) An Irish placename used as a first name.

Cecil [*Siseal*] (m) 'little blind one'. The Roman Martyrology mentions a St Cecil, but its use in Ireland, as in England, mainly results from its being the family name of the Marquess of Salisbury.

Cecilia (f) A form of *Cecily* used in Ireland, where it is more common than *Cecily* itself.

Cecily [*Sisile*] (f) A feminine of Cecil. It was introduced into Ireland by the Normans, where it took the Gaelic form *Sile* (English *Sheila*, q.v.). *Sisile* is a later form.

Celia (f) This is probably a form of *Cecily.*

Celsus (m) St Celsus was a bishop of Armagh in the ninth century. Celsus was used to translate his original name *Kellagh*.

Charles [*Séarlas*] (m) Germanic, 'man'. The first Holy Roman Emperor, Charles the Great (*c.* 742-814), was an early bearer of this name. From France it spread, through royal lines, first to Naples, then Hungary, Germany and Spain. It was an unusual name in Ireland until the time of Charles I (1600-49). His father, James I, named him after a later Holy Roman Emperor, Charles V (1500-58). A form of Charles, *Carlus* from Latin *Carolus,* had been previously introduced by the Norsemen. *Searlas* is the Irish language form and, in Hiberno-English, *Charles* is often pronounced with two syllables. It has been used to anglicise a number of native names, particularly *Cathal,* but also *Calvagh, Cormac, Cahir, Carroll, Sorley* and *Turlough.* Charles Stewart Parnell (1846-91) was a famous nineteenth-century politician. Modern Irish examples are Rev. Charles Denis Mary Joseph Anthony O'Conor, claimant to the Irish throne, and Charles Mitchell, a newscaster on Irish television and radio. Feminine forms include *Carleen, Carol, Caroline* and *Charlot(te).*

Charlot (f) An Irish form of *Charlotte* (Irish, *Searlait*) which is itself a feminine form of *Charles.*

Christian [*Giolla Chríost*] (m, f) The Irish *Giolla Chríost,* 'servant of Christ' was translated into English as Christian, a name which had been in use in England since the twelfth century. Christian is currently increasing in popularity in Ireland. It was originally used as a feminine name, and a modern feminine example has been recorded in Dublin.

Christina [*Chrístíona*] (f) Latin, 'Christian'. Presumably this was introduced into Ireland from England, though the name originally derives from the Continent. It is becoming less popular. *Tina* is a pet form.

Christine [*Cristín*] (f) Another feminine form of *Christian.*

Christopher [*Críostóir*] (m) Greek, 'Christ-bearing'. This name was found in Ireland from the sixteenth century onwards. It is popular today, though not as much as it was formerly. It is often found in its pet form *Christy. Chrystal* is a variant.

Chrystal [*Criostal*] (m) A form of *Christopher.* This name gives rise to the Tyrone surname *MacCrystal.*

Cian (m) 'ancient'. An early Irish name which is still in use today. *Kian* and *Kean* are variants. It was occasionally anglicised as *Cain.*

Clare [*Clár*] (f) Latin 'bright'. A name used in Ireland in honour of St Clare of Assisi (1193-1253). The alternative spelling *Claire* is rarely, if ever, found in Ireland. The Irish county of Clare in Munster is unconnected with the name, and seems to derive either from *clar,* 'plain', or from the Anglo-Norman noble family of *de Clare.*

Claudia (f) Latin, perhaps 'lame one'. This name is occasionally found in Ireland. It was probably introduced from England, where it has been in use since at least the sixteenth century.

Clement [*Cléimeans*] (m) Latin, 'merciful'. A name sometimes found in Ireland. The feminine form *Clementina* is no longer used.

Clive (m) A variant of the English word *cliff.* It originally appeared as an English placename, first recorded in 1327, then as a surname. The popularity of the English statesman and founder of the British Empire in India, Robert Clive (1725-74), led to its use as a first name in England. It has spread to Ireland, where it is now occasionally used.

Clodagh (f) The name of a Tipperary river. One of the Marquesses of Waterford seems to have first used this as a first name for his daughter. It is still used in Ireland.

Clotworthy (m) This peculiar name was once considerably used in Ireland. It was probably originally an English surname, transferred to use as a first name. *Tatty* was a common pet form. Clotworthy Rowley was a Member of the Irish Parliament in 1797. The name now seems to have died out.

Cole [*Comhghall*] (m) 'co-pledge'. St Cole was abbot of Bangor in the sixth century.

Colette (f) A feminine diminutive of *Nicholas,* sometimes used in Ireland.

Colin [*Coileán*] (m) 'pup' or 'cub'. A name used from early times. *Coilin* is an Irish variant. It has been latinised as *Caniculus* and *Catulus.* In Ireland the surname *Ó Coileáin,* anglicised as *Collins,* sprang from it. In England the name has two origins: from Scottish Gaelic *Cailean,* and as a diminutive of *Nicholas.* Withycombe mentions an Irish form *Colán,* but there appears to be no evidence for this. Colin is often used in Ireland today.

Colleen [*Cailín*] (f) 'girl'. This is the ordinary Irish word for a girl used as a first name. It is not frequently encountered in Ireland itself, though it is used in other English-speaking countries.

Colm (m) 'dove'. This name represents the Irish form of *Columba.* It is in use today.

Colman [*Colmán*] (m) 'dovelet'. The Irish form of *Columbanus,* which is used quite extensively today.

Colmcille (m) 'dove of the church'. The nickname of St Columba.

Columba [*Colm*] (m) Latin, 'dove'. The name of the famous Irish saint (*c.* 521-97) who founded the monastery of Iona and whose biography was written by St Adamnan. His name was given to a well-known public school in Rathfarnham. There was also a female Irish saint called *Columba* (Irish, *Colma*).

Columban (m) A form of *Columbanus.*

Columbanus [*Colmán*] (m) A diminutive of *colm* 'dove'. The name of an Irish missionary saint (*c.* 540-615) who preached on the Continent and founded the monasteries of Luxueil and Bobbio. He was the author of a monastic rule. Such French surnames as *Colon* and *Coulon,* as well as the Corsican *Colombi,* are possibly derived from this name. So, Yonge tells us, is the German surname *Kohlmann,* but here she is in error – this surname means 'coalman'.

Comyn [*Comán*] (m) 'little wry one'. A name used in both Ireland and Scotland. It is now often a surname.

Conan [*Cónán*] (m) 'small hound'. Conan the Bald, in Irish legend, was one of the Fianna. St Conan of Assaroe (in the present Co. Galway) lived in the sixth century. The name was also known in Brittany: Conan Meriadech was said to be the ancestor of the dukes of that land. The Bretons introduced it into England at the time of the Norman Invasion. It flourished there for centuries and gave rise to a number of surnames. Sir Arthur Conan Doyle (1859-1930), the creator of Sherlock Holmes, was of Irish parentage. In literature, Conan the Cimmerian, a character invented by Robert E. Howard (1906-36), popularised the name.

Conant (m) Variant of *Conan*.

Concepta (f) A name given in honour of the Immaculate Conception. It is sometimes found in Ireland.

Conchobarre (f) A feminine form of *Connor*.

Congalie (f) A name of uncertain meaning, anglicised as *Constance*.

Conn (m) 'high'. Conn of the Hundred Battles was a legendary Irish monarch. His historicity is doubtful, but he has managed to gain an entry in the *Dictionary of National Biography*. The name Conn is in use in Ireland in modern times. See also *Constantine*.

Connal (f) A name of uncertain meaning, anglicised as *Constance*.

Con(n)or [*Concobhar*] (m) 'hound lover'. An Irish Christian name which gave rise to the surname *O'Con(n)or*, which is one of the most widespread in Ireland today. *Con(n)or* itself is regularly used as a Christian name, but at one time it looked as though it might be replaced by *Cornelius*, which was used to anglicise it. In mythology, Conor mac Nessa was a king of Ulster. Conor Cruise O'Brien is a contemporary statesman and author. Variants are *Conquhare, Constantine, Cornelius, Crogher* and *Crohoore*. *Conchobarre* is a feminine form.

Conquhare (m) Variant of *Conor*.

Constance (f) Latin 'constancy'. This was used to anglicise a number of Gaelic names, e.g. the early Irish feminine name *Buan*, which was said to mean 'constancy in goodness'. See also *Congalie, Connal*.

Constantine [*Consaidín*] (m) Latin, 'constant one'. A name used by the *O'Briens* since the twelfth century. It was also used to anglicise *Cuchonnacht* (now obsolete), *Conn* and *Connor*.

Cooey [*Cumhai*] (m) 'hound of the plain'. A Derry name, anglicised as *Quintin*.

Cooley (m) Variant of *Cullo* (now obsolete).

Cormac (m) Perhaps 'raven'. It has had several English variants: *Cormick, Cormock, Cormocke* and *Cormuck*, and it has given rise to the surnames *MacCormack* and *MacCormick*. Cormac mac Art was said to be an ancient king in Irish legend.

Cormac MacCuilleanan was king of Munster and also a bishop. *Kormak* is the Icelandic form of Cormac – the Norse took Irish slaves to Ireland. *Charles* was used to anglicise the name. In literature, Cormac O'Connor Fahy was the hero of *Ninety-Eight* (1897), a novel by John Hill, and Cormac O'Hagan was the hero of the novel *With Poison and Sword* (1910) by W. M. O'Kane.

Cornelius (m) Latin, perhaps 'horned one'. This name was used to anglicise *Connor*. It now seems to be on the wane. Such pseudo-translations (*Jeremiah* is another example) are now considered old-fashioned.

Covey [*Cúmhéa*] (m) 'hound of Meath'. A name used by the *MacNamaras*.

Crevan [*Criomhthann*] (m) 'fox'. A name which seems to have been chiefly used in Leinster.

Crogher (m) A variant of *Conor*, once used in north-eastern Ireland.

Crohoore (m) A variant of *Conor*, once used in north-eastern Ireland. Pronunciation in modern Gaelic of *Conchobhar*, Irish for Conor, is the same as Crohoore.

Cronan [*Crónán*] (m) 'little dark-brown one'. St Cronan founded the monastery of Roscrea in the seventh century.

He became its first abbot. The name is rarely if ever used nowadays.

Cuchulainn (m) 'hound of Culann'. The name, or rather, the nickname, of the greatest hero of Irish mythology. His real name was *Setanta*, and he obtained the name Cuchulainn by slaying the ferocious hound of Culann and afterwards volunteering to take on the dead creature's duties. He defended Ulster against the forces of Queen Maéve of Connacht, and his exploits are recorded in the epic *Táin Bó Cuailgne*.

Cumania [*Cuman*] (f) The name of a sixth-century Irish saint, said to have been the sister of St Colmcille.

Cyril [*Coireall*] (m) Greek, 'lordly'. A name used in Ireland to anglicise *Kerill*.

D

Dagda [*Daghda*] (m) 'the good god'. This was the name of an important deity of the pagan Irish. According to medieval legend, he was the leader of the Tuatha De Danaan, the traditional early inhabitants of Ireland. Loughead notes Dagda as a given name.

Dahy [*Dáithi*] (m) 'speed', 'agility'. The name of a king of Tara, ancestor of the *O'Dowds*, who, according to legend, raided continental Europe and was struck by lightning at the foot of the Alps. Dahy has often been anglicised as *David*, and it is common as an Irish 'translation' of that name. *Nathy*, the name of an Irish saint, is possibly a variant.

Daireen (f) This name was first used by the Limerick author, F. Frankfort Moore, for the heroine of his novel *Daireen* (1893). It appears to be the author's invention.

Dallan (m) A diminutive of *dall*, 'blind'. St Dallan (died 598) was a bishop of Donaghmore.

Damien (m) A French form of *Damian* (Irish, *Daman*) which perhaps is connected with a Greek word meaning 'to tame'. *Damien* is now quite popular in Ireland.

Dana (f, m) Dana was an important Irish pagan goddess who gave her name to the Tuatha De Danaan, the legendary inhabitants of Ireland. It is also the name of a popular Irish singer, but in her case the name derives from *dana*, 'bold'. There is a masculine name *Dana* which is Teutonic and signifies 'Dane'; this name is borne by the contemporary actor, Dana Andrews.

Daniel (m) Hebrew, 'God is my judge'. A popular name in Ireland. It was used to anglicise the common native name *Donal*, and so it became well established. The Irish forms are *Dainéal* and *Dainial*. Daniel O'Connell (1775-1847), a major Irish political figure in the nineteenth century who secured Catholic Emancipation, further popularised the name. So Irish a name has Daniel become that Spike Milligan used it as the name of the protagonist of his hilarious Irish novel, *Puckoon* (1963).

Darby (m) A form of *Dermot* which occurred in Limerick and Tipperary. It had spread from Ireland to England as early as 1560. Henriette Templeton used the name in her novel *Darby O'Gill and the Good People* which was filmed by Walt Disney as *Darby O'Gill and the Little People*. Darby O'Drive was also a character in William Carleton's novel *Valentine McClutchey* (1845).

Darcy (m) A branch of the *Darcy* family – whose surname comes either from the placename of Arcy-Ste-Restitue or that of Arcy-sur-Cure – came to Ireland in the fourteenth century, and the surname was adopted as a Christian name there.

Darerca (f) The name of a saint associated with Valentia Island who, according to tradition, was the sister of St Patrick. Legend credits her with nineteen children.

Darkey [*Dorchaidhe*] (m) The English form of this name is unusual. *Darcy* has often been substituted for it.

Darragh (m) A name connected in meaning with *dair,* 'oak'. It has been used from time to time in Ireland in modern times, but it is now on the increase.

Darren (m) A name of obscure origin, said to be Irish. It is used in Ireland today. There is a character called Darren in the American television series *Bewitched,* first shown in the 1960s. It is almost certain that this series contributed to the name's recent popularity. According to Rule, it means 'little great one'.

David [*Dáivi*] (m) A Hebrew name of uncertain meaning, once thought to signify 'loved one'. It was used as an equivalent of *Daithi* in Ireland and *Dewi* in Wales, the latter being the real name of St David of Menevia. *Dáibhidh* was a form borne by the eighteenth-century poet O'Bruadair, and *Daibheid* was a form taken from Norman French *Davet* (a diminutive). David is increasingly popular in Ireland today.

Dawn (f) This name, unused before the present century, occurs occasionally in Ireland.

Dé (m) A translation of *Mogue,* used also in Brittany, where it is the name of the village of St Dé.

Deborah (f) Hebrew 'bee'; later, 'eloquence'. A Biblical name adopted by the English Puritans. It was brought to Ireland from England and was used to anglicise the native name, *Gobinet.* It is popular in Ireland today.

Decla (f) An unusual feminine form of *Declan.*

Declan [*Deaglán*] (m) The name of an early Irish saint, which has noticeably increased in popularity in modern times.

Deirdre (f) A name of uncertain meaning, perhaps signifying 'fear', perhaps 'one who rages', or perhaps 'broken-hearted one'. It was borne by the heroine of a tragic Irish legend. Deirdre, the betrothed of the king of Ulster, eloped with one of the three sons of Uisneach. All three sons were slain by the king, and Deirdre was left to mourn them. Two prominent Irish writers have used this legend: W. B. Yeats in his *Deirdre* (1907), and J. M. Synge in his *Deirdre of the Sorrows* (1910). It is popular in Ireland today.

Denis (m) The Greek god of wine was Dionysus, and the name *Dionysius,* 'servant of Dionysus', was used in early times. Denis – sometimes spelt *Dennis* or *Denys* – is a shortened form of this. In Ireland Denis was used to anglicise *Donagh* which established the name. However its popularity has sharply decreased in recent times.

Denise (f) A feminine form of *Denis,* originally from France, but presumably imported into Ireland from England in modern times. The name is now well established in Ireland.

Derek (m) Germanic, 'people ruler'. This is a form of the name *Theodoric.* Old French *Terrick,* Dutch *Dirk* and English *Derrick* are related forms. Derek was introduced into England by Flemings and it occurs there from the fifteenth century onwards. It has been revived in England in modern times and has spread to Ireland, where it is now quite common.

Derforgal (f) This is a variant of a native name, *Dervorgilla.*

Dermitius (m) A latinised form of *Dermot* occasionally

recorded, e.g., there was a Captain Dermitius Coghlan, of King's County and Tipperary, a soldier of the Commonwealth.

Dermod (m) Variant of *Dermot.*

Dermot [*Diarmuid*] (m) 'envy free'. The name of an important hero of Irish legend, who eloped with Grania, the betrothed of Finn MacCool. Dermot MacMurrough was the king of Leinster who invited the Normans into Ireland in the twelfth century. *Darby* was a form of Dermot used in Limerick and Tipperary; *Jarmy* was used by the *O'Kanes* and the *O'Mullans.* It was anglicised as *Jeremiah* in Cork and Kerry, and it has also been anglicised *Jerome* and *Edward.* Dermot is quite popular in Ireland today. *Diarmis* may be a variant. See also *Dermitius, Dermod* and *Kermit.*

Dervla (f) A name used to translate Irish *Dearbhail,* 'true desire'; *Derval* and *Dervilia* are also translations of this name. Dervla Murphy is a contemporary Irish writer and traveller.

Desmond [*Deasún*] (m) An Irish placename, 'South Munster' (i.e. Cork and Kerry), and not, as may be supposed, from Thomond, North Munster. It was first transferred to use as a surname, and then came into use as a first name. It is found frequently today.

Devnet (f) A form of *Dympna.*

Dichu (m) 'great hound'. St Dichu was said to have been the first Irish convert to Christianity made by St Patrick.

Doctor (m) Dunkling says there is an Irish custom of giving this name to the seventh son of a seventh son, but it has not been possible to verify this. However, in Irish folklore, such a person is said to have healing powers.

Dolores (f) Spanish, 'sorrows'. This name is given in honour of the Blessed Virgin who is sometimes referred to as *Maria de los Dolores,* 'Mary of the Sorrows'. The name used to be confined almost exclusively to Catholics but this is no longer the case. It is occasionally used in Ireland today.

Dominic [*Doiminic*] (m) Latin, 'of the Lord'. A name used in Ireland in honour of St Dominic de Guzman (1170-1221). Two unusual Irish forms were *Damhlaic* and *Damhnaic.* The spelling *Dominick* is often used.

Dominica (f) Feminine form of *Dominic.* St Dominica, an early Irish saint, was martyred in Germany.

Donagh [*Donnchadh*] (m) 'brown warrior'. This is a common Irish name, borne by the High King Donagh (died 1064), son of Brian Boru. It has sometimes been anglicised as *Denis* or *Donat. Duncan* was originally a pet form of this name. Donagh O'Malley was a twentieth-century Irish politician.

Donal [*Dónal*] (m) 'world mighty'. A name frequently employed in Ireland, though at one stage it was commonly anglicised as *Daniel.* In Scotland, the Gaelic equivalent, *Domhnall,* has been translated into English as *Donald.* The *O'Donnells* and *MacDonnells* or *MacDonalds* all take their names from *Donal.* Donal of Bangor was an Irish saint.

Donat (m) Latin, 'given'. This was used to translate the native name *Donagh.* St *Donatus* (the Latin form) was said to have been an Irishman. *Donato,* the Italian form, has been noted amongst the Italian community in Ireland.

Donegal (m) The name of an Irish town and county, used as a personal name. In Irish it becomes *Dún na nGall,* which means 'fort of the foreigners'.

Donelle (f) The feminine form of *Donal.*

Donleavy [*Donn Sléibhe*] (m) 'brown of the hill'. A once-popular name, from which the surnames *Donleavy* and *Dunlop* sprang. It was also used in Scotland, where the strange form *Downsleif* is recorded.

Donn (m) 'brown'. This rare name was chiefly used by the *Maguires*.

Doon (f) The Hill of Doon in Lough Mask has provided this unusual first name.

Doreen [*Doireann*] (f) This is perhaps an Irish form of *Dorothy* (Greek, 'God's gift') or a form of the native name *Dorren*, 'sullen'. It was used in Edna Lyall's novel *Doreen* (1894). *Dorothy* itself is sometimes used in Ireland.

D'Orsay (m) An anglicisation of the Irish name *Dorchaidhe*.

Dougal [*Dúghall*] (m) 'dark foreigner'. This Gaelic name is primarily used in Scotland.

Douglas [*Dúghlas*] (m) 'black blue'. Douglas is mainly used in Scotland, though it also occurs in Ireland. Douglas Hyde (1860-1949) was the first President of Ireland (1938-45).

Dowle (m) An unusual form of *Donal*, borne by a member of the *Barry* family of Sandville, Co. Limerick, who died in 1640.

Downett (f) A form of *Dympna*.

Doyle (m) This surname derives from *Dubhghall*, 'dark foreigner', indicating Scandinavian ancestry. Doyle may also indicate ancestry springing from the French towns, Oyle or Ouilly. It has come to be used as a first name.

Duald [*Dualtach*] (m) 'black-jointed'. A name borne by the writer, Dubhaltach MacFirbisigh (1580-1660). It was sometimes anglicised *Dudley*.

Dualtagh (m) Variant of *Duald*.

Dubhdara (m) 'black (man) of the oak'. A West Connacht name.

Dubside [*Dubh Sithe*] (m) 'black of peace'. An early name, borne by a Rector of Iona in the twelfth century.

Dudley (m) Originally this was a surname coming from Dudley in Worcestershire. It became a first name in the nineteenth century, and was used in Ireland to anglicise *Duald*, *Dubhdaleithe* ('black man of the two sides') and *Dubhdara*. It continues in use.

Duff [*Dubh*] (m) 'black'; when used of a man, it means 'black-haired'.

Duvessa [*Dubheasa*] (f) 'dark beauty'. A name used in Ireland in the Middle Ages. The death of one Duvessa O'Farrell was recorded in 1301.

Dwyer (m) An Irish surname which has been recorded as a Christian name in Northern Ireland.

Dymphna (f) Variant of *Dympna*.

Dympna [*Damhnait*] (f) A name perhaps meaning 'befitted'. St Dympna of Tedavnat was an early Irish saint. Another St Dympna of Gheel in Belgium may have been Irish. Both *Dympna* and its variant *Dymphna* are in use today. *Devnet* is another variant.

E

Ea (m) Variant of *Aodh*.

Eachann (m) 'horse lord'. This name was exported to Scotland, where it was anglicised as *Hector* (Irish *Eachtar*), which may mean 'holding fast'.

Ealga (f) 'noble'. Ireland is sometimes referred to as *Inis Ealga*, 'the Noble Isle', which is the source of this unusual name.

Eamon(n) (m) This is the Irish form of *Edmund*, Anglo-Saxon, 'rich protection'; but the name is now frequently used to translate *Edward*. Eamon De Valera (1882-1975) was an important Irish politician and president. The name is currently quite popular. *Aimon* was a spelling variant no longer used. *Iamonn* was another variant used in Derry and Omeath.

Eavan [*Aoibheann*] (f) 'fair form'. A name used in early times which has been revived. Eavan Boland is a contemporary Irish poetess.

Echlin [*Eaclain*] (m) A name used by the *O'Kanes* of Derry. See also *Aichlinn*.

Edana (f) A feminine of *Aidan*.

Edith (f) Anglo-Saxon, 'happy war'. This name has occasionally been used in Ireland. *Editha*, probably a variant, occurs in the *Wallis* family.

Edmund (m) In Ireland this name is usually represented by *Eamonn*, but is sometimes bestowed in its own right. Recently the spelling *Edmond* has become more popular. C. S. Lewis (1898-1963) the Northern-Irish writer, has an Edmund in his Narnian chronicles.

Edward (m) Anglo-Saxon, 'rich guard'. The true Irish form of this name is *Eadbhard*, but this has been largely replaced by *Eamonn*. Edward was introduced after the Norman Invasion (1169). Recently it has sharply declined in popularity.

Egan [*Aodhgan*] (m) 'little fire'. Egan O'Rahilly was an Irish language poet in the seventeenth century. Egan is common nowadays as a surname.

Eileen [*Eibhlin*] (f) This is probably an elaboration of *Evelyn*, rather than a form of *Helen*, as is sometimes supposed. *Eily* is a pet form. The name is frequently encountered in Ireland today, and it has spread abroad. It became common in England and Wales from about the 1920s onwards. A variant, *Aileen*, is sometimes found.

Eilis [*Eilís*] (f) The Irish form of *Elizabeth*. *Eilise* is a variant. It was used, on occasion, to translate *Alice*, *Alicia* and *Letitia* – names wholly unrelated to it. Eilis Dillon is a modern Irish authoress.

Eimar (m) This name has come into use in Ireland in modern times. Its origin is obscure, but, as it does not appear to be used anywhere else, it is presumably Irish. It is unlikely to be connected with Irish *eimh*, 'swift', or with the Germanic name *Einar*, 'chief'.

Elaine (f) A form of *Helen* used in Arthurian romance. Tennyson's *Idylls of the King* (1859-88) led to its modern use, and it is now an established name in Ireland.

Elan (f) This is perhaps a form of *Helen* which is used in Ireland. It was borne by a daughter of Teague O'Meara, of Lismisk, Co. Tipperary, who died in 1636.

Eleanor [*Eileanóir*] (f) The name *Helen* became *Alienor* in Provençal, and this, in turn, was transformed into Eleanor. It became popular in England in Norman times due to Queen Eleanor, wife of Edward I. The Normans brought the name to Ireland. *Eleanora* (Irish *Eilíonóra*) is a variant. Another version perhaps occurs in the name of the Irish martyr, St *Ealanor*.

Elhe [*Ele*] (m) 'bier', 'litter'. The name of the legendary ancestor of the *Healy* family.

Eliza (f) A form of *Elizabeth*, which once enjoyed considerable popularity in Ireland.

Elizabeth [*Eilís*] (f) Hebrew, 'my God is satisfaction'. In the New Testament, St Elizabeth was the mother of John the Baptist. The name was used in the Middle Ages chiefly in honour of St Elizabeth of Hungary (1207-31). It probably first reached Ireland in the variant form of *Isabel*. Elizabeth became extremely popular in Ireland, as well as in England, Wales and Scotland, but its use has sharply declined in modern times. *Beth, Liz, Lizzie, Elsie*, and *Lilibet* are all used as pet forms. *Elisa, Elsa* and *Elspeth* are variants.

Ellen (f) A form of *Helen* which became fashionable in Ireland round about the middle of the century, but between 1950 and 1970 it fell rapidly from favour.

Elli (m) Variant of *Ailbe* (see *Alby*).

Elly (m) Variant of *Ailbe* (see *Alby*).

Elva [*Ailbhe*] (f) A name sometimes anglicised *Olive. Alvy* is an English variant, *Oilbhe* an Irish one.

Emer [*Eimhear*] (f) Emer was the wife of the hero, Cuchulainn, in Irish legend. It has come into use in modern times, no doubt due to the Gaelic Revival and perhaps because of W. B. Yeats' play, *The Only Jealousy of Emer* (1921).

Emily [*Eimile*] (f) The feminine form of a Roman clan name, *Aemilius*, which was to some degree confused with *Amelia*, a different name of Germanic origin. Emily was presumably imported from Britain.

Emma (f) Germanic, 'universal'. This name, much used in England and Wales, is quite popular in Ireland today.

Emmet (m) This was the surname of the renowned eighteenth-century rebel, Robert Emmet. It is sometimes conferred by modern Irish parents on their sons in commemoration of the patriot.

Ena (f) A form of *Ethna*.

Enda [*Éanna*] (m) Perhaps a derivation of *éan*, 'bird', meaning 'birdlike', 'avian'. St Enda (died *c.* 590), one of the most famous Irish saints, is associated with the Aran Islands. The name is in use in modern times.

Eneas (m) A variant of *Aeneas* which has been used to translate Gaelic *Eigneachan* (see *Ignatius*).

Ennis [*Inis*] (f) The name of the capital of Co. Clare, used as a first name.

Eochaidh (m) Because it is so difficult for English speakers to pronounce, this name has declined from the position of popularity it once held in Ireland. There are several more pronounceable variants (e.g. *Achaius, Aghy, Atty, Eoi, Oho, Ogh(i)e, Syka*) which are listed separately. The Latin form, *Equitius*, has been recorded as an independent name.

Eoghan (m) 'well born'. This Celtic name is etymologically identical with Greek *Eugene*, and is often used to translate it. The Welsh name *Eugeuin*, translated into English as *Owen*, has the same meaning – and indeed, in Ireland Owen is sometimes used to translate Eoghan. Eoghan has been translated as *John* in Omeath, due to confusion with *Eoin*. The Scottish *Ewen* may be a form of this name.

Eoi (m) Variant of *Eochaidh*.

Eoin (m) An Irish form of *John*, presumably from Latin *Johannes*. It is probably closely related to Scottish Gaelic *Iain*. Eoin still survives in modern Ireland, but more and more it is being replaced by *Sean* from Norman French *Jehan* which was introduced after the Norman Invasion of 1169, and by the English name *John* itself.

Erc [*Earc*] (m) 'red' or 'speckled'. This name was once frequently found in Munster, but it has now disappeared.

Eric (m) A Germanic name of uncertain meaning, which was revived in England in the nineteenth century. It has occasionally been used in modern Ireland.

Erin(a) (f) The Irish word for Ireland, used as a Christian name. It is employed in the United States, Canada and Australia, but it is not used in Ireland at all.

Ernan [*Earnán*] (m) 'little-experienced one'. This name is used in Ireland as an equivalent of *Ernest*.

Ernest (m) Germanic, 'vigour'. A name used in Ireland to anglicise *Ernan*.

Esther [*Eistir*] (f) A Persian name of unknown meaning, which was used in Ireland to 'translate' *Ashling*. There was an Irish custom of conferring this name on children born at Easter.

Etain (f) According to Irish legend, Etain was the lover of the fairy man, Midir. *Aideen* is a variant. The name was probably made popular by *The Immortal Hour* (1914), an opera by Rutland Boughton based on the legend.

Eth (m) Variant of *Aodh*.

Ethna [*Eithne*] (f) A feminine form of *Aidan. Annie* was used to anglicise it – which at one time resulted in Annie being extremely popular, much more so than *Ann(e)*. Annie is less popular now than it was at the turn of the century; but *Eithne/Ethna* has been revived in modern times. *Ena* and *Etney* are variants.

Etney (f) Variant of *Ethna*.

Eugene (m) Greek, 'well born'. A name used to translate *Eoghan*.

Eunan (m) Variant of *Adamnan*.

Eustace [*Iustas*] (m) Greek, possibly 'fruitful'. A name introduced into Ireland after the Norman Invasion. Since then it has occasionally been used. It was equated with *Iusdas*, a native name for which O'Hart gives the unlikely etymology of 'knowledge desk'.

Eva [*Aoife*] (f) The Latin form of *Eve*. It was used to translate Irish *Aoife*, a name found in legend. It was also the name of the daughter of King Dermot of Leinster, who married Strongbow, the leader of the Norman Invasion. Eva Gore Booth (1870-1926) was an Irish poetess. *Aoife* has become popular in modern times.

Eve [*Éabha*] (f) Perhaps Hebrew, 'lively'. It is not a common name in Ireland.

Eveleen (f) An Irish diminutive of *Eva*.

Evelyn (m, f) A Germanic name, occasionally used in Ireland.

F

Fachnan [*Fachtna*] (m) The name of a sixth-century Irish saint and first bishop of Ros Carbery. *Festus* has been used to anglicise this name; *Faughnan* is a variant.

Fardoragh [*Feardorcha*] (m) 'dark man'. A name which was – fairly popular in the sixteenth century. It was anglicised both as *Frederick* and *Ferdinand*.

Farghy (m) Variant of *Fergus*, perhaps now obsolete.

Farrell (m) Variant of *Fergal*.

Farry [*Fearadhach*] (m) 'manly'. This name was widespread in early times. It has been anglicised as *Ferdinand*.

Faughnan (m) Variant of *Fachnan*.

Feary (m) A form of *Fiachra*.

Fe(c)hin [*Feichin*] (m) 'little raven'. The name of an Irish saint. It was anglicised as *Festus*.

Felim(id) [*Feilim*] (m) 'ever good'. Felim was king of Connacht in the Middle Ages. The Spanish form of the name is *Felime*. Attempts to anglicise it as *Felix* and *Philip* have proved successful, as the name is rarely encountered today. *Phelim(y)* is an alternative spelling.

Felimy (m) Variant of *Felimid*.

Felix (m) Latin, 'happy'. This name was used to anglicise *Felim*, *Phelim* and *Felimid;* e.g. Sir Phelim O'Neill, executed by the English in the seventeenth century, changed his name to *Felix*.

Fenella (f) The Scottish form of *Finola* which is occasionally found in Ireland.

Feories (m) A name which now seems to be obsolete. It is a variant of *Pierce*, presumably from the Irish *Piaras*.

Ferdinand (m) Germanic, 'journey risk'. This name was used in Ireland to anglicise *Farry, Fardoragh, Fergananym,* and *Fergus*.

Fergal [*Fearghall*] (m) 'man of strength'. St Fergal (died 784) was an Irish saint associated with Salzburg, whose name was latinised as *Virgil*. Fergal is still used today. *Farrell* and *Forgael* are variants.

Fergananym [*Fearganainm*] (m) 'nameless man'. This curious name, sometimes anglicised as *Ferdinand*, used to be fairly popular in Ireland. It may sometimes have been applied to unbaptised persons.

Fergus [*Fearghus*] (m) 'man vigour'. An early Gaelic name, still closely associated with Ireland and Scotland. Fergus mac Erca was said to have led the Gaels from Ireland to Scotland in the fifth century. In the eighth century another Irishman, St Fergus, was a bishop in Scotland. *Forcus* was the Pictish equivalent. Later when Irish names were anglicised, Fergus was 'translated' as *Ferdinand* by the wealthy, *Fardy* by those who were not so well-to-do. *Farghy* is a variant noted by Yonge, who also mentions a feminine form, *Fergusiana*. The name continues in use in Ireland, Scotland and even northern England.

Festus (m) This rather strange, Latin name was used to 'translate' *Fachan* and *Fehin*.

ffranck (m) This was used as a middle name in the family of *Rolleston* of ffranckfort and Sandbrook. The double *f* in medieval times was a way of rendering a capital *F*. The earliest traced bearer was James ffranck Rolleston (born 1742).

Fiach (m) 'raven'. Two Irish words for raven, *bran* and *fiach*, were used a Christian names. In the sixteenth century Fiach MacHugh O'Beirne joined forces against the English with Red Hugh O'Donnell after his escape from Dublin Castle.

Fiachra (m) Perhaps a derivative of *fiach*, 'raven'. St Fiacre (died *c.* 670) was said to have been an Irishman, and this may have been his original name. His name was eventually used for a type of coach in Paris. *Feary* is a variant of Fiachra. Macpherson's Fiachere, son of Fingal, may be derived from this name.

Fidelma [*Fideilme*] (f) A name which is quite widespread in modern Ireland.

Finbar [*Fionnbhárr*] (m) 'fair top' or 'fair head'. St Finbar (*c.* 470-548) established a monastery in the south of Ireland, where the City of Cork now stands. The name is still used in Ireland today, e.g. Finbar Nolan is a modern faith healer. *Barry* (Irish *Barra*) is a pet form.

Fineen [*Finín*] (m) 'fair offspring'. A name particularly associated with West Munster. It has been anglicised as *Florence*. *Fineen* is a spelling variant.

Finella (f) Variant of *Finola*.

Fingal (m) A corruption of Irish *Finn* which originated in Scotland and has been made well known by Macpherson's Ossianic poems (1795) and Mendelssohn's *Fingal's Cave* (1830). Fingal occurs as early as the fourteenth century in the works of the Scottish poet, John Barbour (*c.* 1316-95).

Fingar (m) A name formed from *fionn* 'fair-haired.' It is the name of a fifth-century Irish saint.

Fin(n)ian (m) A name formed from *Fionn* 'fair'. St Finian founded the abbey of Moville in the sixth century.

Finlugh [*Fionnlugh*] (m) 'fair winning'. The name of an Irish saint who was a missionary in Scotland in the sixth century. He returned to Ireland to become an abbot.

Finn [*Fionn*] (m) 'fair'. Also *Fynn*. This is the name of one of the great heroes of Irish mythology, Finn MacCool. Mythologists have suggested that he was an aspect of the god Lugh, and that even a place as far away as Vienna (Latin *Vindobona*)derives its name from him. He was the leader of the Fianna, the father of the master-poet Ossian, and the pursuer of Dermot. In folklore Finn was depicted as a giant, but in myth he was of normal stature. He is said to have erected the Giants' Causeway on the Antrim coast.

There is also a Germanic name *Finn,* which Yonge connects with the Irish name, but which probably has an entirely different origin and means 'wise as a Finn' – in the middle ages the Finns were famous for sorcery. *Finni* and *Finnr,* used in medieval Iceland, may come from the Irish Finn. See also *Fingal*.

Finna (f) A name used in medieval Iceland. It is perhaps derived from Irish *fionn*, 'fair'.

Finola [*Fionnuala*] (f) A well-known Irish name, frequently seen nowadays in its shortened form *Nuala*. *Finella* and *Fynballa* are variants. It was 'translated' as *Flora* or *Penelope*. *Fenella* is the form used in Scotland.

Fintan [*Fionntán*] (m) 'little fair one'. St Fintan was a sixth-century abbot of Clonenagh. The name is used in modern times.

Fiona [*Fióna*] (f) This Scottish name was invented in the nineteenth century by the writer, William Sharp, who used it for his pseudonym 'Fiona Macleod'. It comes from Gaelic *fionn*, 'fair'. It has spread from Scotland, becoming particularly popular in Northern Ireland. It is also often found in the Republic.

Fitzgerald [*MacGerailt*] (m) Norman French, 'son of *Gerald*'. The prefix Fitz- is cognate with the modern French *fils*, and readily translated into Irish as Mac. *Fitzgerald* was the name of a prominent Norman noble family in the Middle Ages, a family which included the Earls of Kildare. It is now sometimes used as a first name.

Fitzgibbon (m) A surname used as a first name. It means 'son of *Gibbon*'. (a form of *Gilbert*).

Fitzjames (m) 'son of James'. This name was borne by the Limerick writer Fitz-james O'Brien (1828-62) who emigrated to the United States and was killed in the American Civil War.

Flann (m) 'blood-red', 'red-wat'. An early name which was once quite widespread. It was anglicised as *Florence*. Flann O'Brien was a pen-name used by Brian O'Nolan (1911-66).

Flannan (m) A diminutive of *Flann*, still in use today, but growing less popular.

Flora (f) Latin, derivative of *flos*, 'flower'. Flora was used to translate the Irish name *Blath*, 'flower'. It was also used to translate *Finola*.

Florence (m, f) Latin, 'flowering one'. Florence was once used as a masculine name in England as well as in Ireland; however, its use for boys in England was rare after the seventeenth century. In Ireland its use as a masculine name has persisted, mainly because it was employed to anglicise names such as *Fineen, Fitheal* and *Flann. Flor, Florrie* and *Flurry* are pet forms. As a feminine name it is used to translate *Blathnaid*, derived from *blath*, 'flower'.

Forgael (m) Variant of *Fergal*.

Frances [*Proinséas*] (f) The feminine form of *Francis*, occurring in the latter half of the thirteenth century as Italian *Francesca*, and French *Françoise*. It spread to Ireland where it was once popular, but it has now gone out of fashion. The pet form *Fanny*, occasionally given as an independent name, was used to anglicise the native name *Fainche*.

Francis [*Proinsias*] (m) Italian, *Francesco*, 'Frenchman'. This nickname was given to St Francis of Assisi (1182-1226) who made the name well known throughout Europe. It became widespread in Ireland, as in other countries, but it is less used today.

Frederick (m) Germanic, 'peace ruler'. This name was used in Ireland to anglicise *Fardoragh*.

Fursey [*Fursa*] (m) According to legend St Fursey had a vision of the world to come. His name was used by Mervyn Wall (1908–) in a number of amusing satirical novels.

Fynballa (f) A variant of *Finola*.

Fynn (m) A spelling variant of *Finn*.

G

Gabriel [*Gaibrial*] (m) Hebrew, 'strong man of God'. A name used from time to time in Ireland, e.g. in 1754 an Irishman, Gabriel Redmond, Chevalier de St Louis, became a captain in the French army.

Gael (m) According to medieval Irish legend, this is the name of the hero from whom the Irish race took its name. In fact, the word *Gael* (Old Irish, *Goidel*) is derived from Welsh *Gwyddyl*. *Gathelus* is a variant.

Gale [*Gál*] (m) Various derivations have been given for this name, e.g., Irish 'vapour'; Germanic, 'song'; Danish, 'crow'; and Icelandic, 'furious'.

Gall (m) Perhaps 'rooster'. St Gall (*c.* 550-640) was a follower of St Columbanus. He settled in Switzerland, where the town and canton of Sankt-Gallen were named after him.

Galvin (m) This name is derived either from *gealbhan*, 'bright white', or from *gealbhan*, 'sparrow'.

Gareth [*Gairiad*] (m) In Arthurian romance, Gareth was a brother of Sir Gawaine. The Irish form occurs in the *Lorgaireacht an tSoidigh Naomhtha*, an Irish rendering of a version of the Grail legend. It may derive from a Welsh name or be a form of *Gerald*. The use of Gareth in England in the nineteenth century probably owes much to Tennyson's *Idylls of the King* (1859-88). It is occasionally used in Ireland, where it probably spread from England.

Garrett [*Gearóid*] (m) The name *Gerlad* became *Gearoid* or *Gioroid* in Irish, and was then anglicised as *Garrett* (a name which has no connection with *Gareth*). Garret is one of the more popular Irish names today. The combination *Garrett-Michael* was used on a number of occasions in the *O'Byrne* family.

Gary (m) This is perhaps a form of *Gerald*. It has been used from time to time in Ireland. In the 1930s the American film actor, Gary Cooper, made the name a popular one.

Gaspar (m) A form of *Jasper* occasionally used in Ireland.

Gathelus (m) Variant of *Gael*.

Gavin (m) This name, frequently used in Scotland, but more rarely in Ireland, may come from Teutonic *Gavja*, 'district', or from Welsh *Gwalchmai*, 'May hawk'. It occurs as *Gauvain* in French and *Gawain* in English Arthurian romance.

Gemma (f) Italian (f) Italian, 'gem'. A name used in Ireland to commemorate St Gemma Galgani (died 1903).

Geoffrey [*Seathrún*] (m) This name is Germanic, but it has varying origins, meaning both 'district peace' and 'pledge peace'. The name is sometimes confused with *Godfrey*, to which it is unrelated. The French *Geoffroi* and *Jeoffroi*, Breton *Jaffrez*, became in English Geoffrey and *Jeffrey*. In Ireland, where the name was probably introduced after the Norman Invasion, a variety of forms grew up: *Seafra*, *Seufraid, Seurihu, Seurihru*, and *Siofrai* (from Geoffrey) and *Seathrun* (from a French diminutive of the name). Seathrún Céitinn (in English, Geoffrey Keating) was a priest of the Cromwellian period who wrote a history of Ireland entitled *Foras Feasa ar Éirinn*.

Some of these Gaelic forms have been re-anglicised as *Sheary* and *Sheron*. Geoffrey continues to be used in Ireland today.

George [*Seoirse*] (m) Greek, 'farmer'. The name of the patron saint of England, whose cult was introduced by returning crusaders. George was used by the royal House of Hanover in the eighteenth century, and it came into general use in Ireland at that time. It is now established, though it appears to be less used today. The Portuguese form *Jorge* is borne by Jorge The O'Neill of Clanaboy, claimant to the Irish throne.

Georgina (f) A feminine form of *George*, sometimes found in Ireland.

Gerald [*Gearalt*] (m) Germanic, 'spear rule'. This was introduced to Ireland after the Norman Invasion, but it has tended to give way to *Garrett*. It has also been confused with *Gerard* in both Ireland and Wales. *Gary* is possibly a variant.

Geraldine [*Gearóidín*] (f) The *Fitzgeralds*, earls of Kildare, were known as the *Geraldines*, and in the sixteenth century the poet Surrey saluted Lady Elizabeth Fitzgerald as 'the Fair Geraldine' which possibly started the name. Its popularity may have been increased by its use in Coleridge's *Christabel* (1816). The name is still used in Ireland today.

Gerard [*Gearárd*] (m) Germanic, 'spear hard'. The Normans introduced the name to Ireland, where a certain confusion with *Gerald* arose. It is still quite popular in Ireland today, owing to the influence of St Gerard Majella (died 1755).

Gertrude (f) Germanic, 'spear strength'. A name used in Ireland to anglicise *Grania*.

Gilbert [*Gilibeirt*] (m) Germanic, 'pledge bright'. A name introduced into Ireland by the Normans. It was used in Scotland to anglicise the Gaelic *Gilbride*.

Gilduffe [*Giolla Dubh*] (m) 'black servant'. A name which appears to have been once common in Derry.

Giles [*Éigid*] (m, f) Latin, 'kidlike'. As in England and Scotland, Giles has been used as both a masculine and feminine name. The Irish form, which is taken from an early source, presumably comes from Latin *Aegidius*. At the turn of the century the name was still used for both boys and girls in Co. Donegal, but it is now exclusively a masculine name.

Gill [*Giolla*] (m) An anglicised form of *Giolla* (q.v.) which occurs in the *Joyce* family, e.g. Gill Dubh Joyce (died 1774).

Gillespie (m) 'servant of the bishop'. A Gaelic name sometimes anglicised as *Archibald*. The Irish is *Giolla Easpaig;* the Scottish Gaelic is *Giolleasbuig*.

Gillian (f) A feminine form of *Julian,* name of uncertain meaning. It is used in Ireland in modern times.

Giolla (m) 'servant'. Irish Gaelic *giolla* corresponds to Scottish Gaelic *gille*. Gil was commonly prefixed to names, e.g. *Gilduffe, Gillespie*.

Giolla-na-naomh (m) 'servant of the saints'. This name was anglicised as *Nehemiah*.

Glasny [*Glaisne*] (m) A name formerly used in Ulster.

Gloria (f) Latin, 'glory'. This name was invented by the Irish playwright George Bernard Shaw and used in *You Never Can Tell* (1898). The actress Gloria Swanson, born in the same year, was probably chiefly responsible for spreading the name. Lareina Rule cites *Glori, Gloriana* and *Glory* as variants, but the form Gloriana may derive from Spenser's use of this name in *The Faerie Queene* (1590/6) for a character representing Elizabeth I.

Glorvina (f) This name appears to have been invented by the Irish writer, Lady Morgan, to name the daughter of an Irish prince in her novel *The Wild Irish Girl* (1806). It has occasionally been used as a first name.

Gobinet [*Gobnait*] (f) Derivative of *gob* 'mouth', 'beak', 'bill'. St Gobinet, a saint associated with Ballyvourney, was said to have been born in Clare. The name was anglicised as *Abigail*, with which it was at times used interchangeably. *Gobnat, Gobnet* and *Gubnet* are variants.

Gobnat (f) Variant of *Gobinet*.

Gobnet (f) Variant of *Gobinet*.

Godfrey [*Gofraidh*] (m) Germanic, 'god peace'. A name which was translated into Irish as *Gofraidh, Gothfraidh* and *Gothraidh*. *Gorry* is a variant.

Gordon [*Gordan*] (m) A Scottish surname, thought to be derived from a placename in Berwickshire, which came into use as a first name, first in Scotland then throughout Britain. It became popular in the nineteenth century, chiefly in honour of General Gordon (1833-85).

Gordon was introduced into Ireland from Scotland. The first recorded Irish bearer was a son of Sir Phelim O'Neill, called after the family name of his Scottish grandfather, the Marquess of Huntly.

Gorry (m) Variant of *Godfrey*.

Grace (f) A name used in Ireland to anglicise *Grania*.

Graeme (m) An alternative spelling of *Graham,* recorded in Northern Ireland.

Graham [*Gréachán*] (m) Also *Graeme*. Anglo-Saxon, 'grey home'. The surname of a Scottish family which is now used as a first name. It occurs occasionally in Ireland.

Grania [*Gráinne*] (f) 'grain goddess'. In Irish legend Grania, Finn Mac Cool's betrothed, eloped with Dermot, his follower. Grania Mhaol Ni Mhaolmhaigh, in English, Grace O'Malley was queen of the Western Isles of Ireland in the sixteenth century. The name has been anglicised as *Grace* and *Gertrude*.

Granna (f) Evidently a form of *Grania,* borne by a daughter

of Sir Edward O'Brien, Bt., of Dromoland, who died in 1837.

Gregory [*Greagóir*] (m) Greek, 'watchful one'. The Irish form of the name corresponds to Early English *Gregour,* Scottish *Gregor,* French *Gregoire* and German *Gregor*.

Gruagach (m) An Irish word, deriving ultimately from *gruaig,* 'hair', and meaning literally 'hairy one'. It normally signified 'magician' or 'giant'; but in Omeath, where it was used as a first name, it signified 'hero'.

Gubnet (f) Variant of *Gobinet*.

H

Hamlet (m) This name has been thought to be a form of Germanic *Hamo, Hamon,* 'home', but an alternative etymology has been put forward. The Norsemen, when they came to Ireland, brought with them the name *Olaf,* which was gaelicised as *Amhlaoibh*. It has been suggested that a modified form of this was re-exported to Scandinavia and in due course became Hamlet. Shakespeare has made the name well known, and he gave the variant name, *Hamnet,* to his son.

Hannah (f) A form of *Anne* which was once common in Ireland. It was also used as a pet form of *Johanna* and *Nora*.

Harold [*Aralt*] (m) Germanic, 'army power'. This was introduced into Ireland by the Norsemen, who used the spelling *Harald*. The name was given to Harold's Cross in Dublin.

Hazel (f) A tree name which appears to have been invented in the nineteenth century. It is used from time to time in Ireland.

Heather (f) A plant name which seems to have originated in the nineteenth century, when botanical names became fashionable.

Heber [*Éibhear*] (m) There is a Hebrew name *Heber,* meaning perhaps 'companion', but the Irish Heber is completely unrelated. It may have originated in Cape Clear Island, and it is a phonetic translation into English of the Irish name *Éibhear,* the name of the son of the legendary leader Milesius. Heber was particularly popular in Ulster, and sometimes it was anglicised as *Ivor*.

Hector [*Eachtar*] (m) A Greek name of doubtful meaning which was used to anglicise *Eachann* in Scotland. It occurs occasionally in Ireland.

Helen [*Léan*] (f) Greek, 'bright one'. A name made famous by the legendary Greek beauty. It became popular throughout the Christian world due to St Helena (c. 248-327), mother of Constantine the Great. It is quite frequently bestowed in Ireland, and it is the source of a number of names, e.g. *Elaine* and *Eleanor*. *Nellie,* a pet form, is sometimes used as an independent name.

Helena [*Léana*] (f) The Latin form of *Helen,* used from time to time in Ireland.

Henrietta/Henriette (f) Feminine forms of *Henry,* used occasionally in Ireland in the early part of this century.

Henry [*Anraí*] (m) Germanic, 'home ruler'. A name introduced by the English. It became popular amongst the native population, the Gaelic forms becoming *Anrai, Annraoi, Einri, Hanraoi*. Henry Joy MacCracken was an eighteenth-century Ulster rebel. Today the name is no longer greatly used.

Herbert [*Hoireabard*] (m) Germanic, 'army bright'. This is a rare name in Ireland, but it enjoyed a certain vogue around the turn of the century.

Heremon [*Eireamhón*] (m) In Irish legend, Heremon was the son of Milesius. The name was used on Cape Clear Island, and it was sometimes anglicised as *Irving* or *Irwin*.

Hermon (m) Variant of *Heremon*.

Hewney [*Uaithne*] (m) An early name, sometimes anglicised as *Anthony*. *Oney, Owney* and *Oyney* are variant forms.

Hierlath (m) Variant of *Jarlath*.

Hiero (m) Greek, 'holy'. St Hiero (died 885) was an Irish martyr.

Hilary [*Hioláir*] (m, f) Latin, 'joyful'. A name occasionally used in Ireland. The Irish form may have been influenced by French *Hilaire*.

Hilda [*Hilde*] (f) Anglo-Saxon, probably 'war'. This is not a common name in Ireland.

Hisolda (f) Variant of *Iseult*.

Hodierna (f) A name which is perhaps taken from the Latin liturgy and used for children born about the time of the Epiphany. It has been used in Ireland, e.g. Hodierna de Gernon was granddaughter of the last king of Connacht.

Honor (f) Latin, 'honour'. A name brought to Ireland by the Normans. It became popular, giving rise to the native form *Nora(h)*. *Ohnicio* and *Onora* are variants.

Honora (f) Variant of *Honor*.

Honoria (f) Perhaps a variant of *Honor*. *Hanoria* may be a further variant.

Hubert [*Hoibeard*] (m) Germanic, 'mind bright'. An uncommon name in Ireland. The Gaelic form was sometimes translated *Hugh*.

Hugh [*Aodh*] (m) Germanic, perhaps 'heart'. In both Ireland and Scotland Hugh was used to translate *Aodh*. In Ireland it was also used to translate *Hoibeard*, the Gaelic for *Hubert*. It is now quite widespread.

Humphrey [*Unfrai*] (m) A Germanic folk name *Huni*, 'peace'. Unfrai is the true Irish form, but Humphrey has been used as a translation of *Amhlaoibh*, the Irish form of *Olaf*. Humphrey O'Sullivan (*c.* 1780-1837) was an Irish language diarist. It is not a common name today.

Hyacinth (m) Greek, 'purple'. A name formerly used in Ireland, presumably to translate a native name.

I

Ian [*Ion*] (m) This name represents *Iain*, the Scottish Gaelic form of *John*, cognate with Irish Gaelic *Eoin*. It is ocasionally used in Ireland. The Irish language form, *Ion*, is taken from the diary of Humphrey O'Sullivan (*c.* 1780-1837).

Ibernia (f) Variant of *Hibernia*.

Ida (f) Variant of *Ita*. There is also a Germanic name *Ida*, used in England in the Middle Ages and revived there in the nineteenth century – a revival which may have influenced the increase in use of the Irish *Ida*.

Ierne (f) The Greek name for Ireland. It has been recorded as a given name.

Ignatius [*Éigneachán*] (m) The name Ignatius, sometimes explained as meaning 'fiery one', is in fact of unknown derivation. The Spanish form, *Inigo*, became the form used in Britain, while the Latin *Ignatius* became popular in Ireland, no doubt due to St Ignatius Loyola (1548-98), founder of the Jesuits. It was equated with the native name *Éigneachán* or *Igneachán* which, according to O'Hart,

means 'force person'. St Ignatius' College is a well-known Jesuit school in Galway.

Ina [*Aghna*] (f) Perhaps an Irish form of *Agnes*.

Ion (m) This name may be Greek *Ion*, 'moon man'. It has been explained as a variant of *Ian*, but this seems unlikely; and it is even less likely to be *Ion*, the Basque form of *John*. It was used in the *Trant* family in the nineteenth century.

Irene (f) Greek, 'peace'. A name which was used by the Byzantines and imported into England in the late nineteenth century. It presumably spread from there to Ireland. It is sometimes pronounced with two syllables; sometimes with three, as in the original Greek.

Irial (m) An early name which, Woulfe informs us, was used chiefly by the *O'Farrells, O'Kennedys* and *O'Loughlans*.

Irving (m) Anglo-Saxon, 'sea friend'. A name used to anglicise *Heremon*.

Irwin (m) Variant of *Irving*, also used to anglicise *Heremon*.

Isaac [*Iosóg*] (m) Hebrew, 'he may laugh'. A rare name in Ireland. *The Annals of the Four Masters* note the death of an Isaac O Maolfoghmair in 1235. The name was used in the *Glenny* family of Co. Down. *Iosac* and *Iosoc* are Irish language variants.

Isabel [*Isibéal*] (f) The French seem to have bestowed the translation *Isabelle* on Elizabeth of Hainault, wife of Philip Augustus (1165-1223). King John (1167-1216) married Isabelle of Angouleme, and she brought the name to England. The forms Isabel and *Isabella* took root there, and spread to Ireland, becoming the first versions of *Elizabeth* to be used there. See also *Sybil*.

Isabella (f) A variant of *Isabel* which was very popular in Ireland at the turn of the century, but is much less so now.

Iseult (f) According to Arthurian legend, Iseult, the lover of Tristram (or Tristan), was an Irish princess. The name is perhaps Germanic, 'ice rule'; perhaps Welsh, 'beautiful to see'. Yonge regards it as essentially the same name as *Adsaluta*, the name of a Celtic goddess. Iseult occurs in Ireland in modern times, no doubt because of its Irish associations. *Isolda, Hisolda, Yseult, Ysolte* and *Izett* are variants.

Isleen (f) Variant of *Ashling*.

Ismenia (f) This name may be of Irish origin, and it was certainly used in Ireland up to 1800. *Ismena* is a variant.

Ismey (f) A name of doubtful origin. It is possibly Irish and it was used in Ireland in the eighteenth century. *Ismay* is a variant.

Isolda (f) Variant of *Iseult*.

Ita [*Ide*] (f) 'thirst'. St Ita was associated with Killeedy in Co. Limerick, and her name is used in Ireland today. *Ida* is a variant.

Ivan (m) The Russian, Ukrainian and Bulgarian form of *John*, sometimes used in western countries. It has been recorded in Ireland.

Ivo (m) Germanic, 'yew'. A name, cognate with French *Yves*, which has been used in Ireland in the de Vesci family.

Ivor [*Iomhar*] (m) This name probably comes from Norse *Ivarr*, the name of a number of kings of Dublin. However, there was an Irish saint called *Ibhar* who antedated the Norsemen. Ivor was also used to anglicise *Éibhear* (see *Heber*).

Izett (f) A form of *Iseult*, perhaps peculiar to Ireland. It was recorded in 1891.

J

Jacinta (f) From Greek, 'purple'. This is the Spanish form of a Greek name. It is sometimes found in Ireland.

James [*Séamus*] (m) This name is widely used in Ireland, though recently its use has declined considerably. It is found in both its Irish and English forms, and in its pet form, *Jamie*. Ultimately it is a form of *Jacob*, in Hebrew *Aqob*, of uncertain meaning. In medieval Latin it became *Jacomus*, in Spanish *Jaime*, and in English *James*. For further information on its use in Ireland, see *Seamus*. *Iamus* is an Irish form used in the *Annals of Connacht*.

Jamie (m) Originally a pet form of *James*, chiefly associated with Scotland. On a number of occasions recently it has been given as an independent name in Ireland.

Jana (f) This unusual name is a feminine form of *John*. It was employed in the *Lowther* family of Co. Meath. *Jan,* another feminine form of John, has been noted in Northern Ireland.

Jane [*Sinéad*] (f) A well-known feminine form of *John*, coming ultimately from Old French *Jehane*, and gaelicised as *Sinéad*. Its popularity has declined greatly since 1900, but it is still quite widely used.

Janet [*Sinéidin*] (f) A diminutive of *Jane*.

Janice (f) A form of *Jane* sometimes used in Ireland.

Jarlath [*Iarfhlaith*] (m) 'tributary lord'. St Jarlath (died 550) established the bishopric of Tuam. *Hierlath* is a variant.

Jarmy (m) A form of *Dermot* employed by the *O'Kanes* and the *O'Mullans*. This name is a half-way point between *Dermot* and its anglicisation, *Jeremiah*.

Jason [*Iasan*] (m) Greek, 'healer'. The name of the leader of the Argonauts. It is rapidly becoming a fashionable name in Ireland, and is now widespread.

Jasper [*Geaspar*] (m) A name of unknown meaning. According to tradition it was the name of one of the Magi. It has been used in Ireland, but it is now rare. *Gasper* is a variant.

Jean [*Sine*] (f) A Scottish feminine form of *John* which is used from time to time in Ireland. See also *Sheena*.

Jeffrey (m) Variant of *Geoffrey*.

Jennifer (f) It means 'white wave'. The Cornish form of *Guinevere*, the name of the wife of King Arthur. It is frequently bestowed in Ireland today.

Jeremiah [*Irimias*] (m) Hebrew, 'may God exalt'. The name of an Old Testament prophet, used in Ireland to anglicise *Dermot*. It was once frequently used but it is now much rarer.

Jeremy (m) The English form of *Jeremiah* which has sometimes been used in Ireland.

Jerome (m) Greek, 'holy name'. St Jerome (*c.* 347-419) translated the Bible into the Latin version known as the Vulgate. The true Irish forms are *Cirine* and *Iarom*, but Jerome has generally been used in Ireland as an anglicisation of *Dermot*.

Joan [*Siobhán*] (f) A feminine form of *John*, coming from Latin *Jo(h)anna*. It was brought to Ireland by the Anglo-Normans and was gaelicised as *Siobhán*, of which *Siún* is a somewhat slurred variant.

Joanna (f) A form of *Joan*, once fairly popular, but it has now given way to *Joanne*.

Joanne (f) A recent feminine version of *John*, formed from *Joan* or *Joanna*. It is now thoroughly established in Ireland.

Johanna (f) A feminine form of *John*, once popular but now obsolescent. *Hannah* was a pet form.

John [*Seán*] (m) Hebrew, 'God has favoured'. An enormous number of Irishmen have borne either this name or one of its Irish forms: *Eoin, Sean, Seon, Shaun, Shawn* or *Shane*. Feminine forms of John include *Jane, Jean, Joan, Johanna, Joanna, Shona* and *Jana*.

Jonah [*Íona*] (m) Hebrew, 'dove'. A name occasionally used in Ireland. Jonah Barrington was an eighteenth century Irish writer.

Jonathan [*Ionatán*] (m) Hebrew, 'God's gift'. The first name of the Irish writer, Jonathan Swift (1667-1745). Jonathan Chetwood was a member of the Irish Parliament in 1797. Jonathan is increasingly popular in Ireland today.

Joseph [*Seosamh*] (m) Hebrew, 'God added'. Woulfe notes that this name was only becoming really popular in Ireland in his day – his book, *Irish Names for Children,* appeared in 1923. Its use as a first name is due to St Joseph, husband of the Blessed Virgin. There was an Irish St Joseph, bishop of Tallaght. The usual Irish form is *Seosamh;* others are *Iosaf, Iosep, Ioseph, Seacas, Seosap* and *Seosaph*.

Josephine [*Seosaimhín*] (f) A name which derives from the Empress Josephine (1763-1814), wife of Napoleon, whose real name was *Josepha* (French *Josèphe*).

Joyce (f) A name occasionally used in Ireland. It is a feminine form of the Celtic masculine name *Jodoc,* once used in Brittany.

Judith (f) Hebrew, 'Jewess'. A name used to anglicise *Sile* (see *Sheila*) and *Siobhan*.

Julia [*Iúile*] (f) A Roman name, a feminine of *Julius*, which is of uncertain meaning. It was used to anglicise the Irish names, *Sile* (see *Sheila*) and *Siobhan*.

Julie (f) A pet form of *Juliet*, now sometimes used as an independent name, and becoming increasingly popular.

Juliet (f) A feminine form of *Julius*, popularised by Shakespeare's *Romeo and Juliet*.

Junan/Junanan (m) Variants of *Adamnan*.

Juno (f) A Latin name which may mean 'young', and the name of the queen of the Roman gods. It was used in Ireland to anglicise *Una*, but its true Irish forms are *Iunainn* and *Itúnó*. Sean O'Casey used the name in his play *Juno and the Paycock* (1924).

Justin (m) Latin, 'just'. In Ireland this name was equated with *Saerbhreathach*, 'noble judge'. It is frequently used in the *MacCarthy* family.

Juverna (f) A Latin name for Ireland, used occasionally as a first name.

K

Kane (m) Use of Kane as a first name presumably comes from the surname. *Kane* is a common surname in Ulster, translating the Gaelic *O Cathain*, while is the Isle of Man it translates *MacCathian*. It may sometimes derive from the feminine first name *Keina*, perhaps Welsh, signifying 'beautiful'. At other times, it may derive from the placename *Caen,* or from Anglo-Saxon *Cana*. *Kane* is becoming a popular first name in Australia.

Karen (f) A form of *Katherine*, ultimately of Danish origin. It is now well established in Ireland. The pleasant combination of *Karen-Ann* has been recorded in Northern Ireland.

Kate (f) A pet form of *Katherine* sometimes given as a separate name.

Katherine [*Catraoine*] (f) A Greek name of uncertain meaning, sometimes mistakenly connected with *katharos*, 'pure'. The name was brought to Western Europe in the Middle Ages by returning crusaders, and it became established in Ireland. *Kate* and *Katie* are pet forms which have both been used independently. Other forms include *Catherine, Kathleen, Karen,* and *Catriona*.

Kathleen [*Caitlín*] (f) A form of *Katherine* now closely identified with Ireland. The Spanish form of Katherine was *Catalina;* the Old French form was *Cateline;* and these were presumably related to the Middle English *Catlin,* whence the Irish *Kathleen, Cathleen*.

Kean (m) Variant of *Cian* (see *Cain).*

Keelan (m) Variant of *Killian.*

Keith (m) A Scottish placename, used first as a surname and then as a first name. It has recently become quite popular with Irish parents.

Kellach (m) Variant of *Ceallach,* 'strife' (now obsolete).

Kelly (f) An Irish surname which is now used as a feminine first name. Its meaning is uncertain. In the case of the surname *O'Kelly* it probably derived from *ceallach,* 'strife', but the O' Kellys were distinct from the *MacKellys* of East Connacht.

There is also the possibility that it comes from Kelly in Devon, a placename meaning 'wood', or from a couple of Scottish placenames. There is, in addition, a Manx surname Kelly, of Gaelic origin.

Kennedy [*Cinneide*] (m) Although Wolfe gives this name as meaning 'helmeted head', it in fact means 'ugly head'. It is better known as a surname than as a first name, but it was none the less used as a first name in Ireland in the Middle Ages. King Kennedy of Munster was the father of Brian Boru, as a result of which it came to be employed in the *O'Brien* family.

Kenneth [*Cionaod*] (m) This name is usually associated more with Scotland than Ireland, but it seems to have been quite popular in Ireland during the Middle Ages in the form of *Cinaed.* The Name *Coinneach* (English, *Canice)* was also translated into English as Kenneth. Kenneth Mac Alpine (died *c.* 860) was king of Scots, whose reign united the Picts with the decendants of the Irish settlers in Scotland. *Cinaeth* O Hartagain (died 975) was an Irish poet.

Kenny (m) Variant of *Canice.*

Kerill [*Coireall*] (m) An Irish name which has been anglicised as *Cyril.*

Kermit (m) Variant of *Dermot.*

Kerry (f) An Irish placename now used as a girls' first name. Amongst the Boston Irish it is regarded as a form of *Katherine.*

Kevan [*Caomhán*] (m) 'little handsome one'. A name that was on occasion 'disguised' by Latin *Pulcherius,* 'beautiful one'.

Kevin [*Caoimhín*] (m) 'comely birth'. St Kevin (died *c.* 618), a Leinsterman, founded the monastery of Glendalough. The name is becoming more and more popular in Ireland.

Kian (m) Variant of *Cian.*

Kieran [*Ciarán*] (m) 'little dark one'. St Kieran was an Irish bishop who, it is said, may have antedated St Patrick and been a hermit at Saighiar. St Kieran's birthplace was Cape Clear, a vicinity particularly associated with this first name. Another St Keiran founded the great monastery of Clonmacnoise. The name in both its English and Irish forms is popular today. *Kieron, Queran* and *Kyran* are variants.

Kieron (m) A spelling variant of *Kieran.*

Killian [*Cillian*] (m) A diminutive of *ceallach* 'strife'. St Killian was an early martyr at Wurzburg. The name is still in use in modern times. *Keelan* is a variant.

Kyran (m) Variant of *Kieran.*

Kyras (m) A curious name, perhaps peculiar to Ireland. It may be a form *Cyrus* (=Persian, 'enthroned'). Kyras Tully (died 1637) was dean of Clonfert.

L

Laetitia (f) A variant spelling of *Letitia.*

Laoghaire (m) 'calf-herder'. Laoghaire, king of Tara, was said to have had a confrontation with St Patrick. The name is pronounced something like *Leary.* Dun Laoghaire ('Laoghaire's Fort') is the name of an important town in Ireland, south of Dublin.

Laughlin (m) A spelling variant of *Loughlin.*

Laura (f) Latin, 'laurel'. A name sometimes used in Ireland.

Laurence [*Labhrás*] (m) Latin, 'of Laurentum'. This name was used to translate the name of St *Lorcan* (Laurence) O'Toole (died 1180). Lawrence was introduced into Ireland by the Anglo-Normans and became in Irish *Labhrás.*

Leila [*Lil*] (f) A saint's name of obscure meaning. It is possibly connected with the Laelian gens of Rome, but this seems unlikely. It is a very old name which continues in use today.

Leo [*Leon*] (m) Latin, 'lion'. This name was adopted in Ireland when Gioacchino Vincenzo Pecci (1810-1903) became Pope Leo XIII in 1873. It was readily translated into Irish as *Leon,* the Irish word for a lion, and it is now firmly established.

Letitia (f) Latin, 'joy'. *Laetitia* is also found. In Ireland it is translated as *Eilis,* which is in fact Irish for *Elizabeth.* A variant *Lettice* was recorded in Ireland in 1711.

Lewis (m) The English form of *Louis,* sometimes used in Ireland to anglicise the native names of *Laoiseach* (see *Lysagh*) and *Lughaidh.*

Lewy (m) A phonetic English rendering of the Irish name *Lughaidh.*

Liam (m) The Irish form of *William,* now widespread. It is, of course, the second syllable of William, which was once translated as *Uilliam,* a name also used for the fox, corresponding to *Reynard* in English. The form *Bhullaidh* (pronounced *Wully)* was sometimes used for King William III (1650-1792). Liam was originally a pet form, but it is now established as the Irish translation. *Liam na Lasoige* is an Irish name for the Will o' the Wisp or *ignis fatuus.*

Lily [*Lile*] (f) A plant name coming from the Latin name for the flower.

Linda (f) A name derived from German *Lind,* 'serpent', 'snake', which is now becoming quite popular in Ireland. It is supposed – wrongly – to be connected with Spanish *linda,* 'pretty'. The variant *Lynda* is also found. An early Irish masculine name, *Nathair,* has exactly the same meaning. By tradition the serpent signifies wisdom.

Lisa (f) Originally a pet form of *Elizabeth,* but now an independent name. It is increasingly popular in Ireland today.

Lloyd (m) Welsh, 'grey'. A name sometimes found in Ireland.

Lorcan [*Lorcán*] (m) 'little fierce one'. St Lorcan O'Toole (died 1180) was one of Ireland's most famous saints. He was abbot of Glendalough and later, at the time of the Norman Invasion of Ireland (1169), he was archbishop of Dublin.

Lorna (f) A name invented by R. D. Blackmore for his novel *Lorna Doone* (1869). It is sometimes found in Ireland.

Lorraine (f) A French placename which is quite popular as a first name in Ireland. Lorraine was the birthplace of St Joan of Arc, and the name is associated with her. It was originally known as the Kingdom of Lotharingia, deriving from *Lothair,* son of King Clovis of the Franks, whose name meant 'hear people'. He ruled from 855.

Loughlin [*Lochlainn*] (m) Lochlainn was originally the name of a land in Irish legend, then it was applied to the homeland of the Norsemen. The first name Loughlin may spring originally from *MacLochlainn,* 'son of the Scandinavian'. It became widespread in Ireland. *Lochlann* was a variant in Irish. *Laughlin,* a variant in English, was also used to translate *Leachlainn,* a short form of *Maeleachlainn* (see *Melaghlin, Malachy).* There is a similar Scottish name, *Lachlan,* probably 'heroic', 'warriorlike', from Gaelic *laoch.*

Louis (m) Germanic, 'hear fight'. French *Louis* was translated as *Lewis* in England, but Louis itself was used in Ireland to translate the native names *Lughaidh* and *Lysagh.* It comes from the same root as *Clovis,* the name of a Frankish king. Other variants are *Lodowick, Ludovic,* and *Lutwidge.* In Wales the name was used to anglicise *Llewelyn* (*Lamhailín* in Irish), a name of uncertain meaning.

Louisa (f) A variant of *Louise,* popular at the turn of the century. It has now given way to Louise.

Louise [*Labhaoise*] (f) The feminine form of *Louis* which probably spread to Ireland from England where it was first noted in 1646. The Irish *Labhaoise* indicates that *Louisa* was the earliest form to occur in Ireland – Louisa was the usual form of the name in eighteenth-century England, and it was probably introduced to Ireland at about this time.

Lúcán (m) A derivative of Latin *Lucius* was *Lucianus,* which, as a cognomen, became *Lucanus.* This cognomen was borne by the poet Lucan, author of *De Bello Civilis,* popularly called the *Pharsalia,* and known to Irish readers as *In Cath Catharda.* His name is presumably the origin of the Irish *Lúcán.*

Lucius (m) This name probably comes from Latin *lux,* 'light'. It is firmly established in Ireland, where it is used to anglicise *Lachtna* and *Laoiseach* (see *Lysagh).* The Hibernian Sir Lucius O'Trigger appears in Sheridan's *The Rivals* (1775).

Lucy (f) A feminine form of *Lucius,* and the name of a third-century Sicilian virgin and martyr. In Ireland the name was equated with *Luighseach,* the feminine form of *Lughaidh.* The Italian form *Lucia* has also been noted in Ireland.

Lugh (m) Lugh Lamhfhada ('of the Long Arm') was the name of an early Irish hero of the Tuatha De Danaan who slew Balor of the Evil Eye. It is thought that he may originally have been a deity, perhaps imported from overseas – in the legend he travels to Ireland by boat. Lugh may in fact be identical with the continental Celtic god *Lugos* who gave his name to *Lughdunum* (modern Lyons).

Lughaidh (m) An early name for which the *O'Clery* family seem to have had an especial liking. It was anglicised as

Louis, with which it coincides in pronunciation, and also as *Aloysius* and *Lewis,* the Provencal and English forms of that name.

Luke [*Lúcás*] (m) Greek, 'of Lucania'. A name which owes its popularity to St Luke. In England the name was established by the twelfth century, and it was probably brought from there to Ireland by the Anglo-Normans.

Lysagh [*Laoiseach*] (m) 'of Laois'. Laois is a county of Central Ireland – sometimes known by its English name, Leix – which was formerly called Queen's County. The change of name came after Independence. *Lysagh/ Laoiseach* was anglicised as *Lewis* or *Louis.*

M

Mabbina (f) This curious Irish name is perhaps an elaborate form of *Mabel.* It was used to anglicise *Maeve.*

Mabel [*Maible*] (f) An English form of the Latin name *Amabel,* which probably means 'lovable'. It has been used to anglicise *Maeve.*

Macanisius (m) 'son of Nis'. St Patrick was said to have consecrated St Macanisius (died 514), an early bishop.

Macartan (m) 'son of Cartan'. According to legend St Macartan was made bishop of Clogher by St Patrick.

Macha (f) 'plain'. The name of a legendary queen of Ireland.

Macmahon [*MacMathúna*] (m) An Irish surname used as a first name. The everyday word 'mayonnaise' ultimately derives from this name.

Madeline [*Madailein*] (f) The form of *Magdalen,* 'of Magdala', chiefly used in Ireland. Its English equivalent is *Madeleine.* The name is taken from St Mary Magdalen in the New Testament.

Madog (m) A Welsh form of the Irish name *Mogue,* occasionally found in Ireland.

Maelisa [*Maolíosa*] (m) 'servant of Jesus'. This name is cognate with the Scottish *Malise. Jesus* – Latin, 'God is salvation' (Hebrew *Jehoshua,* Aramaic *Yishu,* Greek *Iesous)* – is not itself used in Ireland, though it is found in some countries. The Irish form is *Íosa.* Jesus is a form of *Joshua* (Irish *Iósua),* a name which has been occasionally used in Ireland. In Hellenistic times Jews named *Joshua* equated the name with *Jason.*

Maeve [*Meadhbh*] (f) Perhaps, 'intoxicating one'. The name of the legendary queen of Connacht, who led an invasion of Ulster and was held at bay by Cuchulain until help arrived. Maeve may originally have been a goddess. Attempts to identify her with the English fairy queen Mab have not proved successful. Connacht was termed *Crioch Mheadhbha* ('Maeve's territory') and *Cuige Meadhbha* ('Maeve's province'). *Meave* is a spelling variant. *Mabbina, Mabel, Margery* and *Maude* have been used as anglicisations, but Maeve is used in its own right in modern times. Maeve Binchy, the *Irish Times* columnist, is a modern example.

Maggie (f) A pet form of *Margaret.* It was occasionally used an as independent name in Ireland in the early part of the twentieth century.

Mago (m) A name used in the Kilrush and Dingle areas. It is now probably obsolete, but it appears to have been a form of *Manus.*

Maguire [*MacUidhir*] (m) A surname of a prominent sept of *Fermanagh* which was used as a first name. *Mac* signifies 'son' and *uidhir* is the genitive of *odhar,* 'dun-coloured'.

Mahon [*Mathghamhain*] (m) 'bear'. Mahon was a medieval king of Munster (died 978), the brother of Brian Boru. The name was often anglicised as *Matthew*. It corresponds to a number of names in other languages: Latin *Ursus*, American-Indian *Hatiya*. Scandinavian *Bjorn* and German *Berno*.

Maille (f) Perhaps this is a native Irish name. It has been translated as *Molly*.

Mailsi (f) Perhaps a native name. It has been translated as *Margery* and *Molly*.

Mairona (f) A diminutive of *Máire*, the Irish for *Mary*.

Maiti (f) Nothing at all is known about this peculiar Irish name, which is pronounced in English as *Matty*. One might tentatively suggest that it is a feminine form of *Matthew*, or a form of *Matilda*.

Majella (f) This name, sometimes found as a first name in modern Ireland, is presumably the surname of St Gerard Majella.

Malachy (m) Hebrew, 'my messenger'. This is the Irish form of the name *Malachi* or *Malachias*. Malachy was used to anglicise *Melaghlin*, the name of two high kings of Ireland, and *Maolmaodhog*, the name of St Malachy (1095-1148), bishop of Armagh. It is still used in Ireland today.

Malcolm [*Maolcholm*] (m) 'servant of St Columba'. This Gaelic name is far more Scottish than Irish, even though it commemorates one of the most celebrated Irish saints. Yonge notes that strange latinisation *Milcolumbus*. Its widespread use in England is modern, but it has been known there from early times: a *Malcolum* is mentioned in the Domesday Book (1086).

Malone (m) An Irish surname meaning 'servant of St John', which at times may have become confused with Muldoon, 'servant of the fort'. Edward Malone (1741-1812) was a famous Irish Shakespearean scholar. Loughead notes its use as a first name.

Malvina (f) Perhaps a derivation of Gaelic *maol*, 'servant' or 'handmaid'. The name is an invention of James Macpherson. In his Ossianic poems (1765) Malvina is the lover of Oscar, grandson of Finn MacCool (see *Finn)*. It has been used as a Christian name.

Manasses (m) Hebrew, 'one who makes forget'. In Derry an unsuccessful attempt was made to use this name to translate *Manus*.

Mane (m) Apparently a form of *Manus*.

Mannix (m) A name used in Ireland to anglicise *Munchin*.

Manus [*Mánús*] (m) Latin, 'great'. Charlemagne (742-814) was known in Latin as *Carolus Magnus*, and Magnus was adopted as a name by the Scandinavians who introduced it to Ireland. In Irish the *g* was eventually left unpronounced. It was particularly popular in Donegal and is still in use to this day. Magnus has been recorded in Northern Ireland. An attempt to anglicise Manus as *Manasses* in the Derry region failed. *Moses* was sometimes used to anglicise it. *Mane* is possibly a variant.

Maolmadhog [*Maolmaodhog*] (m) 'servant of St Mogue'. The Irish name of St *Malachy*.

Marcella [*Mairsile*] (f) A feminine diminutive of *Mark*, probably introduced into Ireland from France.

Margaret [*Mairéad*] (f) Greek 'pearl'. A name introduced into Scotland and England by St Margaret (*c*. 1046-93), queen of Scots, who was born in Hungary, where the name was familiar. The Anglo-Normans introduced it to Ireland and it became very popular. It is now declining sharply. The pet forms are *Peg* and *Peggy* (Irish *Peig* and *Peigi)* and *Maggie*. *Margot* and *Rita* are variants sometimes encountered in Ireland.

Margery (f) From *Margerie*, a French form of *Margaret*. Margery has been used in England since the thirteenth century. It has been also used in Ireland, sometimes to anglicise *Maeve* and *Mailsi*.

Maria [*Máiría*] (f) The Latin form of *Mary*, sometimes used in Ireland.

Marie (f) The French form of *Mary*.

Marion [*Muireann*] (f) A diminutive of *Mary*. In Ireland it was used to anglicise *Muireann*, 'long-haired' (see *Morrin)*.

Mark [*Marcas*] (m) Perhaps a derivative of *Mars*, the name of the Roman god of war, rendered in Irish as *Mars* and *Mart*. Its meaning is uncertain: Greek *marakos*, 'tender'; Latin *mas*, 'male'; and Celtic *marc*, 'horse' have also been suggested as possible origins. The name is international. It was introduced to Ireland by the Anglo-Normans, but it did not become a favourite until modern times. *Marcella* is a feminine diminutive

Marmaduke (m) This name, used also in the north of England, may be of Irish origin. The Domesday Book (1085-6) mentions the name *Melmidoc*, which is possibly an early form, and this readily translates into Irish as *Maelmaedoc*, 'servant of *Maedoc* (=? *Mogue)*.

Martha [*Márta*] (f) This name is possibly a feminine of *mar*, the Aramaic work for 'lord'. It has been used to anglicise *More*.

Martin [*Máirtín*] (m) Probably a derivative of *Mars*. St Martin of Tours (*c*. 316-397) was reputed to be related to St Patrick, and the name became a popular one in Ireland. In England it tended to die out after the Reformation. The earlier Irish form was *Martán*, but Martin was imported by the Normans in the twelfth century.

Martina (f) A feminine form of *Martin*, popular amongst Irish parents of the mid-seventies.

Mary [*Máire*] (f) Probably the most widespread girls' name in Ireland, though at present its popularity is rapidly declining. It represents Hebrew, *Miriam;* Greek, *Mariam;* Latin, *Maria*. It is of uncertain derivation: the Hebrew root may be *rama*, 'long for'.

The name of the Blessed Virgin was little used in Ireland before the seventeenth century, probably due to reverence. Indeed, even today in the Irish language *Máire* is the usual form employed, *Muire* being reserved for the Blessed Virgin. *Miriam*, the name of the sister of Moses in the Old Testament, is occasionally found, as are the Latin and French forms: *Maria, Marie*. Diminutives include *Marion* and *Mairona*. *Molly, Mollie* and *Polly* are pet forms which have been used independently. *Moira* seems to be an attempt to anglicise *Máire*. *Mears* was an Irish form of the name used in Kerry, clearly derived from the English Mary. See also *Maura* and *Maurya*.

Mary is sometimes given as a boys' middle name in Ireland, a custom also found in Spain and Italy.

Matadin (m) Also *Matudan*. A derivative of the early Irish *matad* (modern Irish *mada*), 'dog'. The Norse name *Modan* may have been a variant of this.

Matilda [*Maitilde*] (f) Germanic, 'might strife'. The Normans introduced this name to England, and it spread from there to Ireland.

Matthew [*Matha*] (m) Hebrew, 'God's present'. The name of one of the Apostles. It was translated into Irish as *Matha* and *Maitiú* – the latter, perhaps influenced by French *Matheu*, tended to become confused with *Matthias*, which has the same derivation. Matthew was used in Ireland to anglicise *Mahon*.

Matthias [*Maitias*] (m) A variant of *Matthew* which is sometimes found in Ireland.

Matudan (m) Variant of *Matadin*.

Maude [*Máda*] (f) A Norman form of *Matilda*, coming from Flemish *Mahault*. It was used in Ireland to anglicise *Maeve*.

Maughold (m) 'son of Caldus'. St Patrick is said to have converted St Maughold (died *c.* 488), who became a bishop on the Isle of Man.

Maura (f) A feminine form of Latin *Maurus*, 'Moor'. In Ireland it is regarded as a form of *Mary*.

Maureen [*Máirín*] (f) A diminutive of *Máire*, the Irish for *Mary*. Mary itself is losing ground, but Maureen is increasingly used. It may have been reinforced by *Moreen*, a name of quite different origin. Maureen is frequently used in the United States and England.

Maurice [*Muiris*] (m) Latin, 'Moor'. A name used in Ireland amongst the Anglo-Normans. It has assimilated the native Irish name *Muirgheas*, 'sea choice'. *Moss* and *Mossy* are pet forms.

Maurine (f) Perhaps a variant of *Maureen*.

Maurya (f) A phonetic rendering of *Máire* used by J. M. Synge in his play *Riders to the Sea* (1904).

Maziere (m) A name employed in the *Brady* family. The earliest traced bearer is Sir Maziere Brady, Bt. (1796-1871). The name seems confined to this Irish family.

Meave (f) Variant of *Maeve*.

M(a)el [*Maol*] (m) 'servant'. A name occasionally used in Ireland. It is often found as a prefix in longer names, e.g. *Maelisa*.

Melaghlin [*Maeleachlaihn*] (m) 'servant of St Secundinus'. Melaghlin is the true English form of Maeleachlainn, but *Malachy* was commonly used to translate it, and at present it seems to have completely replaced it. *Miles* was occasionally used as a translation.

Melchior [*Meilseoir*] (m) A name of eastern origin, perhaps meaning 'king'. It was said to have been the name of one of the Magi. In Ireland it was found in the vicinity of Youghal, Co. Cork.

Melissa (f) Greek, 'bee'. A name sometimes found in Ireland.

Merna (f) Variant of *Myrna*.

Meyler (m) A name derived from Welsh *Meilir* which was used to translate *Maelmuire*, 'servant of St Mary'. It now seems to be obsolete.

Miach (m) The name of the son of the pagan Irish god, Diancecht. It is perhaps derived from Latin *medicus*, 'physician'.

Michael [*Micheál*] (m) Hebrew, 'who is like God?' The name given to one of the archangels. In Ireland it only came into use after the sixteenth century, but it then became so common that many people look on it as a particularly Irish name.

The Irish form, Micheál, was given the phonetic rendering of *Meehaul* by James Stephens in his novel *The Crock of Gold* (1912). *Mick* is a common pet form, which in slang has come to mean an Irishman, and in the British Army the Irish Guards are referred to as 'the Micks'. *Mickey*, another pet form, has found fame in Walt Disney's creation, Mickey Mouse. Disney had the name's Irish associations in mind when he gave it to his celebrated character. *Mike* is an international pet form. Less common is *Mikey*, a form used in T. H. White's hilarious Irish novel, *The Elephant and the Kangaroo* (1947). *Miche* is a rare pet form.

Michan (m) St Michan was a Dublin monk. His name was given to St Michan's Church in the city.

Michelle (f) A French feminine version of *Michael* which seems popular amongst modern Irish parents. *Michele* is an alternative spelling. *Michaela*, another feminine form of Michael, also occurs.

Miles (m) A name of unknown meaning. It was used in Ireland as the equivalent of *Melaghlin*, *Maelmuire* and *Maolmordha*. *Meidhligh* was a Derry form of Miles, recasting the name into Irish. *Myles* is a spelling variant.

Milesius [*Mile*] (m) The name of the legendary leader of the invasion of Ireland by the Celts or Milesians. He was called *Míle Easpáin*, which may represent Latin *Miles Hispaniae*, 'soldier of Spain'.

Milo (m) The Old German form of *Miles*, used in Ireland to anglicise the same names.

Miranda (f) Latin, 'admirable'. This name was invented by Shakespeare for his play *The Tempest*. It is occasionally used in Ireland.

Mogue [*Maodhóg*] (m) A pet form of *Aidan* given to St Aidan of Ferns (died 626). The name was adopted into Welsh as *Madog*. In Ireland it was anglicised as *Aidan* by Protestants, and *Moses* by Catholics.

Moina (f) Boyer lists this as an Irish name, meaning perhaps 'noble'. She gives *Moyna* as an alternative spelling.

Moira (f) This seems to be an anglicised spelling of *Máire*. The name has spread to England. It was used as the name of a character in the novel *The Way Women Love* (1877) by E. Owens Blackburn. *Moyra* is a variant.

Molan [*Maolanfaidh*] (m) 'servant of storm'. The name of St Molan of Lismore (died 697).

Molly [*Maili*] (f) Originally a pet form of *Mary*, but now sometimes used independently. Molly was used to translate the native names *Maille* and *Mailsi*.

Mona(t) [*Muadhnait*] (f) 'little noble one'. A name used in its own right and also as a pet form of *Monica*.

Monica [*Moncha*] (f) The meaning of this name is uncertain; it is perhaps Greek 'alone' or Latin 'counsellor'. St Monica was the mother of St Augustine of Hippo (335-430). *Mona* is a pet form.

More [*Mór*] (f) 'great'. Once a widespread Irish name. It has been anglicised as *Agnes*, *Mary* and *Martha*.

Moreen [*Móirín*] (f) A diminutive of *More* which perhaps became confused with *Maureen*.

Morgan (m) Welsh, perhaps 'sea-born'. In Ireland this name was used to anglicise the native names, *Murchadh* and its West Connacht variant, *Brochadh*.

Morna [*Muirne*] (f) 'affection', 'beloved'. This was the name of Morna Dunroon, heroine of Harriet Jay's novel *The Dark Colleen* (1876). It has been used as a first name. *Myrna* is a variant, popular in the United States.

Morolt (m) In Arthurian legend Morolt was the brother of Iseult, princess of Ireland. The name is perhaps a form of *Murrough*.

Morrin [*Múireann*] (f) 'long haired'. This early Irish name has been anglicised as *Marion,* or even *Madge,* a pet form of *Margaret. Muirinn* was an Irish language variant.

Mortimer (m) Originally a surname, Mortimer derives from Mortemer, a place name in Normandy. In Ireland it is used to anglicise *Murtagh* and *Murrough.*

Moses [*Maoise*] (m) A name, possibly of Egyptian origin, signifying 'child'. It was used in Ireland to anglicise *Mogue* and *Manus.* Amongst the Anglo-Irish, Moses was used in the *Hill* family.

Moyra (f) A spelling variant of *Moira.*

Mugain (f) A feminine form of *mogh,* 'slave'. This was the name of a queen or goddess in Irish mythology.

Mulroona [*Maolruanaidh*] (m) A name used by the *O'Carroll* family, princes of Ely O'Carroll.

Munchin [*Mainchin*] (m) 'little monk'. St Munchin is associated with Limerick. *Mannix* was used as an anglicisation of this name.

Muriel (f) In Ireland this is the English form of *Muirgheal,* 'sea bright'. Muriel can also be traced to medieval Brittany and Normandy. It is probably Celtic; Yonge suggests that it comes from Greek and means 'myrrh', but this seems unlikely.

Murphy (m) 'sea warrior'. A widespread Irish surname. It means 'grandson of *Muirchu*', which is a combination of *muir,* 'sea' and *cu,* 'hound' (figuratively 'warrior'). It has now come to be used as a first name.

Murrough [*Murchadh*] (m) 'sea warrior'. An early name, once very widespread. *Mortimer* was used as an anglicisation. *Morolt* is perhaps a variant.

Murtagh [*Muircheartach*] (m) 'sea expert'. A royal name in Ireland, the name of three kings of Tara, and a prince known as Muircheartach of the Leather Cloaks. *Mortimer* was used to anglicise it.

Myles (m) An alternative spelling of *Miles.* Brian O'Nolan (1911-66) used the pen-name Myles na Gopaleen – a name originally created by Dion Boucicault (1822-90) – for a number of his works and for his *Irish Times* column.

Myrna (f) Another form of *Morna.* Though Irish in origin, this name seems to be more used in the United States. *Merna* is a variant.

N

Naal (m) The name of an early Irish saint. His name is also given as *Natalis,* a Latin word meaning 'birth'. Naal may be a form of this word.

Nancy [*Nainsí*] (f) A pet form of *Anne* which is now sometimes used as an independent name.

Natasha (f) A Russian form of *Natalie.*

Nehemiah (m) Hebrew, 'God's consolation'. In Ireland this name was used to anglicise *Giolla-na-Naomh. Nehemias* Donnellan was archbishop of Tuam.

Neil (m) A form of *Niall.* It is used more in Scotland, but it is increasing in Ireland. *Neal* is a variant.

Nelda (f) A feminine form of *Neil* or *Niall.*

Nellie (f) A pet form of *Helen* which has occasionally been used as an independent name in Ireland.

Nessa (f) Originally, this was a pet form of *Agnes,* but it is now used as an independent name in Ireland.

Nessan [*Neasan*] (m) A name which was perhaps originally connected with the word *neas,* 'stoat'.

Nevan [*Naomhan*] (m) 'little saint'. A rare name in modern Ireland.

Niadh (m) 'champion'. St Niadh was venerated in Meath, and his name was given as a Christian name.

Niall (m) A derivative of *néall,* 'cloud', and the name of one of the most famous kings of Tara, Niall of the Nine Hostages, the founder of the Ui Neill dynasty of Irish kings. The *O'Neills,* a branch of that family, descend from Niall Black-Knee, who fell fighting against the Scandinavians in 917. Although used today, the name is yielding ground to its Scottish form, *Neil.* In Irish Niall rhymes with 'real'; in English it rhymes with 'phial'.

Niamh (f) 'bright'. In Irish mythology, Niamh, princess of the Land of Promise, departed with Ossian, son of Finn MacCool, for the Otherworld. The name is rapidly increasing in popularity in Ireland today. *Niav* is an anglicised spelling.

Nicholas [*Nicolas*] (m) Greek, 'victory people'. This name has been popular in Ireland since the Middle Ages. It is still quite frequently used.

Nicola (f) A feminine form of *Nicholas.* The original feminine form was *Nicole* – Nicola is in fact the masculine form used in Italy, where it has replaced the more masculine-sounding *Niccolo.* Nicola is now the established feminine form in Ireland.

Nigel (m) The history of this name is complex. The Scandinavians bore the Irish name *Niall* to Iceland where it became *Njal,* a form which 'returned' to Scandinavia, and from there went to Normandy where it was latinised as *Nigellus.* Nigel dates from the fifteenth century, and it has become the everyday English form. It is occasionally used in Ireland, but it is most used in Scotland, where it also occurs as *Neil.*

Noel [*Nollaig*] (m) Noel is French for 'Christmas', and the Irish Nollaig translates it exactly. The name enjoyed great popularity in Ireland in mid-century, but it is now declining.

Noelle [*Nollaig*] (f) French, 'Christmas'. A feminine form of *Noel.*

Nora(h) [*Nora*] (f) A form of *Honora,* of Irish origin. Nora is the commoner spelling, but the name's popularity is declining today. *Honoria,* a name particularly popular in the nineteenth century, may have been an elaboration of Nora(h) rather than a name taken directly from Latin. Nora was used by Ibsen in his play *A Doll's House* (1879). *Nonie* and *Hannah* are pet forms.

Noreen [*Nóirín*] (f) A diminutive of *Nora* which occurs from time to time as an independent name.

Norlene (f) An elaboration of *Nora.*

Nuala (f) A short form of *Fionnuala* which was popular round about the middle of the century, but it is now little used.

O

Odanodan (m) Variant of *Adamnan.*

Odran (m) Variant of *Oran.*

Ogh(i)e (m) Variant of *Eochaidh.*

Ohnicio (f) An Irish variant of *Honora.*

Oho (m) Variant of *Eochaidh.*

Olga (f) A Russian name, ultimately derived from Germanic, 'holy'. It is rare in Ireland.

Olive (f) Latin, 'olive'. This name was used in Ireland to anglicise *Elva.* See also *Olivia.*

Oliver [*Oilibhéar*] (m) Perhaps a form of *Olaf* (see *Auliffe*); or perhaps from Old French, 'olive tree', or Old German,

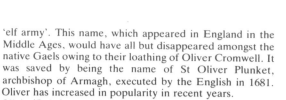

'elf army'. This name, which appeared in England in the Middle Ages, would have all but disappeared amongst the native Gaels owing to their loathing of Oliver Cromwell. It was saved by being the name of St Oliver Plunket, archbishop of Armagh, executed by the English in 1681. Oliver has increased in popularity in recent years.

Olivia (f) A form of Olive used by Shakespeare in *Twelfth Night*. It became an established name in England in the eighteenth century, and it probably spread from there to Ireland, where use of the name is currently increasing.

Ona (f) Variant of *Una*.

Onan (m) A form of *Adamnan* found in Derry.

Oney (m) A form of *Hewney*.

Onora (f) A form of *Honora* used in Ireland, where it was recorded as early as 1634.

Oona(gh) (f) Variant of *Una*.

Oran [*Odhrán*] (m) A diminutive of *odhar*, 'green' or 'dun'. *Odran* is a variant.

Orinthia (f) This name was invented by the Irish playwright, George Bernard Shaw, for use in *The Apple Cart* (1929). It has since passed into general usage.

Orla [*Orfhlaith*] (f) 'golden lady'. A name which is increasing in popularity. It may also be spelt *Orlagh*. *Aurnia* is a variant.

Orna(t) [*Odharnait*] (f) A diminutive of *odhar*, 'dun' or 'green'.

Oscar (m) The name of a hero of legend, the grandson of Finn MacCool. Some writers assume that this is the Germanic name *Oscar*, 'divine spear', introduced into Ireland by the Scandinavians, but this is unlikely. The Finn legends probably antedate the Vikings, and a likelier derivation is Irish *oscar*, 'champion warrior'. The word in Irish can also mean 'jewel'. The use of the name in the Swedish royal family comes from the Gaelic source. The House of Bernadotte adopted it at Napoleon's instance – the Emperor had a predilection for Macpherson's Ossianic poems (1765). The Irish writer, Oscar Wilde (1854-1900) was named after a Swedish king.

Ossian [*Oisín*] (m) 'fawn'. The name of the son of the legendary hero, Finn MacCool, whose mother was said to have spent part of her existence as a deer. Ossian was supposed to have lived for a time in the Land of Promise. The Scottish writer, Macpherson, described his adventures in his Ossianic poems (1765) where the deeds of the Fianna are set entirely in Scotland.

Ounan (m) Variant of *Adamnan*.

Owen (m) A name used in Ireland to anglicise *Eoghan*, to which it equates phonetically. In Wales it represents *Euguein*. Both names mean 'well born'.

Ownah (f) Variant of *Una*.

Owney (m) Variant of *Hewney*.

Oynie (m) Variant of *Hewney*.

P

Pamela (f) Greek, 'all honey'. A name invented by Sir Philip Sidney (1554-86). It was popularised by Samuel Richardson's novel *Pamela* (1740), and this resulted in its use as a first name.

Parlan (m) Variant of *Partholon*.

Partholon [*Parthalón*] (m) The name of a legendary invader of early Ireland – the first, so tradition has it, to come there after the Flood. His followers are referred to as the Partholonians. *Bartholomew, Barclay* and *Berkley* have all been employed to anglicise Partholon. It is still in use today. *Parlan* is a variant.

Patricia [*Pádraigín*] (f) Latin, 'noble'. The feminine form of *Patrick*, and a name which appears to have been known in early times. According to legend St Patricia died in Naples *c.* 665. The name is commonly supposed to have been recreated in eighteenth-century Scotland, but the evidence for this is doubtful. However, it has greatly increased in popularity in modern times, perhaps due to its royal bearer, Princess Patricia of Connaught. The Irish have, of course, welcomed the female equivalent of the names of their patron; it has been gaelicised as *Pádraigín*, formerly used only as a diminutive of *Pádraig*. The pet forms are *Pat* and *Paddy* – the latter is rather rare.

Patrick [*Pádraig*] (m) Latin, 'noble'. The Latin adjective *patricius* signified membership of the patricians, the aristocracy of ancient Rome. Although a name of Latin derivation, Patrick is regarded as the national name of Ireland. St Patrick (*c.* 385-461), patron saint of Ireland, was an early missionary to the country. It has, in fact, been suggested that there may have been more than one early Christian preacher with this name.

At first the name was not used in Ireland, presumably out of reverence, but compounds such as *Gilpatrick* and *Maelpatrick* were found. In due course the Irish started using Patrick on its own. It was established by the seventeenth century, when Patrick Sarsfield was the Jacobite earl of Lucan.

At one time there was an attempt to amalgamate Patrick with *Peter*. While this did not meet with success, St Patrick's Day is now sometimes called *Peadar's (Peter's) Day*.

The usual Irish form of Patrick is *Pádraig*. Variants include *Padraic, Patric* and *Peyton. Pha(e)drig* was a rather unsatisfactory variant. *Pat, Paddy, Patsy* and *Pa* are pet forms in Ireland; *Pate* and *Patie* were used in Scotland. *Pádraigín*, an Irish diminutive, is now also used to translate *Patricia*. Patrick is often given in conjunction with *Joseph*, and bearers are sometimes called *Pa Joe*.

The surname *Fitzpatrick* is a Norman form of the Irish *Mac an Giolla Pádraig*, 'son of the servant of Patrick'.

Patrick Pearse, the rebel leader of 1916, no doubt added to the name's popularity.

Paul [*Pól*] (m) Latin *paulus*, 'little'. The Roman name of *Saul* (Hebrew, 'asked for'; Irish, *Sol*), one of the foremost early Christians. Paul had its beginnings amongst the Aemilian gens, a tribe noted for their smallness. The name is used in Ireland, as in other Christian countries. It has become very popular in modern times.

Paula (f) A feminine of *Paul,* sometimes used in Ireland.

Pauline [*Póilín*] (f) A feminine form of *Paul* from its derivative, *Paulinus*.

Penelope (f) A Greek name of uncertain meaning, borne by the wife of Odysseus. In Ireland it was used to anglicise *Finola*. *Penny* and *Nappy* are short forms.

Perce (m) Presumably a variant of *Pierce*, itself a variant of *Peter*. It was borne by one of the *Butler* family, Lord Dunboyne, the third son of Edward Butler, who was referred to as both Perce and Peter.

Peregrine (m) Latin, 'wanderer', 'pilgrim'. This name has its origin in the seventh century in Italy where a hermit, said to have been an Irish prince, was known as *il pellegrin;* he was later canonised as St Peregrine, *Pellegrino* in Italian. Peregrine occurs in England from the thirteenth century onwards, and it was used in Ireland to anglicise *Cuchoigcriche,* 'hound of the border', a Westmeath and Offaly name (now obsolete).

Peter [*Peadar*] (m) According to the New Testament, *Cephas* (Aramaic, 'rock') was the name bestowed by Christ upon the Apostle Simon. This was translated into Greek as *Petros,* intended as a masculine form of *petra,* 'rock'. The Norman form *Piers/Pierce* was the usual one in Ireland until comparatively modern times, but nowadays Peter is popular. At one stage there was an unsuccessful attempt to amalgamate Peter with *Patrick.* The Irish form *Peadar* strongly resembles the Welsh *Pedr.*

Phadrig (m) Variant of *Patrick,* doubtless from *Phadraig,* the vocative of *Padraig.*

Phaedrig (m) Variant of *Patrick.* Sir Phaedrig Lucius Ambrose O'Brien, baron of Inchiquin and claimant to the Irish throne, is a contemporary example.

Phelan (m) A diminutive of *faol,* ('wolf'). This is more common as a surname, but it has been given as a first name.

Phelim(y) (m) Variant of *Felim(id).*

Phiala (f) The name of a fifth-century Irish saint who was killed in Cornwall.

Philip [*Pilib*] (m) Greek, 'lover of horses'. The name of a number of kings of Macedonia, notably Philip II (382-336 B C), the father of Alexander the Great. It spread throughout the Near East in the Hellenic Era. St Philip was one of the Apostles. The name was established in Ireland by the Anglo-Normans and it is popular today. *Filib* and *Filip* are Irish language variants.

Philomena (f) Greek, 'loved'. The supposed relics of a saint of this name were discovered in 1802. The name became popular in Ireland, but, when the Vatican suppressed the cultus, a sharp drop in the number of Irish girls given this name occurred.

Phyllis (f) Greek, 'leafy'. An ancient name which became popular in England at about the turn of the century. It was doubtless exported from there to Ireland.

Pierce [*Piaras*] (m) The Norman French form of *Pierre* (the French for *Peter)* was *Piers,* and this was once the usual form in England, where Peter was unknown in the early Middle Ages. The English brought Piers/Pierce to Ireland and there the Gaelic forms *Piaras* and *Fiaras* sprang up, the latter giving rise to the surnames *Kerrisk, Kierse* and *MacKerrisk.* The name has been used in modern times. *Feories* was formerly a variant.

Piers (m) Variant of *Pierce.*

Polly [*Paili*] (f) A pet form of *Mary* (via *Molly*) which is now sometimes used as an independent name.

Q

Quentin (m) Variant of *Quintin.*

Queran (m) Variant of *Kieran.*

Quinn (m) An Irish surname meaning 'counsel', which is sometimes used as a Christian name.

Quintin (m) Latin, 'fifth'. This name was used in Ireland, together with its variants *Quentin* and *Quinton,* to anglicise *Cooey.*

Quinton (m) Variant of *Quintin.*

R

Rachel [*Ráichéal*] (f) Hebrew, 'ewe'. An Old Testament name which has become established in Ireland in modern times.

Ralph [*Rádhulbh*] (m) Germanic, 'counsel wolf'. The Irish form corresponds to Anglo-Saxon *Raedwulf,* Old Norse *Radulfr.* It was common amongst the medieval Anglo-Normans in Ireland. *Ralf* in Irish is a personal name used for the Cromwellian soldier.

Ranalt (f) A name dating from the twelfth century: Ranalt, daughter of Awley O'Farrell, king of Conmacne, married Hugh O'Connor, the last king of Connacht.

Randal(l) (m) Anglo-Saxon, 'shield wolf'. A name used to anglicise *Raghnall,* itself the Irish form of *Reginald.*

Randolph [*Rannulbh*] (m) In Ireland this name represents the Frankish *Randulf,* 'shield wolf', whereas in England it is a form of *Randal.*

Raymond [*Réamonn*] (m) Germanic, 'counsel protection'. A name brought to England by the Normans. It spread from there to Ireland, where it is a popular name today. See also *Redmond.*

Rebecca (f) Hebrew, perhaps 'heifer'. An Old Testament name which has occasionally been used in Ireland. *Rebekah,* an alternative spelling, has also been noted, though this is much rarer.

Redmond (m) An Irish form of *Raymond,* sometimes encountered in modern times. John Redmond, an Irish politician in the early part of the twentieth century, may have influenced usage. *Redmund,* presumably a spelling variant, has also been noted.

Regina (f) Latin, 'queen'. A name used in Ireland as the equivalent of the native name *Riona.*

Reginald [*Rá(gh)nall*] (m) Germanic, 'power might'. A name brought to Ireland by both the Scandinavians, who used the form *Rognvaldr,* and the Anglo-Normans, who employed the form *Ragenald. Reynold* was a Middle English form.

Renan (m) Variant of *Ronan.*

Renny [*Rathnait*] (f) 'little prosperous one'. A name which may now be obsolete. *Ranait* is an Irish language variant.

Revelin [*Roibhilín*] (m) A name of Ulster origin, found in the Co. Down area. It was sometimes anglicised as *Ro(w)land.*

Richard [*Risteard*] (m) Germanic, 'ruler hard'. A popular name in medieval England. It was introduced into Ireland and became established there. Richard Steele (1672-1729) was an Irish essayist, and Richard Brinsley Sheridan (1751-1816) was a famous Irish playwright. It is a popular name in Ireland today.

Rickard [*Riocárd*] (m) An Irish variant of *Richard;* cf. Old German *Ricohard.* The name continues to be used on a small scale in Ireland.

Ringan (m) An Irish form of *Ninian,* the name of the saintly British missionary and bishop of Whithorn (died *c.* 432).

Riona [*Rioghnach*] (f) Perhaps 'queenly', derived from *rioghan,* 'queen'. *Regina* was used to translate this name.

Robert [*Roibeárd*] (m) Germanic, 'fame bright'. This name was *Robert* in French, *Ruprecht* (English *Rupert*) in German. It was frequently used in Ireland amongst the Anglo-Normans, and *Roibeard, Ribeart, Ribirt* and *Riobart* were Irish language forms. *Robin* (Irish *Roibin*) was

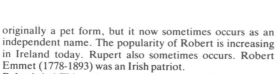

originally a pet form, but it now sometimes occurs as an independent name. The popularity of Robert is increasing in Ireland today. Rupert also sometimes occurs. Robert Emmet (1778-1893) was an Irish patriot.

Robuck (m) This curious name has been used in the *Galway* family: it was borne by Robert *Kinvan* (died 1635), son of Robert Kinvan.

Roderick (m) Germanic, 'fame rule'. A name used in Ireland to anglicise *Rory*.

Rodney (m) Anglo-Saxon, 'reed island'. A name which is found from time to time in Ireland.

Roger (m) Germanic, 'fame spear'. Roger was used in Ireland to anglicise *Rory*. Roger Casement (1864-1916) was an Irish patriot.

Roland [*Rólann*] (m) Germanic, 'fame land'. According to medieval legend Roland was a peer of Charlemagne who died at Roncesvalles. The Italians made the name *Orlando*, and in this form it was used by the poet Ariosto (1474-1533). It was introduced into Ireland by the English, and was occasionally used to anglicise *Revelin*. *Rowland* is a spelling variant. In fiction, the name was used in Walter Sweetman's *Roland Ryan: an Irish sketch* (1896).

Rolf [*Rodhulbh*] (m) Germanic, 'fame wolf'. A name used in medieval Ireland, but it is now rare, if not obsolete. It derives from Old German *Hrodulf* and Old Norse *Hrolfr*, whence English Rolf. The name is sometimes confused with *Ralph*.

Ronald (m) *Rögnvaldr,* a Norse name (of which *Reginald* is a modern variant) became *Raonull* amongst the Gaels of Scotland, from which came English Ronald, a name still used in modern Ireland.

Ronan [*Rónán*] (m) 'little seal'. Ronan, king of Leinster, was the subject of a tragic Irish legend. He was deceived by his second wife into killing his first son. *St Ronan's Well* (1823) was the title of a novel by Sir Walter Scott. The name is known in France, sometimes in its variant form *Renan*. It is increasingly popular in Ireland, and it has also been recorded in Canada.

Ronat (f) A name, now obsolete, derived from *ron*, 'seal'. The seal is an important animal in Celtic folklore.

Rory [*Ruairí*] (m) A derivative of *rua*, 'red', 'rufous', borne by the last high king of Ireland, Rory O'Conor (reigned 1166-70). It is still used in Ireland, and the Gaelic forms *Ruaidri, Ruaraidh* have been recently recorded. Rory O'More was a seventeenth-century Irish patriot. *Roderick* and *Roger* were used to anglicise Rory.

Rosaleen [*Róisín*] (f) An Irish diminutive of *Rose*. *Róisín Dubh*, 'Dark Rosaleen', was used as a figurative name for Ireland in a celebrated poem. The name is quite widespread today, often in its Irish form.

Rose [*Róis*] (f) This name generally derives from Old German *hros*, 'horse', although in the case of St Rose of Lima (1586-1617) it derives from *rosa*, 'rose', and it is almost always associated with the flower today. The forms *Rohais, Roese* and *Roesia* appear amongst the Normans in England, and they probably introduced the name into Ireland, where it became widespread.

Ross [*Ros*] (m) 'promontory'. A name which was common in South Ulster. Ross MacMahon was archbishop of Armagh and a leading opponent of Cromwell. The name continues in use today.

Rossa (m) A name given in honour of Jeremiah O'Donovan Rossa, the nineteenth-century Irish politician.

Rowan [*Ruadhán*] (m) 'little red one'. An Irish name still in use today, e.g. the television reporter, Rowan Hand. Rowan can also be a Teutonic name, signifying 'mountain ash'.

Rowland (m) Variant spelling of *Roland*.

Roy (m) Gaelic *ruadh*, 'red', unconnected with French *roi*, 'king'. A name which originated in Scotland and spread from there to England and Ireland.

Ruth [*Rút*] (f) A Biblical name of unknown derivation. It is becoming increasingly popular in Ireland.

Ryan (m) 'little king'. This Irish surname is much used as a Christian name in North America, e.g. the film actor, Ryan O'Neal. It has been recorded as a Christian name in Ireland itself.

S

Sabia (f) A name used to translate *Sive*.

Sabina [*Saidhbhín*] (f) Irish *Saidhbhín*, a diminutive of *Sadhbh* (English *Sive),* became in translation *Sabina*, a Latin name meaning 'Sabine woman'. Sabina was also used to translate *Síle* (see *Sheila*).

Saibhne (m) A name, perhaps an Irish form of *Simon*, which was once used in Omeath. It is now probably obsolete.

Samantha (f) Aramaic, 'listener'. Like Darren, this name has probably spread amongst watchers of the American television series, *Bewitched*.

Samhaoir (f) In legend, Samhaoir was Finn MacCool's daughter. It is also, in Irish, the name of the Morning Star River in Co. Limerick, and an early name for the River Erne.

Samuel (m) A Hebrew name of uncertain meaning, perhaps 'name of God'. It was used in Ireland to translate *Sorley*. Samuel is widespread in Northern Ireland. *Sam* and *Sammy* are common diminutives. Samuel Becket (1906–) the Irish writer and Nobel Prize winner is a contemporary example.

Sandra (f) This name was originally a short form of *Alessandra*, the Italian for *Alexandra*. It occurs from time to time in Ireland.

Sara(h) (f) Hebrew, 'princess'. In the Old Testament Sarah was the wife of Abraham. The name was used frequently in Ireland, sometimes to anglicise the native names *Sorcha, Sive* and *Saraid*.

Saraid (f) 'excellent'. This name has been anglicised as *Sarah*.

Savage (m) An unusual first name used in the *Parsons* family.

Scoheen [*Scoithín*] (m) Perhaps a diminutive of *scoth*, 'flower'. St Scoheen was a sixth-century Irish saint.

Scota (f) Latin, 'Irishwoman'. Medieval legend places two women of this name amongst the progenitors of the Irish race: Scota, wife of Niul, and Scota, wife of Milesius. In the early Middle Ages *Scotia* was a name for Ireland, and *Scotus* of which Scota is the feminine, signified 'Irishman'. The term 'Scot' was applied to Irish settlers in Caledonia, who later gave their name to the whole country.

Seamus (m) The Irish form of *James*, itself derived from *Jacob*. *Seamus* is used by the Gaels of both Ireland and Scotland. The latter tend to favour the spelling *Seumus*, which is also found in Ireland. The vocative, *Sheamais*, is phonetically rendered by the Scots as *Hamish*. Both James and Seamus are popular names in Ireland today, though, as can happen to extremely popular names, James is no longer nearly so frequently bestowed as it once was.

James Joyce (1882-1941) was a leading Irish writer. James Connolly was an Irish rebel executed in 1916. In English the pet forms are *Jim, Jimmy (Jem, Jemser* are occasionally found in the Dublin area). *Simi* is an Irish form of Jimmy.

Seamus has been phonetically rendered *Shamus* and, less successfully, *Shemus. Shay* is a frequent modern pet form. *Seamus rua* ('Red Shamus') is a name applied in Irish to the fox.

Sean (m) The Irish form of *John.* There was actually an earlier form, *Eoin* (cf. Scots Gaelic *Iain)* derived from Latin *Johannes.* The early medieval Irish philosopher, Johannes Scotus Eriugena, may have borne this form of the name. Eoin is still used today, but Sean is normally thought of as the Irish form; compare Welsh *Evan* and *Sion.* In the Gaelic-speaking areas of Scotland, Sean has not replaced *Iain,* but the lexicographer Edward Dwelly has noted it as a name which occurs in folklore there.

Sean is derived from French *Jehan/Jean,* introduced by the Normans. It is sometimes phonetically rendered in English as *Shaun* or *Shawn.* It has also been anglicised *Shane,* a form associated with Shane the Proud, chief of the *O'Neills,* a leading Irish prince in Elizabethan times.

Sean has been reinforced by *Séon,* another form of John. *Seainin,* a diminutive, is also used to name a fish, the thornback. Sean O'Casey (1880-1964), the Irish dramatist, is a recent example of the name. Sean is used outside Ireland and it has been made internationally famous by the Scottish actor, Sean Connery.

John, Sean, Eoin and Shane are all very popular today, though John is sharply declining. John itself has been borne by a number of Irish playwrights, including John Millington Synge (1871-1909) and the contemporary playwright, John B. Keane.

Jack, the English pet form is also much employed. It comes from *Jackin,* a form of *Jankin,* itself a form of *Jehan* and *Jan* (the latter is a variant of John). Jack Cade (died 1450) was an Irishman who led an uprising in medieval England.

Selia (f) Variant of *Sheila.*

Senan [*Séanán*] (m) A diminutive of *sean,* 'old'. *Sinon* and *Sinan* are variants.

Shamus (m) A phonetic form of *Seamus.*

Shane (m) A form of *Sean* which is used in Ireland today. Shane O'Neill (died 1567) was the principal chief of Ulster in his day.

Shannon (m, f) The name of the longest river in Ireland, which is listed by various authorities as a masculine and feminine name, but there is no evidence for its use in Ireland itself.

Sharon (f) Hebrew, 'the plain'. A name which seems well established in Ireland today.

Shasta (m) One of the various names invented by C. S. Lewis (1898-1963), the Northern Irish writer, in his Narnian chronicles. Although these names have not yet passed into common usage, they may be of interest to parents seeking unusual names for their children. The name Shasta itself may come from Mt Shasta in the United States. Other names from this series include *Caspian* (m) *Tirian* (m) *Rilian* (m) and *Aravis* (f).

Shaun (m) An alternative spelling of *Sean.*

Shauna (f) A feminine form of *Sean/Shaun.*

Shawn (m) Variant of *Sean.*

Shawndelle (f) A feminine form of *Shawn* which was coined in Canada.

Sheary (m) An Irish form of *Geoffrey.*

Sheela(gh) (f) Variant of *Sheila.*

Sheena [*Síne*] (f) The French feminine form of *John* was *Jeanne* which became *Jean* in Scotland, giving rise to Gaelic *Sin(e).* The name is also found in Ireland, particularly in the vicinity of Derry, though nowadays it has become more widespread.

Sheila [*Síle*] (f) Síle was originally an Irish form of *Cecilia, Cecily* or *Celia,* and it was variously anglicised as *Julia, Judith* and *Sabina.* However, it is chiefly in the anglicised form Sheila – or its spelling variants, *Sheela* and *Sheelagh* – that the name is used today. It remains quite common. *Selia* is a further variant. In Australia Sheila is used as a common noun to mean 'girl'.

Shelley (f) This name was originally a surname, coming from one or more of the places called Shelley in Yorkshire, Essex and Suffolk. It probably reached Ireland through the popularity of the film actress, Shelley Winters.

Shemus (m) A form of *Seamus.*

Sheron (m) An Irish form of *Geoffrey,* through Gaelic *Seathrun.*

Shiel [*Siadhal*] (m) An early Irish name mentioned by Woulfe; but, despite this, it has not been resurrected.

Shirley (f) English, 'shire meadow'. Originally this was a surname and masculine first name particularly associated with Yorkshire. It was probably first used as a girls' name by Charlotte Brontë in her novel *Shirley* (1849). This and recently, presumably, the fame of the film actress Shirley Temple, spread the name widely.

Shona (f) A feminine form of *John* which is sometimes found in Ireland.

Sidney (m, f) As a feminine name in Ireland this is probably a form of *Sidony,* a name once given in honour of the Winding Sheet of Christ. It is not common. Sidney is also found as a masculine name, in which case it comes from a surname which was in Latin *de Sancto Dionysio,* 'of St Denis'.

Simon [*Síomón*] (m) Greek, 'snub-nosed'. In all probability this name was equated with the Hebrew name *Simeon* (in Irish, *Suimeon),* 'hearkening'. Simon or Simeon was the original name of St Peter. Irish language variants are *Síómónn, Siomun* and possibly *Saibhne.* In addition, the name was used as an equivalent for *Sivney.* Simon is popular in Ireland today and the feminine form, *Simone,* sometimes also occurs.

Sinan (m) Variant of *Senan.*

Sinead (f) The Irish form of *Jane,* a common feminine of *John.* It has become very popular indeed within recent years. The actress Sinead Cusack, is a contemporary example.

Sinon (m) Variant of *Senan.*

Siobhán (f) The Irish form of *Joan* (which is sometimes rather sloppily rendered *Siún* in Irish), a name which was introduced into Ireland by the Anglo-Normans. *Siobhán* has been anglicised as *Judith* and *Julia.* Its popularity has increased greatly since mid-century. The actress, Siobhán MacKenna, is a modern example.

Sitric (m) Perhaps Norse, 'conquering security'. A name

borne by medieval kings of Dublin, notably Sitric Silkenbeard. It has given rise to the surname *Kitterick*, *MacKitterick*.

Sive [*Sadhbh*] (f) 'goodness'. An early name which, over the years, has been variously anglicised as *Sabia*, *Sophia*, *Sarah*, etc. *Sabha* was a form used in Connacht; another form *Sadbha* was employed in Ulster.

Sivney [*Suibhne*] (m) 'well-going'. An early name borne by the protagonist of the medieval romance *Buile Suibhne Geilt* ('The Madness of Suibhne the Lunatic'), of which Flann O'Brien made use in his novel *At Swim-Two-Birds* (1939). Suibhne is essentially the same name as the surname *Sweeney*. It was translated as *Sivney* (formerly as *Swifne*), and sometimes anglicised as *Simon*.

Siany [*Sláine*] (f) 'health'. An early name favoured by the O'Briens. It was exported to France, where it became *Slania* and *Slanie*.

So-Domina (f) Latin *domina*, 'lady', with the Irish prefix *so-*, 'good'. A name formerly used in Ireland.

Solomon [*Solamh*] (m) A Hebrew name of uncertain meaning, which has occasionally been used in Ulster.

Sonya (f0 The Russian form of *Sophia*. Both Sonya and its spelling variant, *Sonja*, have been noted in Ireland in modern times.

Sophia (f) Greek, 'wisdom'. This name was used to anglicise the Irish name *Sive*.

Sorcha (f) An early name, which was anglicised as *Sarah*. It has once again returned into use in its own right.

Sorley [*Somhairle*] (m) Old Norse *Sumerlidi*, 'viking'. A name which was translated as *Samuel* or *Charles*. It was used amongst the *MacDonnells*, e.g., Sorley MacDonnell the Yellow, grandfather of Red Hugh O'Donnell. The name became *Somerled* in Scotland.

Standish (m) Anglo-Saxon, 'rocky valley'. This name was used to anglicise the native name *Aneslis*.

Stanislaus (m) Slavic, 'camp glory'. A name used in Ireland to anglicise *Aneslis*.

Stanley [*Stainléigh*] (m) A first name of recent origin, transferred from the surname. It is used in both Ireland and England.

Stephen [*Stiofán*] (m) Greek, 'crown'. The name of the first recorded Christian martyr (died *c*. A D 36). It was used in Ireland by the Normans, who probably introduced it to the country. There are many Irish forms: today *Stiofán* is the usual form, but in Woulfe's time *Steafán* was probably commoner. The spelling *Steven* is also found.

Susan [*Súsanna*] (f) Hebrew, 'lily'. A name introduced into Ireland by the Anglo-Normans. It has become very popular in modern times.

Suzanne (f) A form of *Susan* which is well established in Ireland.

Sybil [*Síbéal*] (f) In Ireland this name generally represents a short form of *Isabel* (cf. Early English *Zabel*) rather than *Sibyl* (sometimes spelt *Sybil*), the name applied to oracular priestesses in ancient times.

Syka (m) A form of *Eochaidh*.

Sylvester [*Sailbheastar*] (m) A derivative of Latin *silva*, 'wood'. It is occasionally found in Ireland.

Synan (m) Variant of *Senan*.

T

Taber [*Tobar*] (m) 'well'. A rare name, noted by Loughead.

Tadhg (m) 'poet'. An early name. The English forms are *Teige* and *Teague* – the latter is used as a term of opprobrium by Ulster Protestants for Catholics. The name was anglicised as *Timothy* (which accounts for the great popularity of that name in Ireland) and also as *Thaddeus*, *Theodore*, *Theodosius* and *Toby*. *Thady* is a variant form, taken from *Thaddeus*. Both Tadhg and Timothy occur in modern times. The incorrect Irish spelling *Tadgh* has also been noted. Another recorded variant is *Tighe;* and one wonders if the mysterious name *Tian*, listed by Boyer as an Irish name of uncertain meaning, is a further variant.

Tadleigh (m) Variant of *Tadhg*.

Tara [*Teamhair*] (f) The name of a hill in Central Ireland, a seat of kingship in early times, which is now used as a feminine first name. However, sometimes the name Tara may be a form of *Tamar(a)* (Hebrew, 'palm').

Teague (m) An anglicised form of *Tadhg*.

Terence (m) A Latin name of uncertain meaning, and the name of the Roman poet Terence (*c*. 195-159 BC) who was of African origin. It was used in Ireland to anglicise *Turlough* and so became very popular.

Teresa [*Toiréasa*] (f) A name meaning perhaps 'corn carrying', or possibly connected with one of the two Greek islands names Therasia. The name was once confined to Europe south of the Pyrenees, but St Teresa of Avila (1515-82) spread it far and wide. In Ireland it was identified with a native name variously rendered *Treasa* and *Treise*, meaning 'strength'. *Tracy* is a variant.

Thaddeus (m) Aramaic, 'praise'. The name of one of the Apostles, thought to be identical with St Jude. The name tended to be used more in Eastern than in Western Europe, e.g. Russian *Fadei*. In Ireland it was used to represent the native *Tadhg*.

Thady (m) A form of *Thaddeus* peculiar to Ireland, where it became widespread as an anglicisation of *Tadhg*.

Theobald [*Tiobóid*] (m) Germanic, 'people bold'. A name introduced into Ireland by the Normans. It also occurred in the form *Tibbot*. *Tioboid* has been anglicised as *Toby*. Theobald Wolfe Tone was an eighteenth-century Irish patriot.

Theodore [*Thadóir*] (m) Greek, 'gift of God'. This name was brought to Western Europe by the Venetians, although it may have existed in Wales from early times, giving rise to the Welsh name *Tewdwr*. In Ireland it was used to anglicise *Tadhg*.

Theodosius (m) Apparently a Spanish form of Greek *Theodotus*, 'God given'. It was used in Ireland to anglicise *Tadhg*.

Thérèse (f) The French form of Teresa, made well known by St Thérèse of Lisieux (1873-97). It is used in Ireland today.

Thomas [*Tomás*] (m) Aramaic, 'twin'. An international name, borne by one of the Apostles, and also by St Thomas a Becket (1118-70), which made it popular amongst the Normans in Ireland. The name became widespread, but it has lost its hold recently. It has been used to anglicise *Tomhas*.

Tibbot (m) An Irish form of *Theobald*, which also occurs in Irish as *Teaboid* and *Tioboid*. The son of Grace O'Malley (see *Grania*) was called Tibbot of the Ship (he was born at sea). The form Tibbot may be of English origin as *Tibbott* was recorded in England in 1699.

Tiernan [*Tiarnán*] (m) A diminutive of *tiarna*, 'lord'.

Tierney [*Tiarnach*] (m) 'lordly'. The name of an Irish compiler of annals in the Middle Ages.

Tigris (f) Latin and Greek *tigris*, 'tiger'. By tradition St Tigris is St Patrick's sister.

Timothy (m) Greek, 'honour God'. An early Greek name, borne by a musician of Alexander the Great. It was adopted in England after the Reformation, and presumably it came from there to Ireland, where it was used to anglicise *Tadhg* and so became common. It has also been used to anglicise *Tomaltagh*. The true Irish forms are *Tiomoid* and *Tiamhdha*.

Tina (f) Originally this was a pet form of *Christina, Christine* and *Clementina,* but it is now sometimes given as an independent name.

Toal (m) Variant of *Tully*.

Toby [*Tóibí*] (m) Hebrew, 'God is good'. Toby is the usual English form of this Hebrew name. *Tobias*, another form, has been used in Ireland, e.g. a Tobias Brown of Cork was listed as a soldier of the Commonwealth. The name enjoyed considerable popularity in Europe in the Middle Ages. When it reached Ireland it was used to anglicise two names: *Tioboid* (an Irish form of *Theobald*) and *Tadhg*.

Tomaltagh [*Tomaltach*] (m) An early name which has been anglicised as *Timothy*. *Tumelty* is a variant.

Tomhas (m) A name used in the *O'Dowd* family, anglicised as *Thomas*.

Tracy (f) A form of *Teresa* which is sometimes used in Ireland. It has perhaps been influenced by the surname *Tracey*: indeed, *Tracey* is a spelling variant.

Tully [*Tuathal*] (m) 'people mighty'. An early name, still in use, particularly in its Irish form. *Toal* is a variant.

Tumelty (m) A form of *Tomaltagh*.

Turlough [*Toirdhealbhach*] (m) This name perhaps means 'shaped like Thor'. Thor (Irish *Tomhar)* was a Norse god whose name may be connected with 'thunder'. Turlough was the name of two kings who reigned in the tenth and eleventh centuries, Turlough I O'Brien and Turlough II O'Conor. *Tirloch* is a spelling variant. In literature, there is an Irish St Toirdhealbhach in T. H. White's *The Once and Future King* (1938-58). The name is normally pronounced *Turlock*, but the pronunciation *Traylock* sometimes occurs. It was anglicised *Terence*, which popularised that name.

Tyrone (m) An Irish name of a county in Ulster. The name signifies 'Eoghan's land' and has been used as a first name, e.g. the director Tyrone Guthrie (1900-71).

U

Uileos (m) An Irish name rendered *Ulysses* in English.

Ulicia (f) A rare feminine of *Ulick*.

Ulick [*Uileog*] (m) This name is regarded by Woulfe as a diminutive of *Uilliam*, the Irish for *William*. However, it may be a form of Norwegian *Hugleik*, 'mind reward'. *Uilleac* and *Uillioc* are variants. The name is in use today.

Ultan [*Ultán*] (m) This unusual name may be a derivative of *Ulaidh*, the Irish word for Ulster.

Ulysses (m) The Romans used the name *Ulixes*, perhaps from Etruscan *Uluxe,* for the Greek *Odysseus*, which is of uncertain meaning. They may then have used Ulysses to increase the names' resemblance to each other. In Ireland it was used to anglicise *Ulick*. James Joyce's *Ulysses* (1922) is a modern parallel of Homer's *Odyssey* set in Dublin, where Leopold Bloom takes the part of the wandering Ulysses, and Stephen Daedalus represents Telemachus, his son.

Una [*Úna*] (f) An early name, which at one stage was frequently anglicised as *Winifred*, but which is now once again popular in its own right. It was supposedly connected with *uan*, 'lamb', and it has on occasion been anglicised as *Agnes* or *Unity*. In England Una is sometimes the Latin word for 'one', taken from the character in the first book in Spenser's *Faerie Queene* (1590). However, as Spenser was resident for a time in Ireland, he may have been influenced by the Irish name. The name is pronounced *Oona* in Ireland, *Yoona* in England. *Ona, Oona(gh), Ownah* and *Wony* are variants.

Unity (f) A virtue name of the kind which became common amongst English Puritans. In Ireland it was used to anglicise the native *Una*.

Ursula (f) A diminutive of Latin *ursa*, 'she-bear'. It is quite popular in Ireland.

V

Valentine [*Vailintín*] (m) Latin, 'healthy'. A name used from time to time in Ireland, but at present it is declining. An Irish example in the seventeenth century was Valentine Greatrakes, who was reputed to be able to heal scrofula by touch.

Valerie (f) The French form of the Latin name *Valeria*, 'healthy'. It is sometimes found in Ireland today.

Vanessa (f) A name invented by the Irish writer, Jonathan Swift (1667-1745), to use for Esther Vanhomrigh. It has now spread beyond the shores of Ireland – the English actress, Vanessa Redgrave (1937–), has probably helped with its recent dissemination – and it is used quite frequently in Britain, Canada and Australia. Yonge, writing in the last century, does not mention it at all, indicating that it became widespread only in modern times.

Veronica (f) Latin, 'true image'. A name sometimes found in Ireland. It is given out of reverence for Veronica who is supposed to have wiped the face of Christ on the way to His Crucifixion.

Vevina (f) A form of the Gaelic name *Bébhinn* ('sweet lady') used by Macpherson in his Ossianic poems (1765).

Victor (m) Latin, 'conqueror'. A name which was more or less confined to Italy in the form *Vittore,* until after the French Revolution. It came into use in England in the nineteenth century (isolated examples had occurred before). Queen Victoria's similar name may have had an influence, though *Victoria* is not the feminine of Victor: it is the feminine of *Victorius*. In Ireland, Victor was used to anglicise *Buagh*.

Victoria [*Victeoiria*] (f) Latin, 'victory'. A name introduced into Ireland from England, where it came into general use only in the nineteenth century. Quite popular around 1900, it later declined, as it was considered too English in a time of Nationalist fervour. However, it is now making a comeback.

Vincent [*Uinseann*] (m) Latin, 'conquering'. This name was brought to Ireland by the Normans. The French priest St Vincent de Paul (1576-1669) probably added to its popularity. *Uinsionn* is a variant Irish form. It now seems to be used less and less.

Vivienne (f) Latin, 'living'. This name originally sprang up in the French language, perhaps due to confusion with Celtic *Ninian. Vivian,* another form, was used in Ireland to anglicise *Bébhinn* ('sweet lady') of which *Bevin* is the true translation. Vivian has also been recorded as a masculine name in Ireland.

W

Walter [*Ualtar*] (m) Germanic, 'rule folk'. The name of a prince of Aquitaine in legend, which was introduced to Ireland by the Normans. *Thaiter* was a peculiar Irish form, which now seems obsolete.

Walters [*Bhaltair*] (m) A variant of *Walter* borne by one, Bhaltair O'Toole, in the twelfth century. His name was variously translated as Walters and Walter.

Whiltierna [*Faoiltiarna*] (f) An early name, a combination of *faol,* 'wolf', and *tiarna,* 'lord', which sounds somewhat masculine for a woman's name.

William [*Liam*] (m) Germanic, 'will helmet'. A name frequently used by the Normans in medieval Ireland. It became very popular and remains so today. In Irish it became first *Uilliam,* then it was contracted to *Liam.* In modern times William is more frequently bestowed than the Irish Liam. William Butler Yeats (1865-1839) was an influential playwright and poet.

Winfred (m) This unusual name appears to be used in Ireland as a masculine form of *Winifred.* Indeed, Winifred itself was registered as a masculine name in Cork at the turn of the century. The name is unlikely to be connected with the Teutonic name *Winfred,* 'friend peace'.

Winifred (f) A name derived from *Wenefreda,* the Latin form of Welsh *Grewfrwei,* 'blessed reconciliation'. In Ireland it was used to anglicise the native name *Una,* perhaps because Una had a variant *Wony* which may have been thought identical with *Winnie,* the pet form of Winifred. As Winifred becomes less popular in modern Ireland, Una becomes more so.

Withypoll (f) This curious name, which may well be peculiar to Ireland, occurs in the pedigree of the *Losse* family of Dublin. It possibly comes from English *withy,* 'twig', 'willow' and *poll,* 'head'.

Wony (f) A form of *Una.*

Y

Y (m) This must surely be one of the world's shortest names. Actually, it is a form of *Aodh* which occurs in fifteenth-century documents.

Yseult (f) Variant of *Iseult.*

Ysolte (f) Variant of *Iseult.*

Yvonne (f) A French name, ultimately Germanic, signifying 'yew'. It is now fairly common in Ireland. *Evonne,* a possible variant, was registered in Ireland in 1975, and *Yvette,* a cognate name, also occurs.

Z

Zaira (f) This name was invented by the Irish writer C. R. Maturin, who used it in his novel *Women; or, pour et contre* (1818).

Zephan (m) This name is listed by Weidenham as that of an Irish saint.

Zinna (f) An unusual feminine name which occurs in the *Toler-Aylward* family of Shankhill Castle.

BOOK II

IRISH FAMILY NAMES

by Ida Grehan

Introduction

The Irish are a remarkably literary people. Writing — or talking about writing — is one of their main industries. Their intense interest in genealogy could be said to have been their first step along the road to literature. Pedigrees are about people. From earliest days the Irish could recite the descent of their families from ancient kings and chieftains. Reciting the litany of names provided the poets and the musicians with an endless flow of stories as heroic characters were recalled, Malachy who lost his collar of gold; Cormac MacCarthy who built the miniature church on the Rock of Cashel; Cearbhal, the warlike, Brian Boru's swordsman, who gave his name to the O Carrolls; Clerieach, Clark, progenitor of the O Clearys who helped compile the *Annals of the Four Masters* with its invaluable genealogical information.

The hewers of wood and drawers of water who had no names assumed the surnames of their chieftains — hence the importance of an authenticated pedigree.

Nicknames became respectable. Cruitín (hunchback) became MacCurtin. Dochartaigh meant 'obstructive' which, at one time, the O Dohertys were. The Norsemen the natives dubbed Dubhgall (dark stranger), are now the numerous Doyles. MacNamara, from the Irish which means 'hound of the sea', aptly described this sept on the seacoast of Clare. Ceallachain, meaning 'strife', probably described an earlier breed of O Callaghans. Conchobhair, 'hero' or 'champion', suited the Connacht O Connors who were High Kings of Ireland. The O Donnells of Tyrconnell, whose name means 'world mighty', are descendants of King Niall of the Nine Hostages, progenitor of many leading families, including the O Neills.

In Austria, where the Irish were very early missionaries, they are still known as Scots, a name they got from the Romans when they raided Britain from Ireland.

Hereditary surnames came spontaneously and compartatively early to Ireland — between the 10th and the 11th centuries. The prefix Mac meant 'son of', while O could signify either grandson, or earlier ancestor. Fitz, from the French 'fils', also meant 'son of'. A girl used Ni before her father's name, while her mother prefixed Ban.

During the centuries when the Irish and their Catholic religion were suppressed they were forced to drop these prefixes and to translate their names into English, which has led to some confusion such as MacAodhagain (Egan) becoming Keegan, or MacMathghamhna (MacMahon) becoming Vaughan, and many more.

Beginning with the Celts from Spain and then the Vikings who swept down from Scandinavia in their long boats to raid the coast, pillage the monasteries and found cities, Ireland absorbed a diversity of settlers. Unfortunately the Romans never got to Ireland. The Normans made the greatest impact with their fine stone buildings and their continental vitality and connections. Their names have long since become accepted as Irish. What Dillon, or Power, or FitzGerald would think he was anything other?

The sept, rather than the clan, was the Irish dynastic system. It comprised a group whose immediate ancestors had a common name and lived in the same locality. Chieftaincies were not hereditary — which often led to bloodshed or putting out of eyes: a maimed chieftain would not be acceptable.

With the easing of the discriminatory laws against the native Irish and a growing confidence in their own individuality, the prefix Mac and O began to be resumed in the late 19th century.

To trace a family back 1,000 years is to see the panorama of Irish history. To trace several families is to learn world history. Driven abroad by sword or famine the Irish fought on every side on battlefields in Europe, Russia and America north and south. They spread the gospel, filled high legal and political office, developed countries and commerce. They were journalists, dramatists, actors and labourers on the railroads and in the mines. Only recently have they begun to surface on an international level in music and painting, arts difficult for a suppressed people to follow.

There are millions more Irish men and women in Britain and the Americas, Australia, Argentina and Canada, than there are in Ireland. Eighty out of a possible 3,500 names is a modest offering. It is attempted in the hope of revealing a versatile race and giving a factual and balanced story of the island of Ireland through the vicissitudes of its leading families.

The Irish Genealogical Office which was established in 1552 has its new headquarters in Kildare Street, Dublin. The Chief Herald deals with an ever-increasing number of enquiries from abroad, especially from the USA and Australia, from people who are anxious to trace their roots and have sufficient documentary records of their families to enable them to do their research. There are also a number of professional research companies who will do this work for a specific fee.

Because a great many of Ireland's aristocratic families went abroad, their records and pedigrees are to be found mainly in the archives of France, Austria and Spain. These valuable historic documents are being explored and microfilmed for the National Library of Ireland, which should add considerably to research possibilities.

Ahearne *Ó hEachtighearna*
Hearne

Barry
Barrymore

Ahearne is practically the only Irish name spelled with the first letter of the alphabet. Originally it was Ó hEachtighearna, meaning 'lord of the horse' The family was one of the very many descendants of the High King, Brian Boru. They were of the Dal gCáis (Dalcassians), an important sept in very early times in the counties of Clare and Limerick.

In time the name took many forms, of which Hearne is commonest today. Hearne is also to be found in England so that, lacking exact genealogical information, some Hearnes could be of English origin. Fleeing from religious persecution in the 17th and 18th centuries, many Ahernes found a new life in France, in the church, in the colleges and in the royal courts.

In 1754 a Limerick man, John Aheron, was author and illustrator of the first book on Irish architecture to be printed in Ireland. Another John who spelled his name Aherne was a United Irishman and a friend of Wolfe Tone. When he had to flee Ireland he became an officer in Napoleon's army.

In the 18th century, sometimes changing from Ahearne to Herne or Hearne, many emigrated to Canada, the USA and Australia.

The Barrys came from Wales with the Anglo-Norman invasion in 1170. They soon possessed a vast area of Co. Cork. There were so many Barrys that, to distinguish one from the other, they were known as Barry Mór (the Senior), Barry Óg (the Young), Barry Roe (the Red), Barry Maol (the Bald) and Barry Liadir (the Strong). They acquired titles such as Earl of Barrymore and Viscount of Buttevant. This Tipperary town got its name from the French 'boutez-en-avant' ('strike forward'), the rallying cry of the Barrys in their many battles.

Several Barrys were prominent in the arts and medicine. James Barry was a distinguished painter in London. The stage was strong in the Barry blood from 16th-century actor/dramatists to the trio of Barrymore stage and film actors of Philadelphia.

A Wexford man, John Barry, is revered as 'the father of the American Navy'.

Like so many of the nobility of the 18th and 19th centuries, the Barrys squandered their money, drinking and gambling until most of their splendid houses were gone.

A hunting lodge, Fota Island (outside Cork city) remains, taken over by Cork University. It is beautifully preserved and the furnishings include many Irish paintings.

During the Irish war of independence there were two Barry patriots, Kevin Barry and Commander Tom Barry.

Also: **Aheron**, see above
Barrett, see page 81

Beirne *Ó Beirne*

Blake
Caddell

Beirne, with or without the Ó, should never be confused with Byrne although they may sound alike. Beirne is thought to have originated from the Norse Bjorn.

The Beirnes settled around Co. Roscommon, where they formed an important sept. They do not appear in the records until about the 18th century, when two brothers from a family living in County Meath were sent to Rome to study for the priesthood. They returned home and went different ways. One became a parish priest while the other became a famous Archbishop of Meath of the Established Church. Beirnes are well recorded on the army rolls of France, Spain and America, where an Ó Beirne took a major part in the American Civil War. Their armorial bearings are particularly colourful. In the centre is an orange tree with a green lizard sitting at the base and, on one side, a red cross. A band of blue tops the shield with a silver crescent and a smiling sun.

When they came with the Normans through Wales the Blake's name was Caddell. An especially dark-hued member of the family was nicknamed 'Le Blaca' (the Black). Thus the Blake name evolved. They settled in Galway city and county where, for hundreds of years, they were rich landowners and merchants and were numbered among the famous '14 Tribes of Galway'. Many of them were mayors and sheriffs of that city. They built castles all around Connacht, some of which survive. Apart from being statesmen they were also soldiers, going on the crusades and also taking part in Irish uprisings, including the decisive Battle of Kinsale.

An 18th-century Blake who inherited an enormous fortune got through it in a few years.

A Blake of Wicklow in the 19th century chartered a ship on which he sailed with his family and friends to Canada. There he was the progenitor of a succession of Toronto lawyers.

A branch of the Blake family settled in Co. Kildare where there are three Blakestowns.

In the west of Ireland there are Blake families of Gaelic origin whose name, Ó Blathmhaic, was anglicised to Blowick and then to Blake.

Boland *Ó Beolláin*
Bolan

The Bolands get their name from a Norwegian who came to Ireland very long ago. In Irish it is Ó Beolláin, while in English it used to be O Dolan. One branch of the family which claims descent from Mahon, one of King Brian Boru's brothers, went to Clare where they lived around Lough Derg. Ballybolan (the town of the Bolans) perpetuates their name. The other family settled in Sligo with their headquarters at Doonalton.

Little is recorded of the Bolands until the 20th century when they took part in the struggle for independence. A mission to America to collect funds and promote the Irish Republic internationally did very well. A Bolshevik party from Russia, who were doing far from well, asked for a loan of $20,000, offering what they said were some of the crown jewels as security. Harry Boland, who was with the delegation, gave the jewels to his mother for safe keeping. Harry was killed during the civil war. When Eamon de Valera came to power the Boland family gave him the jewels. It was not until 1948 that they were finally ransomed in London by the Russian Embassy there.

Frederick Boland was Irish Ambassador in London in the 1950s and also President of the United Nations. Eavan Boland, his daughter, is one of Ireland's leading poets. One of the oldest bakeries in Dublin, Boland's Mills, was the focus of much action during the Rising of 1916.

Boyle *Ó Baoighill*
O Boyle

There are two Boyle families, both of whom have made an impact on Ireland. In Irish Boyle is Ó Baoighill, which possibly means 'having profitable pledges'. They were a leading sept in Donegal, where their chieftain was duly inaugurated. The O Boyles of Boylagh owned much land in Co. Derry and had their castle at Desart in Co. Armagh.

Richard Boyle, who came as an 'adventurer' from England in the 16th century, has become known as 'the first colonial millionaire', the 1st Earl of Cork and the father of 15 children, most of whom — or their descendants — are among the Boyles featured in the *Dictionary of National Biography*. A scientific invention, Boyle's Law, was the work of one of his sons — the only untitled member of this opportunistic family. Richard Boyle 'acquired' the lands of most of the leading Irish families in Munster. When Sir Walter Raleigh was executed he bought his Waterford estate. At one time he made Lismore Castle there his principal seat.

In the 19th century Boyles from the north of Ireland began to go abroad; one to India and Japan to construct railroads; another to New York where he was a sculptor.

William Boyle was among the earliest dramatists to write for the infant Abbey Theatre in Dublin.

In recent years the Boyles have begun to resume their O prefix.

Brady, see page 81
Breen, see page 81
Brennan, see page 81

Browne
Brown   le Brun

Burke
Bourke   de Burgo

The Irish Brownes have made their mark in history since they came with the Normans in the 12th century, when they were known as le Brun. They settled in Galway, married into the leading families and joined the '14 Tribes of Galway'.

A Browne from England was granted a huge area of Kerry by Elizabeth I. Ross Castle by the lakes of Killarney was Browne property. Lord Castle-rosse, journalist and *bon viveur*, was the last of the Brownes to live in Kerry.

The Brownes spread through Ireland and went abroad in great numbers following the ill-fated Stuart monarchy. A soldier of fortune from Co. Limerick served in Russia where he rose to become Count George Browne at the court of Catherine the Great. A close relative was a Field Marshal in the Austrian army and a Count of the Empire.

William Brown from Co. Mayo was a founder of the Argentine navy. In America the Irish Browns were prominent in the army, science, the church, politics, education and commerce.

One of Ireland's rare cardinals was a Tipperary Browne.

Westport House in Co. Mayo, home of the Marquesses of Sligo of the Browne family, is in the stately home business and is managed by the heir, Lord Altamont. It is rich in the artefacts of Irish history and is visited by thousands every year.

The Burkes descend from William the Conqueror and are the most numerous and most thoroughly integrated of all the Normans who came to Ireland in the 12th century. Originally their name was de Burgo (of the borough).

They were granted vast areas of O Conor land in Connacht. They multiplied fast and divided into a number of septs. The two senior were distinguished as MacWilliam Uachtar of Galway and MacWilliam Iochtar of Mayo.

Although a Burke is credited with building Galway city, they were not accepted into the '14 Tribes of Galway'. They were prominent in Anglo-Irish politics and exchanged their Gaelic chieftaincy of Clanricarde for the royal titles of Earl and Marquess of Clanricarde.

The most famous Burke is Edmund, a Dublin-born writer and orator who was a privy councillor in London at the time of the French Revolution.

During the exodus to Europe in the 17th century, there was a Regiment of Burke serving in France. They also went in great numbers to America and Australia.

Irish family pedigrees and the study of genealogy owe a great debt to the Tipperary family of Burke who founded *Burke's Peerage* and *Burke's Landed Gentry*. A descendant, Sir Bernard Burke, once held the office today styled Chief Herald of the Irish Genealogical Office.

Buckley, see page 81

Butler

Cahill   *MacCathail*

The Butlers were one of the most outstanding of the Norman-Irish families. When Theobald Fitzwalter was created Chief Butler of Ireland by Herny II in 1177 the family came to be known as Butler. As they grew in importance they were created Earls of Ormond, the most important of many titles conferred on them. From their fortress at Gowran and, later, Kilkenny Castle, they feuded constantly with their neighbours and powerful rivals, the FitzGeralds, Earls of Kildare.

Anne Boleyn, one of the wives of Henry VIII and mother of Elizabeth I, was of Butler descent. The famous poet, William Butler Yeats, was also a kinsman.

The 7th Marquess and 31st Chief Butler lives in America. At the splendid Kilkenny Castle which the Butlers have handed over to the nation they gather from all over the world every three years for their family rally. A Butler archive has been set up in the castle tower. There are still Butlers in Europe, descendants of the 'Wild Geese'.

Butler is a very common name both in England and in Ireland. Lacking an authentic pedigree it would be impossible for anyone of the name to trace his ancestry to the Ormonds — or any other branch of this extensive family. Ulster is the only province the prolific Butlers failed to populate.

Cahill is one of the earliest recorded surnames. Originally a first name, Cathail is the Irish form of Charles which signifies 'valour'.

The first to bear this name was an important sept in south Galway in the very early times. Several distinct septs who developed independently spread to Munster, where there are no less than three Ballycahills in Co. Tipperary. There is also a Ballycahill in Co. Galway and another in Co. Clare — their original territory.

There are records of a 10th-century O Cahill martyr. The only other notable Cahill was a 19th-century crusading priest who collected in the USA for Catholic institutions in Ireland in the period of the Famine and Catholic Emancipation. In World War I three sons of the Ballyragget family in Co. Kildare were killed in action in France.

Cahill remains the most numerous name in Munster. The O prefix appears to have been dropped completely.

Byrne, see **O Byrne**, page 67

Caddell, see **Blake**, page 42

Callaghan, see **O Callaghan**, page 68

Carey, see page 81

Casey, see **O Casey**, page 82

Carroll *Ó Cearbhaill*
MacCarvill

The O Carrolls trace their ancestry to a 3rd-century King of Munster, Oilioll Olum. Their name comes from Cearbhal (warlike champion), one of King Brian Boru's leading swordsmen at the Battle of Clontarf in 1014. Until the arrival of the Normans in 1170 there had been six different O Carroll septs headed by O Carroll Ely (Tipperary and Offaly) and O Carroll Oriel (Monaghan and Louth).

Much of their Tipperary territory was annexed by their powerful neighbours, the Norman Butlers. They were dispersed to various parts of the country, most particularly to Co. Offaly.

Father John Gleeson's *History of the Ely O Carroll Territory* was reprinted in 1982.

They were early churchmen who founded monasteries. They married into the royal blood of Ireland and England. They were incessant fighters, and fled with the 'Wild Geese' to Europe where they put their swords to use in the armies of France and other countries.

In the 20th century they founded Ireland's biggest tobacco industry, P. J. Carroll Ltd of Dundalk, Co. Louth.

An Ely O Carroll went to America at the end of the 17th century and was progenitor of a line of aristocratic and prominent American Carrolls who called their Maryland home Carrollton Manor.

O is their most numerous prefix but there is a separate MacCarroll sept which, in Ulster, has been anglicised to MacCarvill.

Clery *Ó Cleirigh*
Cleary Clarke

Cleary is of some antiquity, dating from an early 9th-century Cléireach of the lineage of King Guaire of Connacht, renowned for his hospitality. His well-restored Dunguaire Castle on Galway Bay hosts medieval banquets in the summer.

Cléireach is the Irish work for 'clerk'. Early in the 16th century a family of O Clerys were instrumental in compiling a most valuable Irish manuscript, *The Annals of the Four Masters*. It was written mostly by a Franciscan monk in the ruined friary of Donegal.

The Clerys had been driven from Connacht to Ulster where they were poets, churchmen and *brehons* (lawgivers).

When the use of Gaelic names was forbidden the name was anglicised to Clarke. Lacking a family tradition or an official pedigree it is now impossible to distinguish between the Irish Clarkes who were O Clery and the many immigrant English Clarkes. Time has led to a happy integration and no one would question the Irishness of Thomas Clarke, one of the leaders of the 1916 Rising and first signatory to the Proclamation of the Irish Republic, Austin Clarke, the poet or Harry Clarke, the stained glass artist.

Two daughters of a Clery in Marseilles became Julie, Queen of Spain, and Desiree, Queen of Norway and Sweden, in Napoleonic times.

Collins *Ó Coileáin*

There are very many of the name in England as well as in Ireland. Collins is an anglicisation of the Irish Ó Coileáin (whelp or young creature).

Until they were driven away by the Anglo-Norman invasion, the Ó Coileáin had been lords of the barony of Connello in Co. Limerick. They went further south to settle in West Cork, where the majority of the Collins are now to be found.

There were distinguished ecclesiastical Collins, including a patriot Jesuit who was hung in 1602, and a Dominican who led an attack on Bunratty Castle in 1647. An Ó Coileáin poet earned the epithet 'The Silver Tongue of Munster'.

An early emigrant, a Collins from Offaly, was a governor of Tasmania and a founder of Sydney. Another, who exchanged Wicklow for London, bred several generations of painters and authors, including Wilkie Collins who wrote *The Moonstone*.

There have been comparatively few Irish explorers, but a Collins has been recorded in the Arctic. In America a Collins line represented a family of shipowners who left Ireland in 1635.

The hero of the Collins family is Michael, 'The Big Fellow', whose promising political life was cut short in the civil war in 1922.

Connolly *Ó Conghaile*

Conghaile, the original Gaelic version of Connolly, means 'valorous'. They were an ancient sept of Connacht who in time separated and dispersed as three distinct families. They are still mainly based around counties Cork, Meath and Monaghan, where they were one of the 'Four Tribes of Tara'. In Monaghan, about 1591, Tirlogh O Connola is recorded as being chief of his name.

Because of his dazzling wealth the most famous Connolly was an early 18th-century William Connelly from Donegal whose family paved the way to success by conforming to the religion of the Establishment. A lawyer, he bought and sold the lands lost by the old Gaelic families exiled following the Battle of the Boyne. He was speaker in the Irish House of Commons. He began the building of the splendid Co. Kildare mansion, Castletown, now the headquarters of the very active Irish Georgian Society.

'Little Mo', the meteoric USA tennis star of the 50s, was a Connolly.

The patriot James Connolly, born in Scotland, was an Irish trade union pioneer and commanded the Republican army in Dublin. He signed the Proclamation of the Irish Republic just before his execution.

Connell, see **O Connell**, page 68

Also see page 81 for:
Conroy
Conway
Cooney
Corcoran
Costello
Coughlan
Crowley

Cullen *Ó Cuillin*

Curtin *Mac Cuirtin*
MacCurtin   Curtayne

Cullen in Irish is Ó Cuillin (holly tree). They were once a numerous clan in Wicklow until driven away by the O Byrnes and O Tooles. They moved to Co. Kildare, and there many have remained, giving their name to the town of Kilcullen.

They were in Wexford, too, recorded in the late 16th century as being gentry of Cullenstown.

This comparatively simple name has worked its way through an astonishing number of variations including Cullion, Culhoun, MacCullen and Cullinane. It could also be connected with a Scottish clan.

They were remarkable for their powerful clergymen, particularly bishops. There were a number of Cullen castles and mansions in the midlands, including ruined Liscarton Castle, once home of relatives of Ireland's first cardinal, Cardinal Paul Cullen.

In the early 19th century many sailed for the Argentine.

They were also prominent administrators in Australia. A shrub, *eucalyptus cullenii*, is named after a Cullen horticulturist there.

O rather than the Mac is thought to be the correct Irish prefix to this name, although Mac is more likely to be found now. At one time the name in Irish was Cruitín (hunchback).

Originally the MacCruitíns' territory was on the Atlantic seaboard between Ennistymon and Corcomroe Abbey in Co. Clare. A MacCurtin who was chief of his sept was one of a long line of medieval scholars, poets and bards; a succession of them were hereditary bards to the aristocratic O Briens of nearby Thomond. Scattered by various internal battles, the Mac Curtins were dispersed around the country, especially to Limerick, Cork and, later, Dublin.

The MacCurtin family were prominent in France during the Revolution. One was a signatory to the National Convention, while a Major General Curtin was a leader of the Royalist opposition army.

A Cork man, Tomás MacCurtain, who commanded the Cork Brigade during the war of independence and was later Lord Mayor of Cork, was brutally murdered in 1920 by misguided militia.

Cummins, see page 81
Curran, see page 81

Cusack *Cíomhsóg*

The Cusacks came from Guienne, a province of France, in 1211 in the wake of the Anglo-Norman invasion and were rewarded with a considerable acreage of Kildare and Meath. They integrated wholeheartedly with their Irish neighbours, and fought their way also to new possessions in Mayo, where they were known as MacIosóg.

They were on the side of James II at the Battle of the Boyne, and subsequently sailed with the many refugees to France to serve in the armies of Europe. One Cusack who had soldiered in Flanders turned to privateering on the high seas.

A distinguished and fashionable Dublin surgeon was the uncle of Margaret Cusack, 'the nun of Kenmare', a very emancipated and high-minded woman who dramatically changed her religious allegiance several times.

The Gaelic Athletic Association was founded in 1884 largely through the inspiration of Michael Cusack from Clare.

Cyril Cusack is a much acclaimed actor of stage and screen who is ably followed by his daughters.

Daly *Ó Dálaigh*

In Irish the name is Ó Dálaigh, which was the word for a meeting place, as in Dail Eireann.

The Ó Dálaigh ancestry goes back to the 4th century, to Niall of the Nine Hostages, the High King who had his palace at Tara, Co. Meath, and from whom descend also the O Neills and the O Donnells.

They are very prominent in records dating from the 12th to the 18th century, when their extraordinary genius for bardic literature was manifest in the bardic school set up by Cuconnacht Ó Dálaigh in Westmeath.

From the 11th to the 17th century they were hereditary poets and minstrels to most of the leading families.

Their outstanding churchman was a Dominican friar, Daniel, who, fleeing religious persecution, went to Europe where he founded colleges in Louvain and Lisbon.

From a Daly family, Barons of Dunsanele and Clan Conal in Co. Galway, came six mayors of the city of Galway. This family emigrated to the colonies, America and Australia, where they distinguished themselves as administrators and, in Britain, in the army.

In the 1970s Chief Justice Cearbhaill Ó Dálaigh of County Wicklow was with the Court of Justice of the European Economic Community and, afterwards, for a brief period, President of the Republic of Ireland.

See page 81 for:
Delany
Dempsey
Devine
Devlin

Dillon

The Dillons are a widespread and well-recorded family who in the 800 years since their arrival from Brittany as de Leon have merged indistinguishably with the Irish. They were granted great acreages where they prospered and grew so numerous that their lands around Longford, Westmeath and Kilkenny were called Dillon's Country.

Offshoots of the family went to Mayo and Sligo, where the head of that family was Viscount Dillon of Costello-Gallen. The Dillons acquired many peerages and played an active role in the tangle of 17th-century Anglo-Irish politics. They built many castles but lost them and their land because of their adherance to Catholicism.

Following the devastation perpetrated by the Cromwellians they fled to France, where they raised a Regiment of Dillon in which Irish refugees distinguished themselves. During the French Revolution Theobald, Count Dillon, a Field Marshal of France who had fought in the American War of Independence, was its colonel.

Portlick Castle, Glasson, Co. Meath, is one of the best preserved of their remaining castles. Clonbrock House in Ballinasloe, Galway, where the Dillons had lived since 1575, was sold a few years ago and its invaluable archives were presented by Luke Dillon-Mahon to the nation.

Doherty *Ó Dochartaigh*

There are many variants of O Doherty of which Doherty is the most usual. In Irish it is Ó Dochartaigh, which is supposed to mean 'obstructive'. They are descended from the powerful 4th-century King Niall of the Nine Hostages. Their earliest headquarters was the Inishowen Peninsula in Donegal.

Their promising but foolish chief, Cahir Ó Doherty, in an ill-conceived rebellion attacked Derry and was massacred. This uprising let to the Plantation of Scottish settlers in the six counties of Ulster, laying the base for continuing strife.

Cahir's brother joined the 'Wild Geese' in their flight to Europe. His accredited descendant is in Cadiz, Spain and styles himself 'The O Doherty'.

From colonial resistance in Ireland the O Dohertys fled to Scotland and England where they merged successfully. Later they emigrated to Australia and north America.

The O Dohertys are still plentiful in Donegal where, since 1981, they have been planning a clan rally for 1985. Already there has been a clan rally in the USA, where there is an O Doherty Family Research Association.

Dolan, see page 81

Donoghue *Ó Donnchadha*
Dunphy

There are a variety of ways in which this important and numerous Irish patronymic can be spelled. In Irish it is Ó Donnchadha, coming from the personal name Donnchadh (Donogh).

At first there were O Donoghue septs in Cork and Kerry, where Ross Castle was their fortress on Lough Lene, Killarney. Other septs moved up to Galway, Kilkenny and Cavan, where their descendants are usually Donohue. They claim descent from a King of Munster who fought at Clontarf in 1014.

In Kerry their chieftain was O Donoghue Mór of Ross Castle, while the other was O Donoghue of the Glens, also in Kerry. His descendant is styled 'The O Donoghue', one of approximately fifteen chieftains who have been officially recognised as such.

A 12th-century O Donoghue founded the beautiful Jerpoint Abbey in Co. Kilkenny. A namesake of the present O Donoghue, Geoffrey O Donoghue of the Glens, was a revered 17th-century poet and scholar at Glenflesk, Killarney.

In Kilkenny some of the O Donoghue sept changed their name to the more high-sounding Dunphy. In the 18th century the O Donoghues were with the Irish diaspora who served in the continental armies. Ironically, the last Spaniard to rule Mexico bore the name Juan O Donju.

Doyle *Ó Dubhghaill*

When the Norsemen came to Ireland about the 9th century they were called dubh-ghall (dark foreigner). In Irish Doyle is Dubhghall and it is assumed that they were Norsemen, which seems to be borne out by the fact that this very numerous name is so prevalent on the south-east coast, particularly around Wexford.

They are not mentioned in the ancient Irish genealogies. However, from the 17th century on they feature, particularly in the armies of Europe and, later, Britain, where at one time there were six Doyles from Kilkenny all with the rank of major general.

There were many distinguished Doyle ecclesiastics. Arthur Conan Doyle, the inventor of the great detective Sherlock Holmes, was the descendant of a famous family of artists and writers who had originated from Dublin.

In comparatively recent times Jack Doyle, 'the Gorgeous Gael', blazed a starry trail across the boxing rings, the footlights and the divorce courts.

Donovan, see **O Donovan**, page 70
Doran, see page 81
Dowling, see page 81

Driscoll, see **O Driscoll**, page 82

Duffy *Ó Dubthaigh*

The Irish Ó Dubhthaig gives a clue to this name. Dubh means 'black'. Little is recorded of their origins except that in the 7th century they were prominent in the church in Monaghan. At that time, too, the patron saint of Raphoe in Donegal was Dubhtach. In Ulster the name has been transformed to Dowey.

Exceptionally gifted craftsmen, in the 12th century they enriched monasteries and churches working for the High King, Turlough O Conor.

In Roscommon there was such a multitude of Duffys there is a town there called Lissyduffy.

In the 19th century Sir Charles Gavan Duffy was the progenitor of a succession of able lawyers. He went to Australia where he was Premier of Victoria and left many distinguished descendants. His daughter founded Dublin's famous Irish language school.

An ex-Irish army officer and garda, General Eoin O Duffy, organised an Irish brigade to fight for Franco during the Spanish Civil War.

In the 19th century James Duffy founded a Dublin publishing firm which is still in existence. Duffy's is one of the oldest circuses still touring the Irish roads.

Duggan, see page 81

Dunne *Ó Duinn*
Dunn

Although there are Dunnes in England, it is a very numerous Irish name and means 'brown'. The sept predominated in the midlands, in Leix, where at one time they were Lords of Iregan, one of the important families in Leinster.

In the 12th century the chief poet of Leinster was Giolla-na-Naomh O Dunn.

They were very active in the Jacobite wars, and afterwards they emigrated to the USA, where they served in the church, the law and the army.

In Ulster the more usual form of the name is Dunn.

A five times President of the Royal College of Physicians in Ireland came from Scotland in the 17th century. Sir Patrick Dun's Hospital in Dublin is his lasting memorial.

In recent years Dunne's Stores, a countrywide chain store group, has become a household word.

Dunphy, see **Donaghue**, page 51
Dwyer, see **O Dwyer**, page 82

Egan *Mac Aodhagáin*
Keegan

MacAodhagáin means 'son of Aodh' (anglicised to Hugh). Seldom using their Mac prefix, in modern times the name has become Egan. Their origins are in Galway, Roscommon and Leitrim. They were scattered to Tipperary, Kilkenny and Offaly.

For generations they had held the hereditary office of *ollav* or lawyer to the ruling families. Following the destruction of the old Gaelic order they held high office in the church, while also taking part in many battles.

Two Pierce Egans, father and son, were popular writers in 19th-century London. Another London-born Egan who styled himself 'The MacEgan', though not officially accredited, was a painter of distinction.

In the USA there were many Egans, one of whom became known as 'the Dean of the Diplomatic Corps'.

When Irish names had to be changed to their nearest English equivalent Egan sometimes became Keegan, especially in Dublin and Wicklow.

Thanks to a family of lawyers in Castlebar, Redwood Castle in Lorrha, Tipperary, has been beautifully restored and is the setting for Clan MacEgan rallies.

FitzGerald

Fitz means 'son' and since Maurice, son of Gerald, came with the Norman invaders in 1170 the FitzGeralds proliferated and became one of the most powerful families. Their leaders were the Fitzgeralds, Earls of Kildare and Dukes of Leinster, and the Fitzgeralds who were Earls of Desmond (Kerry and Cork).

In the 16th century Garret Mór, 8th Earl of Kildare, was for 40 years regarded in all but name as King of Ireland. The Earls of Desmond were in rebellion for many terrible years and became extinct when the 16th Earl was killed in Elizabethan times.

They built splendid castles, a number of which are still in good condition. In succeeding generations many FitzGeralds who opposed English rule were imprisoned or executed in the Tower of London.

An early Earl of Desmond created his three illegitimate sons Knight of Glin, Knight of Kerry and the (no longer surviving) White Knight.

The FitzGeralds have seldom been out of politics. A modern Garret FitzGerald has been three times Taoiseach (Prime Minister).

See page 81 for:
Fagan
Fahy
Fallon

Farrell, see **O Farrell**, page 71

Flaherty, see **O Flaherty**, page 71

See page 81 for:
Fitzpatrick
Flanagan
Flynn
Fogarty
Foley
Gaffney

Gallagher *Ó Gallchobhair*

The Gallaghers, who were one of the principal septs of Donegal, are still very numerous there. They claimed absolute seniority over the Cineal Connail, the royal family of Connall Gulban, son of the great 4th-century King Niall of the Nine Hostages.

A translation from the Irish for their name, gallchobhair (foreign help), was possibly acquired in the three centuries when they were marshalls in the armies of the O Donnells.

Their notabilities in the main were clerical. Six O Gallaghers were Bishop of Raphoe in Donegal.

Redmond O Gallagher, Bishop of Derry, helped the Armada sailors wrecked off Donegal and was executed by the English.

Frank Gallagher, a journalist who fought in the civil war, was the first editor of De Valera's newspaper, the *Irish Press*. Patrick Gallagher of Donegal, known as 'Paddy the Cope', initiated the idea of co-operative farming.

Guinness *MagAonghusa*
Magennis

In 1894 sixteen different versions were recorded of the ancient Ulster surname, MagAonghusa. It means 'son of Aonghus' (one choice). Their ancestry goes back to a 5th-century chief of Dal Araidhe. By the 12th century they had become lords of Iveagh in County Down, where they had their fortress at Rathfriland.

Although they played along with the Elizabethans, they were with Hugh O Neill at the victorious Battle of the Yellow Ford in 1598.

They survived disastrous defeat at Kinsale and had their 22,000 acres restored. Magennis of Iveagh was created Viscount. They had several distinguished bishops in the family, both Catholic and Protestant. A Viscount Iveagh sat in the 'Patriot Parliament' in 1689, the last such until 1922. Shortly after the Battle of the Boyne the Magennis's joined the exodus to serve in the armies of Austria, France, Spain and later, America.

The Guinness name has been stamped on the Irish consciousness since 1759, when Arthur Guinness set up his enormously successful brewery by the River Liffey in Dublin. The Guinness family endeared themselves by their generous contributions in charitable institutions. The company, affectionately known as 'Uncle Arthur', was one of the corner stones of the Irish economy.

Healy *Ó hÉildhe*
Hely

Hennessy *Ó hAonghusa*
Hensey Henchy

The modern Healy/Hely is an amalgam of two distinct septs, Ó hEildhe (éildhe means 'claimant') whose chieftains were centred on Lough Arrow in Co. Sligo, and Ó hÉilaighthe (éaladhach means 'ingenious') who settled in Donoughmore in Co. Cork.

They were all dispossessed of their lands by the Cromwellians. Even before that crucial period Healys had gone abroad for their education, especially for the priesthood.

When John Hely of Cork married a Hutchinson heiress he added her name to his and began a line of distinguished Hely Hutchinsons who were Earls of Donoughmore. The first John Hely Hutchinson was Provost of Trinity College Dublin. In 1974 the elderly Earl and Countess of Donoughmore were abducted for a while from their ancestral home, Knocklofty, in County Tipperary. They have since sold Knocklofty.

In the 18th and 19th centuries there were a number of prominent painters in the Healy family, including a stained glass artist. Tim Healy of Bantry was a journalist, wit and politician in London. He was the first Governor General of the Irish Free State from 1922 to 1928. Ulster born Cahir Healy has been described as 'one of the sanest and most farseeing leaders of the northern nationalists'.

Ó hAonghusa comes from a personal name, Aonghus or Angus. There are as many places called Ballyhennessy in Connacht and Munster as there were branches of this family who have totally discarded the O prefix, gradually transforming their name to Hennessy, Hensey and Henchy.

The leading sept were in Offaly, near Kilbeggan. Another sept had their lands on the borders between Meath and Dublin. With the arrival of the Normans in 1170 they fled to Limerick, Tipperary and Cork where the majority of the name is still to be found.

One of their strongholds, Ballymacmoy near Mallow, Co. Cork, has only recently been abandoned by the Hennessys.

They served with great distinction in the French army and at the court, where they were given titles of nobility. It was an Irish member of this martial family, retired from the French army, who discovered the formula for the brandy of Cognac which continues to keep their name before the public. They also had an eye for horses and one of their French thoroughbreds won the Triple Crown in the Hennessy Gold Cup.

A member of the distinguished Pope Hennessy family of Cork, an MP for Westmeath, was the first Catholic Conservative member to hold an Irish seat.

Hearne/Herne, see **Ahearne**, page 41
Hegarty, see **O Hegarty**, page 82

Hickey, see page 81

Higgins *Ó hUigin*

Although there are also Higgins of British origin, in Ireland the name is an ancient one, a translation from the Irish Ó hUigín (uigín meaning 'knowledge'). Earlier, they were a branch of the Westmeath O Neills. Many of them moved away to Co. Sligo where, until recently, they owned much land.

From the 13th to the 17th century there were eight Ó hUigín poets, including one who was also a bishop. Following the submergence of the poets and bards the O Higgins changed to medicine and the sciences, where they excelled.

One of the Meath family was an 18th-century Viceroy of Peru. His son, the famous Bernardo O Higgins, Liberator of Chile, was its first President. Their name is commemorated in Chile in the province called O Higgins.

Two Higgins qualify for the list of Irish eccentrics. One, a divinity graduate of Dublin, preached sedition in London, where he also kept a house of ill fame. The other, 'The Sham Squire', followed every means of accumulating money; changing his religion, marrying an heiress, gambling, journalism, informing.

Many Higgins sailed for Australia. A son of a Co. Down family was Attorney General there.

The founder of the Civic Guards, patriot and lawyer Kevin O Higgins, was assassinated in 1927.

Hogan *Ó hOgáin*

Óg is Irish for 'young'. An Ó hOgáin sept descends from the celebrated 10th-century King of Ireland, Brian Boru. They were of the Dalcassian people who inhabited Thomond, around Clare and Limerick. They divided to spread across Tipperary, where their chieftain has his fortress at Nenagh.

The Hogans lost their lands under the Cromwellians but had some re-granted by Charles II.

In 1691 'Galloping Hogan' became the hero of Sarsfield's destruction of the Williamite siege train at Ballyneety.

Later some went to Europe. There was a Hogan surgeon in the Irish brigade in France, and they were with T. J. Meagher in the Irish-American brigades in the Civil War of the 1860s.

John Hogan from Waterford reached great eminence as a sculptor in Rome, only driven home by the revolution of 1848 to enrich Ireland with his beautiful statues.

In the 19th century the Hogans contributed to literature. Edmund, a Jesuit priest, edited books on Irish place names and biographies. Michael, 'the Bard of Thomond', wrote popular verse. Austin Hogan of Clare founded the Transport Workers Union of America, while another man from Clare, Patrick Hogan, patriot, trade unionist and writer, was a senator and speaker in Dáil Éireann.

Hoey, see **Keogh**, page 58
Hoy, see **Keogh**, page 58
Jennings, see page 81

Joyce

The Joyce name has been deeply embedded in Connacht since they arrived there by sea in the wake of the Norman invaders. Joyce comes from the French personal name Joy. They quickly intermarried with strong local families like the O Briens, Princes of Thomond.

A huge clan, they owned vast territory in the barony of Ross (Co. Galway), known today as Joyce's Country, and were admitted into the elite of the '14 Tribes of Galway'. There were Joyce bishops and crusaders to the Holy Land. One who was captured en route was shown buried treasure by an eagle. When he escaped with this wealth he used it to build the walls of Galway city.

A Joyce captured in the Middle East learned the art of gold and silver smithing. It is he who is credited with the origins of the Claddagh ring.

A family literary strain is epitomised in James Joyce, playwright, poet, musician and author of *Ulysses*.

During World War II the infamous William Joyce broadcast Nazi propaganda from Germany. Of mixed Irish-English-American background, his English affiliations caused him to be hanged for treason when he was captured after the war.

Kavanagh *Caomhánach*

Cavanagh

The Kavanaghs are direct descendants of Diarmuid MacMurrough, 12th-century King of Leinster, who initiated the Anglo-Norman invasion. He sent his son Donal to be educated at Wexford with the monks at Kilcavan (Cill Caomhan, i.e. St Kevin's Church). Perhaps to distinguish him from the other Donals the King's son was called Caomhanach, anglicised to Kavanagh.

Donal, alias Kevin/Kavanagh, was not chosen to succeed as king. He was compensated with large areas of Wexford and Carlow, still the base of the numerous Kavanaghs.

Art MacMurrough, the first to style himself Kavanagh, was King of Leinster for 42 years. He fought hard to oust the invaders. His struggle was continued by a succession of McMurrough Kavanagh kings until the time of Henry VIII.

Art McMurrough Kavanagh, a direct descendant of Leinster kings and a 13th child, was born lacking legs or arms. Thanks to the devotion of his mother he grew to be an athlete, sportsman and scholar. He became heir to the great Borris estate, married, fathered seven children, and was an MP. He has inspired many books.

A man from a Monaghan farm, Patrick Kavanagh, is one of the leading 20th-century Irish poets.

Castles at Enniscorthy and Ferns, Borris House and the Kavanagh drinking horn in Trinity College Dublin are tangible reminders of these kings of Leinster.

Keane *Ó Cathain*
Kane

Keogh *MacEochaidh*
Kehoe   Hoey   Hoy

The Keane/Kane family were originally Mac Cathain of West Clare, Ó Cahain of Ulster and Ó Céin of Munster. In time their anglicisation as Keane, or Kane, made their topographical origins difficult to define. Their name derives from the personal name Cian.

Blosky O Kane, who slew the heir to the throne in the 12th century, was the forefather of the MacCloskeys. Aibhne Ó Catháin's descendants became the McEvinneys.

The Kanes tend to be numerous in Ulster while the Keanes are usually to be found in Munster and Connacht.

For centuries, both at home and far afield, the Kanes/Keanes were active military men. In the 18th century there were 14 O Keane brothers serving in Europe.

In the 19th century, Kanes and Keanes were prominent in the sciences, architecture and the arts. The great acting family of Edmund Kean and his son Charles had their origins in Waterford. The popular playwright-publican, John B. Keane, is a Kerryman.

John Keane and James Keane, at different periods, were two of many Irish-Americans who filled the post of Bishop of Dubuque in Iowa, USA.

MacEochaidh—it needs an Irish speaker to pronounce it—was anglicised to Keogh, pronounced Kee-oh. Eochaidh, a personal name, was adopted by a family which comprised three distinct septs. Their territory was Limerick and Ballymackeogh; the second sept were lords of Moyfinn around Athlone and Roscommon (known as Keogh's Country); the third sept, the MacKeoghs of Leinster, is the most recorded. They were related to the O Byrnes, for whom they were hereditary bards. In 1534 Maolmuire MacKeogh was the finest poet in Leinster, one of a line of poets of the name.

Following the Norman invasion they moved south to Wexford, where they are now more usually known as Kehoe.

John Keogh of Dublin was an early pioneer of Catholic Emancipation. William Keogh of Keoghville, Galway, a wealthy judge, fell foul of the Fenians and the Home Rulers, who hounded him out of Ireland.

Myles Keogh of Carlow has become an American folk hero for his part in the disastrous incident at the Little Big Horn.

In some cases Keogh was anglicised to O Hoey or Hoy. They were of the sept which was descended from the early kings of Ulster.

Another offshoot who were Limerick landowners spelled their name K'Eogh. They also had property in Holland and Switzerland.

Kirwan *Ó Ciardubháin*

The origins of the Kirwans go back to Heremon of the Milesians who probably came from Spain. In Irish their name is Ciardubháin ("black"). Louth was one of their earlier settlements. When they moved to Galway, with the Darcys, they were the only native families accepted into the '14 Tribes of Galway'.

They have a long history of eminent ecclesiastics, both Catholic and Protestant. As priests and soldiers they had close connections with Europe. Richard Kirwan of Cregg Castle, Galway, who was 6ft 4in. tall, was with Dillon's Regiment at Fontenoy. His fondness for duelling caused his dismissal from the French army, whereupon he changed to the Austrian army. In the 18th century there were a number of Kirwan medical men in France. James Kirwan was a physician to the indolent Louis XV.

From Château Kirwan in the Medoc comes the prestigious French wine which still bears their name.

A Dublin Kirwan precipitated the 1803 revolution and was executed with Robert Emmet.

Richard Kirwan of the Cregg Castle family was an amazingly versatile man, a true eccentric. He left the Jesuits and, in time, became a most learned member of the Royal Dublin Society and was first President of the Royal Irish Academy.

Lacy *de Léis*
de Lacy

The de Lacys took their name from Lascy in Normandy, from which they came to conquer England and then Ireland.

The founder of this once great Norman family was Hugh de Lacy, who was given 800,000 acres in Meath, deposing the royal O Melaghlins (now known as MacLaughlin). Hugh married Rose, daughter of O Conor, King of Connacht, and built castles, including Trim Castle by the River Boyne.

His son, Walter, acquired land in Co. Down and was created Earl of Ulster by the English. Realising the de Lacys were growing too powerful, King John expelled them to Scotland for a while. In the 16th century the de Lacys joined with the native Irish in the struggle to expel the Elizabethan usurpers.

A strongly military family, when they had to leave Ireland with the 'Wild Geese' they joined the Irish brigades in France. Peter Lacy of Limerick, following the Battle of the Boyne, went to Poland and Russia, where Peter the Great employed him to train the élite of his army. As Peter, Count Lacy, after 50 years in Russia, he retired to his estates there. His son, Count Franz Moritz, born in St Petersburgh, served the Empress of Austria as Field Marshal. There are still Lacys in Russia.

Although the de Lacys have long since left their ancestral estates at Ballingarry, Bruff and Bruree they are still numerous in all four provinces.

Lynch *Ó Loingsigh*

Lynch, one of the most numerous and distinguished Irish surnames, is a fusion of two different races. One forebear was de Lynch who came with the Normans. The other was Labradh Longseach (mariner), who in the 6th century BC was King of Ireland. These Lynches settled in Clare, Sligo and Limerick, with a branch in Donegal.

The Norman Lynches were leaders of the '14 Tribes of Galway'. From 1484–1654 Galway city had 84 Lynch mayors. To protect their families and their wealth they built strong castles in Connemara and in Galway city.

Dominic Lynch founded a school there, attended by thousands of scholars. His son was Archdeacon of Tuam and an historian. He had to flee to France and Spain with many other learned Irish priests.

The Blosse Lynch family of Co. Mayo (the Blosse came from a marriage) were 19th-century travellers and merchants who explored the Euphrates, the Tigris in Persia and sailed into Baghdad.

The Lynches went to Australia, the Argentine and Chile, where Patrick Lynch is remembered as 'the foremost Chilean naval hero'. Elizabeth Lynch and the Paraguayan dictator, Francisco Lopez II, held sway there for a dozen years.

Thomas Lynch, a plantation owner, signed the American Declaration of Independence.

Jack Lynch of Cork, who won six All-Ireland medals for hurling and Gaelic football, was Taoiseach for two terms in the 1970s.

See page 81 for:
Lyons
MacAuley
MacAuliffe
MacBride

MacCabe *Mac Cába*

In the middle ages Irish chieftains imported fighting men from Scotland to augment their forces. Many of these mercenaries, known as gallowglasses, were the MacCabes who came from Inis Gall (the Isles of the Norsemen) in the Hebrides. They served the O Reillys and the O Rourkes of Leitrim and Cavan. It is thought their name comes from the peculiar hats they wore; caba means 'hat' or 'cap'.

They remained in Ireland to found their own sept. One of these, Cathaoir MacCabe, was a close friend of Turlough O Carolan, the greatest of the MacCabe bards. O Carolan offended MacCabe by writing a premature lament on his death. When O Carolan died Cathaoir wrote a beautiful lament for him.

A Belfast MacCabe prevented the shipowners there from using their vessels for the slave trade. His son, William Putnam MacCable, who was very active during the 1798 rising, eluded all his pursuers because of his uncanny talent for disguise. He escaped to Normandy where he followed his father's business by setting up a cotton mill.

They can boast a cardinal; Edward Cardinal MacCabe (1816-1885).

Eugene MacCabe, a Monaghan farmer, wrote a number of popular plays which were performed at Dublin's Abbey Theatre.

MacCann, see page 82

MacCarthy *MacCarthaigh*

MacCarthy is one of the most ancient and numerous surnames in Ireland, going back to a 3rd-century King of Munster. The surname derives from Carthac, a 12th-century descendant.

A MacCarthy king and bishop, Cormac, built the much admired chapel on the holy Rock of Cashel, still known as Cormac's chapel. The MacCarthys were good builders, and the remains of their fine castles are to be found all over Munster.

Blarney is the most famous, and there lived Cormac MacCarthy, whose evasive answers to Queen Elizabeth's letters demanding his submission roused her to call his protestations 'blarney'. So started the legend that kissing the Blarney Stone would convey eloquence. There was no lack of eloquence in the MacCarthy family, from whom has come a succession of poets and writers.

Florence MacCarthy, Lord of Carberry, dared to strengthen his territories by marrying his cousin, Lady Ellen of the Clan Carthy, which also displeased the English monarch. Florence was eventually incarcarated in the Tower of London, where he spent 37 years occupied with writing a history of Ireland, published 200 years after his death.

In Ireland the Muckross estate, by the Lakes of Killarney — once the home of the MacCarthy Mór — is looked after now by the state and is open to the public.

MacCarroll, see **Carroll**, page 46
MacCarvill, see **Carroll**, page 46
MacConmara, see **MacNamara**, page 64
MacCormack, see page 82
MacCurtin, see **Curtin**, page 48

MacDermot *MacDiarmada*
MacDermott Kermode

The brother of Muiredach Mullethan, King of Connacht in the 8th century, Maelruanaidh Mór (Mulrooney) was Prince of Moylurg in Roscommon. It was from a 12th-century descendant, Dermot, King of Moylurg, that they adopted the surname Dermot (free man).

Their territories in Roscommon and Sligo were known as 'MacDermot's Country'. They built their fortress on the legendary island of Lough Cé. A 16th-century chieftain, Brian MacDermot, instigated the writing of the *Annals of Lough Cé*, now in Trinity College Dublin.

In ancient times there were three MacDermot septs; those who descended from Muiredach Mullethan, forebears of the kingly O Conors of Connacht; the MacDermottroes whose seat was at Alderford, Roscommon; the MacDermotts who were chiefs of Airtech. Following the ill-fated Stuarts they lost much of their property and their chief seat moved to Coolavin in Sligo. The only Irish family to have a princely title, they are also chiefs of their name. Although their kinsmen went abroad, the Princes of Coolavin remained in Ireland where, in the 19th century, they reached high office. The present Prince of Coolavin, 'The MacDermot', Sir Dermot MacDermot, a former ambassador in the British Diplomatic Service, has compiled their history for his family.

There are variations in the spelling of MacDermot, but the most unusual and rare is Kermode.

MacEgan, see **Egan**, page 53

See page 82 for:
    MacElroy
    MacEvoy
    MacGee
    MacGovern

MacGrath *MacRaith*
Magraith Magraw

Maguire *MagUidhir*
MacGuire McGuire

There are several variations in the modern spelling of this numerous name, which originally was MacRaith. Raith, a first name, means 'prosperity'. There were two septs. In Donegal and Fermanagh the Macgraths were hereditary guardians of Saint Daveog's monastery at Lough Derg. They lived in Termon Castle, near Pettigo. The other sept were from Clare and Limerick, where the MacGraths were poets and their patrons were the kingly O Briens of Thomond. They were also presidents of the famous school for bards at Cahir, Tipperary.

The notorious, avaricious Myler Magrath came from the Donegal sept. Originally a Franciscan friar, he trimmed his beliefs to whatever religion suited his ambition. He was Anglican Bishop of Cashel during Elizabeth's reign. At one time he held four bishoprics, both Catholic and Anglican. He married twice and lived to be 100 years old. His son, Edmund, acted as a spy for the Cromwellians who confiscated much of the McGrath possessions and burned their castle outside Waterford.

One of those who helped to build up the Irish economy was Joseph McGrath, a veteran of the Rising and a government minister. He was one of the founders of the Irish Hospitals Sweepstakes and he helped to revive the old Waterford crystal industry.

The Macguire name is first recorded in 956, but it was not until the 14th century that they became the most prominent of the Fermanagh septs. The name comes from the Irish, MagUidhir (Mag meaning 'Mac'), and means 'pale coloured'. They were kinsmen of the kingly O Neills and the princely O Connells of Ulster. From the 15th century a succession of learned Maguire bishops is recorded.

The Maguire stronghold was on Lough Erne, where they were Barons of Enniskillen. Their greatest chieftain, Hugh Maguire, led the Irish army which defeated the English at the Battle of the Yellow Ford. A descendant, Conor, notorious for his bungling of the Ulster nobles' plot to capture Dublin castle, was subsequently executed in the Tower of London.

Many of the Maguires followed the exodus to Europe where their aristocratic lineage was recognised by the French court.

Thomas Maguire (d. 1889) was the first Roman Catholic to be made a Fellow of Trinity College, where he was Professor of Moral Philosophy.

There were many distinguished Maguires in the USA. Those who spell the name MacGuire, or McGuire, usually originated in Connacht. One of these was chief surgeon to Stonewall Jackson, and Professor at Virginia Medical College.

Enniskillen Castle, their Fermanagh stronghold, is in good repair and there are several remains of their seats in that area.

MacGuire, see **Maguire**, page 62

See page 82 for:

MacHugh	**MacNulty**
MacIrnerney	**MacQuaid**
MacKee	**MacQuillan**
MacLoughlin	**MacSweeney**
MacManus	**Madden**
MacNally	**Magee**

Magennis, see **Guinness**, page 54

Maher, see page 82

MacKenna *Mac Cionaoith*

MacMahon *Mac Mathghamhna*
Mohan   Vaughan

In Irish the name is MacCionaoda, meaning 'son of Cionaoid'. Who this was is not known, for little is recorded of the MacKennas until comparatively recently. An Ulster family, they were lords of Truagh, the present Trough in County Monaghan.

The most outstanding characteristic of the MacKennas is their literary talent. Theobald MacKenna, a political moderate at the time of Wolfe Tone, wrote tirelessly promoting parliamentary reform and Catholic Emancipation. In the late 19th century there were three Stephen MacKenna writers, two novelists and one journalist who had fought for the Greeks and translated Plautinus. Lambert MacKenna, a Jesuit priest, edited many books in the Irish language on bardic poetry and history.

The most colourful of the MacKennas was John (later Juan) from Tyrone who studied engineering in Spain and went to South America where the viceroy, Ambrosio O Higgins, made good use of his skills in the defence of Peru. John MacKenna died later following a dramatic duel in Buenos Aires.

The talented MacKennas are also well known for acting. Siobhan McKenna is the doyenne of Irish actresses, and T. P. McKenna is a popular stage, screen and TV actor.

Martin McKenna left Kilkenny for Australia to become a successful brewer, farmer and founder of a big family in Kyneton, Victoria.

MacKeogh, see **Keogh**, page 58

MacMahon (in modern Irish MacMahuna, meaning 'son of a bear') represents two distinct septs. One descends from the royal O Briens and was of Corcabaskin, Clare, while the other sept were known as Lords of Oriel in Louth and Monaghan. The two chieftaincies became extinct in the 18th century with the deaths of Teige of Corcabaskin at Kinsale and Hugh Óge of Oriel who was hung at Tyburn.

Hugh Óge's cousin, Heber MacMahon, was a European-educated bishop, a member of the Catholic Confederation and a poet. He was also an army general – for which he had to suffer martyrdom.

Folklore credits Máire Rua (Red) MacMahon with diverse amorous attachments. In the records she had one husband who died young. Then she chose to marry Conor O Brien and together they built the handsome castle of Lemaneagh in Clare. When he was killed, to protect her large family and property she ruthessly married a Cromwellian. She managed to elude a charge of murder.

The outstanding MacMahon is Edmonde Patrice, a descendant of an ennobled family of France who had fled there with the 'Wild Geese'. A brilliant professional soldier, this field marshal was for six years President of France.

Of the numerous MacMahons who emigrated to Australia one was Prime Minister from 1971-2.

When Mac is dropped from MacMahon it indicates an entirely different name, one which can also be Mohan and which, at some time, was also transformed to Vaughan.

MacNamara
MacConmara

Malone   *Ó Maoileoin*

MacNamara means 'son of the hound of the sea'. Their territory was the far west coast of Clare and their ancestor, Cas, was the first chieftain of the powerful Dalcassians. The MacMahons had the right to inaugurate the O Brien chieftains or kings.

The MacNamaras became compulsive builders — 57 castles, fortresses and abbeys are credited to them in Clare, including Quin Abbey and the famous castles of Bunratty and Knappogue.

There were two septs. The MacNamara Fion (fair) held the chiefdom of Clancullen West, while MacNamara Reagh (swarthy) was chief of the East. Their titles and possessions were wrested from them by the marauding Cromwellians, which drove them to seek outlets in Europe and the new world.

They were natural seamen. Count MacNamara, a commodore of the French fleet and diplomat in the Far East, was assassinated there in the backlash from the French Revolution because of his royalist connections.

Donnchadha Ruadh MacConmara was educated for the priesthood in Rome, but was expelled. He turned to teaching and poetry, for which he has become best known. He travelled much and had many wild adventures, changed his religion to suit his prospects and lived to be 95.

One of the MacNamara houses, at Ennistymon, is now the Falls Hotel. Here was born Caitlin, wife of Dylan Thomas, and her father, Francis, poet and eccentric.

The Malone name comes from Maoileoin, which meant 'one who served St John'. Early Malone history is centred on Offaly, where they had their estate at Ballynahown. They were kinsmen of the O Conors, who were kings in nearby Connacht.

Clonmacnoise, the great ecclesiastical seat of learning, was in their territory and a number of Malones presided there as abbots or bishops. The Malones who supported James II had to flee to Europe, where they can be traced in the armies and in the records of France and Spain. In Italy William Malone was a President of the Irish College in Rome.

The Malones of Baronstown changed to the Anglican faith, which saved them from losing their lands in Westmeath.

Of two Sylvester Malones, both priests, one was a church historian and Irish language enthusiast, while the second went to Brooklyn where he worked for the relief of the victims arriving on famine ships.

Walter Malone, who also went to the USA, wrote the epic poem on the Mississippi river where the American Indians were cruelly treated by the Spaniards.

'Molly Malone' is one of Dublin's outstanding characters, and every Dubliner can sing the popular ditty describing how she 'Wheeled her wheelbarrow through streets broad and narrow, Singing cockles and mussels, alive, alive oh!'

MacMurrough, see **Murphy**, page 66
Magouran, see page 82
Mahon, see **MacMahon**, page 63
Mahoney, see **O Mahoney**, page 73

Martain, see **Martin**, page 65

Martin *Ó Martain*
Martyn   Gilmartin

The Irish Martins were kinsmen of the O Neills of Tyrone. MacGiolla Martin was anglicised to Gilmartin. Giolla Earnáin O Martain (d. 1218) was an important bard and, later, there were two bishops of the name. The Martins of Connacht, the most prominent family of this name, claim descent from Olyver Martin, a Norman Crusader.

The Martins were one of the '14 Tribes of Galway' and they owned 200,000 acres in Connemara with an avenue of 30 miles to Ballynahinch Castle. Richard Martin's father had turned Protestant so that his son could sit in parliament and urge Catholic Emancipation. In his younger days Richard was known as 'Hairtrigger Dick' because of his constant duelling. This changed to 'Humanity Dick' when he got an act through parliament protecting animals and founded the Royal Society for the Prevention of Cruelty to Animals.

His granddaughter, Mary Laetitia, the 'Princess of Connemara', turned from a glittering success in London to care for her father's tenants during the Famine. He died from the famine fever and she died, penniless, aged 35, in the USA.

A kinswoman, Violet Martin of Ross, was Edith Somerville's collaborator in writing the *Experiences of an Irish RM*.

Edward Martyn of Tulira Castle founded the Feis Ceoil and became part of the Irish literary renaissance which included W.B. Yeats and George Moore.

The Martins who went to Australia produced a Prime Minister who held the post three times.

Moore *Ó Mórdha*

Moore, or in Irish Ó Mórdha, means 'noble'. They descend from Conal Cearnach, one of the chieftains of the legendary Knights of the Red Branch. Their territory was Leix, and in the Cistercian Abbey they founded is the tomb of their last chieftain, Malachi O More.

Today Moore is a common name, both in England and Ireland. There were also Moores who arrived with the Normans and it would be difficult now to disentangle the original Ó Mórdha and the Norman-English Moores.

The O Moores were a warrior people who defended their territory against the colonialists. In 1183 Conor O More defeated the Earl of Essex, sent by Queen Elizabeth to quell the Irish.

There are Moores who descend from an English soldier who had estates at Mellifont in Meath. About 1767 Field Marshal Sir Charles Moore, 6th Earl and 1st Marquess of Drogheda, built Moore Abbey in Kildare.

One of the earliest economists was an 18th-century Moore, while another Moor became John Wesley's right-hand man. The most celebrated is Thomas Moore, poet and musician.

Moore Hall in Connacht was the home of a distinguished line financed by wine trading.

Murphy *Ó Morchoe*

Ó Morchoe, or Murphy, the most numerous Irish name, means 'sea warrior'. There were several septs in Tyrone, Sligo and Wexford, where they were kings of Leinster. Dermot MacMurrough, the most famous Murphy, invited the Normans into Ireland. His brother, Murrough, is the eponymous ancestor of all the Wexford Murphys, including their present, accredited chieftain, 'The Ó Morchoe', who farms in Wexford.

Some of the Wexford sept moved west to Cork, where Daibhi Ó Murchu, the blind harper, played for Grace O Malley, the pirate queen. Seán Ó Murchadha was the last of the Blarney bards.

A singularly talented family, they have produced innumerable artists, sculptors, writers and a very famous actor and playwright, Arthur Murphy. Two heroic Wexford priests, both named Michael, lost their lives there in the 1798 rising.

One of the daughters of a shoemaker who emigrated to France, Marie Louise Murphy, was the French painter Boucher's favourite model until she became mistress to Louis XV.

Several branches of the Cork family who were brewers and distillers merged and, later, joined with Powers and Jamesons, the whiskey distillers. Irish Distillers Ltd, the biggest distillers in Ireland, still have Murphys on the board.

The Murphys in America are more numerous than in Ireland. They are also plentiful in Australia.

Nugent *Nuinseann*

The name Nugent, originated in the 10th century in the French town of Nogent, from which the family moved to Ireland in the 12th century. They settled in Westmeath, where they were created Barons of Delvin, their principal stronghold. They formed new septs, one of which had its headquarters at Aghavarton Castle in Cork.

The Nugents are an outstanding military family. Some identified with the Irish while others held to the English rule, several acting as lord deputies.

Sir Christopher, 14th Baron Delvin, compiled *A Primer of the Irish Language* to help Elizabeth I understand the Irish. It did little good, for he spent much of his life imprisoned in Dublin Castle.

The term 'to nugentsize' originated with Robert Nugent, a poet, who made a nice life for himself by marrying wealthy widows, which craftily paved the way to a peerage from George III, to whom he loaned money.

Abroad the Nugents distinguished themselves in many wars. One fought at Fontenoy, another became a governor of Prague. Laval, Prince Count Nugent, field marshal and Knight of the Golden Fleece, is buried in his home at Fiume.

An illustrious exception was Christopher Nugent of Meath, who followed medicine and contributed to the cure of hydrophobia.

Ballinlough Castle in Westmeath is one of the fine houses still in Nugent occupation.

Many members of this family have settled in Canada.

Neill, see **O Neill**, page 74

O Brien

The O Briens take their name from the 10th-century Brian Boru who was High King of Ireland. A very powerful and numerous sept in Clare and Limerick, they spread far and wide and still predominate in Munster. Their history fills volumes, beginning with the saga of their contentions with the Normans and the Tudors. They were granted many titles of nobility; Earls of Thomond, Viscounts Clare, Earls of Inchiquin.

The 6th Earl of Thomond, 'Murrough of the Burnings', earned his second title for his siding with the Cromwellians in the ravaging. Repenting years later, he journeyed to Rome to expunge his atrocities.

Other more constructive Earls of Thomond built abbeys and fine castles, including Dromoland.

In the Battle of the Boyne they were active on both sides, the losing O Briens (the Viscounts Clare) fleeing to France where they founded Clare's Dragoons.

In Ireland by the 18th century they were parliamentarians, urging legislative independence for Ireland. Foremost among these was William Smith O Brien of Dromoland, whose nationalist views included the taking up of arms which led to his banishment for a while to Australia.

A number of O Briens chose the sea. The 3rd Marquis of Thomond was an admiral in the British navy. Captain Jeremiah O Brien and several of his brothers were in the American navy at the time of the revolution and it was they who opened the naval hostilities by capturing several of the English ships.

O Beirne, see **Beirne**, page 42
O Boyle, see **Boyle**, page 43

O Byrne *Ó Broin*

Byrne

With or without the O prefix, Byrne counts as one of the most numerous Irish names. Ó Broin, the Irish version, comes from Branach (raven), a son of Maolmordha, 11th-century King of Leinster. Kildare was Ó Broin country until they were driven south to the mountains of Wicklow by the encroaching Anglo-Normans.

They settled in Crioch Bhranach (O Byrne's Country), with Ballinacor as their headquarters. Their warrior chieftain, Fiach MacHugh O Byrne, followed the O Byrne tradition, waging guerrilla warfare against the English. Later, he was killed and his head was impaled outside Dublin Castle. A collection of poetry eulogising the O Byrnes, *Leabhar Branach,* is in the library of Trinity College Dublin.

Joining the exodus in 1691 they went to France, where they served in the army. Because of their aristocratic lineage a number of them were imprisoned and guillotined in Paris during the Revolution. O Byrnes were among the leading citizens of Bordeaux, where one family had a vineyard.

There were distinguished O Byrne bishops and surgeons in the USA. Donn-Byrne, the novelist, born in New York, returned to Ireland where he wrote patriotic Irish novels which had great success.

Gay Byrne is a well known Irish television personality.

The O Beirnes, whose territory is Connacht, are a completely distinct sept from the O Byrnes.

O Callaghan *Ó Ceallacháin*

This name probably came from Ceallachan, 10th-century King of Munster and chieftain of the Eoghanact (a consortium of the leading families of Munster). Ceallachain means 'strife', which aptly describes this King of Munster who led plundering expeditions to the surrounding counties. He is also famed for killing Cinneide, father of the future king Brian Boru.

Just before the devastations of Cromwell, Colonel Donogh O Callaghan was a member of the Irish Confederation of Kilkenny. He was outlawed and had to seek refuge in France.

In the 18th century Cornelius O Callaghan of Tipperary was created Baron Lismore, one of the rare native Irishmen to be so honoured.

Father Jeremiah O Callaghan travelled through England and Europe vehemently preaching justice. In north America, where he finally settled, he was affectionately known as the 'Apostle of Vermont'.

In the 19th century in New York Edmund Bailey O Callaghan, a scholarly doctor, published a comprehensive *History of New York* — the first of its kind. The *History of the Irish Brigades in the Service of France* by John Cornelius O Callaghan is a thorough documentation of the 'Wild Geese' and their posterity.

Many Callaghans settled in Spain. Don Juan O Callaghan, a Barcelona lawyer, is the authenticated chief of his name.

O Connell *Ó Conaill*

The O Connells boast a pedigree dating back to a High King c. 280 BC. The name appears to have evolved from the ancient British or Celtic first name, Cunovalos.

The O Connells came from several distinct septs sited in Derry, Galway and Munster. Their chieftains had their castle at Ballycarberry near Cahirciveen. When it was broken up by the Cromwellians they began their long association with France and Austria. They were of a distinctively military cast.

When Muircheartach O Connell joined the Austrian army he changed his name, understandably, to Moritz. The Empress Maria Theresa appointed him Imperial Chamberlain. His kinsman, Count Daniel O Connell, had fought with the Prussians against Maria Theresa.

Another kinsman, Sir Maurice O Connell, was transferred at the time of the Revolution from the French to the British army. He was given a command in Australia, where he married the daughter of Captain Bligh of *The Bounty*.

Daniel Charles Count O Connell served in many armies. In France he was admitted to the nobility but had to flee the Revolution. His nephew was the 'Liberator', Daniel O Connell of Cahirciveen, a lawyer and orator, who roused the people to demand — and get — Catholic Emancipation.

The many O Connell scholars and clerics have been somewhat eclipsed by the soldiers and politicians. Father Daniel O Connell, a kinsman of the 'Liberator' and a Jesuit, is recognised internationally as an astronomer and seismologist.

O Casey, see page 82
O Cleary, see **Clery**, page 46

O Connor *Ó Conchobhair*
O Conor

The O Connors hold pedigrees going back to the 2nd century. Conchobhair, meaning 'hero' or 'champion', was the 10th century King of Connacht from whom they took their name. There were, however, at least six O Conor septs, not necessarily in the same line as Conchobhair. Among these were O Conor of Corcomroe in Clare, O Connor Faly of Offaly, O Connor Kerry, chief of the Munster O Connors, and O Connor Keenaght of Ulster. The O Conors of Connacht were the royal and predominant line. In the 12th century Turlough Mór O Conor was High King of Ireland.

Their family mansion, Clonalis near Roscommon, is a unique treasury of Irish relics and archives which have been professionally classified. When others fled from colonial oppression, the O Conors remained in their remote Belanagare fastness, the Connacht family seat which preceded Clonalis. The chiefs of this family style themselves O Conor Don.

In the 18th century there was a succession of O Conor scholars and antiquarians who collected and translated Irish manuscripts, many now in the Royal Irish Academy.

Space does not allow for a proper account of the eminent O Connors, among them writers, artists, soldiers, priests, politicians and diplomats. There was a Napoleonic general and a general with Simon Bolivar, a physician to the King of Poland, a governor of Zambia and another of Civita Vecchia, and a Charles O Connor of New York who declined an offer for presidency of the USA in the 19th century.

O Donnell *Ó Domhnaill*

The O Donnells are one of the eminent families whose forefather was Niall of the Nine Hostages. Tirconnell, meaning 'Connell's territory' (now Donegal) was their base, and from Domhnaill (world mighty) they took their name. Their chieftains were inaugurated on the Rock of Doon near Letterkenny.

Theirs is a history of battle. They built strongholds around Donegal and defended them first from their neighbours, the O Neills, and then, in a losing battle, from the Tudors.

As a youth the O Donnell heir, the great Red Hugh, was abducted and imprisoned in Dublin Castle. His escape through the snow-covered Wicklow mountains is one of the great sagas. He was a leader in the triumphant battle of the Yellow Ford, but died in Spain following the exodus after Kinsale.

The O Donnells established an Austrian line with a Major General Henry, Count O Donnell. Count Joseph, his son, was finance minister following Napoleon's depredations. Another O Donnell count was aide-de-camp to the Emperor Franz Josef. Their kinsmen reached the highest rank in Spain — Prime Minister in 1858.

Many O Donnells have been illustrious churchmen, including the 'Apostle of Newfoundland' and Cardinal Peter O Donnell in Ireland. Their present chieftain is a Franciscan missionary whose heir will come from the Duke of Tetuan's family in Spain. Clan rallies are held at intervals. The next is due in Donegal in 1985.

O Dea, see page 82

O Donovan *Ó Donnabhain*

O Farrell *Ó Fearghaill*
More O Ferrall

The O Donovan pedigree goes back to Callaghan, a 10th-century King of Munster. From his son, Donnabhain, came the family name (donn meaning 'brown' and dubhann meaning 'black').

A noble race in Munster, they were chieftains in Carbery. Their extensive territory followed Limerick's River Maigue. Brugh Riogh ('royal residence') was the explanatory name of their stronghold until the Normans drove them south to Cork where they acquired more possessions and are still very numerous.

Because of their adherence to the doomed Stuarts they were outlawed and lost their wealth. In France, where they found careers in the army, O Donovan's Infantry was a regiment to be reckoned with. Because they were aristocrats they suffered sadly during the French Revolution.

Another O Donovan family of Kilkenny who claimed descent from Eoghan, a 3rd-century King of Munster, produced one of the most celebrated historians, John O Donovan. He published an *Irish Grammar* and translated and edited the first complete edition of the *Annals of the Four Masters*.

Jeremiah O Donovan, the revered patriot O Donovan Rossa (red), emigrated to America, driven out by his Fenian activities.

The classic short story writer, Frank O Connor was, in fact, born Michael Ó Donovan of Cork city

Weight throwing was a Gaelic sport 3,000 years ago. In the last century an O Donovan in America was world and USA champion.

Ó Fearghaill means 'man of great valour', an auspicious sobriquet inherited from a Lord of Annaly of the family which also named the town of Longford where their base was Longphuirt Ui Fhearghaill (O Farrell's Fort).

The O Farrells multiplied and divided into two septs; O Farrell Boy (buidhe means 'yellow') and O Farrell Bán (bán means 'white'). In the *Annals of the Four Masters* they are accorded much space.

When they married into the Moore family they founded their own illustrious sept — the More O Ferralls.

Many went to Europe; one was a Spanish diplomat; another was a Major General in the Austrian army. Several O Farrells were in the service of the King of Sardinia until he was overthrown by Napoleon.

Richard More Ó Ferrall, MP, Lord of the Treasury, First Secretary to the Admiralty and the first civilian governor of Malta, gave up this glittering career in 1850, disagreeing with the Prime Minister's opposition to the liberalisation of Catholicism in England.

For decades the BBC and the British film and television industry were dominated by George More O Ferrall, who had studied acting before becoming joint producer of the first television programme ever made. He later directed many films and plays.

Of the two branches of the More O Ferrall family one was based at Balyna, Kildare, originally the Moore family home. The other, at Kildangan near Monasterevan, Kildare, is celebrated for its rare gardens and blood stock.

O Doherty, see **Doherty**, page 50
O Dowd, see page 82
O Driscoll, see page 82
O Duffy, see **Duffy**, page 52
O Dwyer, see page 82

O Flaherty   *Ó Flaithbheartaigh*

The O Flahertys boast a genealogy going back at least 3,000 years. They were sea faring people of Connacht and in earlier days they were the enemies of the elitist '14 Tribes of Galway', who dubbed them 'the Ferocious O Flahertys'. They carried on a continuous warfare against their neighbours, the Burkes, and the royal O Conors. In time they defeated the Burkes and acquired much territory between Lough Corrib and the Atlantic, where they were styled Lords of Iar (West) Connacht. Aughnanure Castle near Oughterard, Galway, is a majestic ruin tinged with stories of bloody O Flaherty revenge killings.

The pirate Queen Granuaile (*see* O Malley) had, as her first husband, Donal an Chogaidh (of the battles) O Flaherty, but he succumbed early to his lust for battle. The last O Flaherty chieftain, Roderick of Moycullen, died in a miserable cabin but left an invaluable history written by himself.

During World War II the 'Scarlet Pimpernel of the Vatican' was a Kerry O Flaherty priest who helped allied soldiers to escape from German-occupied Italy.

The O Flaherty prowess in modern times is celebrated in Liam O Flaherty, novelist, playwright, short story writer and formerly, man of Aran. Robert Flaherty, son of an Irish emigré, made documentary films in the USA including *Man of Aran*.

In Ulster a different form of Irish is spoken, which accounts for O Flaherty, who was styled Lord of Aileach in Donegal, having his name transformed to O Laverty.

O Grady   *Ó Grádaigh*

Ó Grádaigh means 'illustrious' and their pedigree shows the O Gradys to be of Dalcassian sept, kinsmen of the royal O Briens. Their territories circled Clare and they had their fortress on Inis Cealtra (Holy Island) on Lough Derg. A ruined O Grady castle testifies to their settlements in Clare, as does Lough O Grady near Scarriff.

Their neighbours, the O Briens, dispersed them to Limerick, where the present chief of the name, Lieutenant Colonel Gerard Vigors de Courcy O Grady, lives at Killballyowen.

During the frenetic period of Henry VIII's rule an O Grady changed his faith and his name to the less Irish sounding Brady in order to keep his lands. His son was the first Protestant Bishop of Meath.

The family has long since reverted to its original name. Darby O Grady, who lost his lands during another penal purge, had them restored to him following his marriage to Sir Thomas Standish's daughter. In gratitude, there has been a male or female Standish in succeeding generations of the family until the present day.

A Standish O Grady who was an Attorney General was created Viscount Guillamore. His nephew was the distinguished Standish O Grady, engineer in America and then, on his return to Ireland, a most remarkable antiquarian and compiler of Irish manuscripts. Another Standish O Grady was the famous writer of heroic Irish folk stories. In America an O Grady, married to a black American lady, was the great grandfather of Cassius Clay, alias Muhammed Ali.

O Keeffe *Ó Caoimh*

O Kelly *Ó Ceallaigh*

Art O Caom, son of Fionghuine, the King of Munster who died in 902, gave his name to the O Keeffes whose territory was around Glanmore and Fermoy in Cork. When they were uprooted by the Normans they moved south to the Duhallow county where their surroundings came to be called Pobble O Keeffe (O Keeffe country). Caom means 'noble' or 'gentle'.

Their celebrated poet, Owen O Keeffe, who was president of the Cork bards, was also a parish priest of Doneraile.

Following the submergence of the old Gaelic order, the O Keeffes began to feature in the army lists in France. There were many O Keeffe officers, and as they settled in France their name was gradually eroded to Cuif.

Those who managed to survive at home were able to use their talents with the easing of the penal laws. One artist O Keeffe, following training in Dublin, got the signature of approval in London with an exhibition at the Royal Academy.

His brother, John, was an actor and dramatist. When he first went to London his name lacked the O prefix, as was usual then. As a successful playwright and song writer he gained the confidence to show his Irish origins by returning the O to Keeffe.

When John Lanigan of Tipperary married an O Keeffe heiress they combined their names. The Lanigan O Keeffe families have a definite legal tradition. Some have gone to Australia, others to Rhodesia, now Zimbabwe.

The O Kellys derive their name from Ceallach, a celebrated 9th-century chieftain. Ceallach, meaning 'war' or 'contention', was at one time an apt cognomen for the O Kellys who, after the Murphys, have the most numerous name in Ireland.

For centuries their territories included much of Galway and Roscommon, known as 'O Kelly's Country'. At one time the O Kellys had become so prolific they spread out into eight different septs.

In 1351 the O Kelly chief invited all the musicians and poets to spend Christmas with him — a gesture which originated the expression 'O Kelly's Welcome'. Murtough O Kelly, the Archbishop of Tuam who compiled the historic *Book of the O Kellys,* was one of many distinguished O Kelly churchmen. Malachy O Kelly led the horrendous inter-tribal massacre at Knocktoe in 1499 when the leading Irish families fought each other.

The O Kellys who fled with the 'Wild Geese' were distinguished in the Irish regiments of France. The enduring dynasty who were honoured with the title Count of the Holy Roman Empire began when the Austrian Empress Maria Theresa conferred it on Dillon John Kelly.

The ballad 'Kelly the Boy from Killann' refers to a Kelly killed in the 1798 rising in Wexford. Sean Kelly, of Carrick-on-Suir, continues to win awards as an international cyclist. The much-lamented Grace of Monaco was a Kelly from America, where there are far more Kellys than in Ireland. Not the least of their representatives in Australia was the gangster Ned Kelly.

O Kennedy   *Ó Cinneide*

O Mahony   *Ó Mahúna*

There is a Kennedy clan in Scotland also who, very far back, may have been related to the Irish Kennedys. They were certainly kinsmen of King Brian Boru, from whose brother, Dunchad, they descend. Cean Éidig, which means 'ugly head', was the father of Brian and Dunchad and it is from him that the name originated.

For a long time the O Kennedys were settled in Clare, near Killaloe. The O Briens and the MacNamaras drove them away to Tipperary and Kilkenny, then known as Ormond. For 400 years they were Lords of Ormond and grew so mighty they divided into several new septs. For a long time they held out against the Butler-led encroachment of the Normans. These stirring times are recorded in the *Ormond Deeds*, (c. 1579), which were presented to John F. Kennedy during his 1963 visit.

By c. 1746 the combination of the Butlers and Cromwellians had deprived them of their 20,000 acres and their castles. They flocked to France to join the Irish Brigades. In Spain their name was adapted to Quenedy.

In the 19th and 20th centuries the Kennedys have been distinguished in the church, medicine, the law and the navy. There was a popular songwriter too: Jimmy Kennedy of 'Red Sails in the Sunset' fame. The Kennedy Road crossing from Simla to Tibet commemorates the engineer who built it.

Towering over all are the Kennedys who sailed from Dunganstown to Boston, from whom sprang John F. Kennedy, President of the USA.

The O Mahony name comes from Mathghamhan, son of Cian Mac Mael Muda, a 10th-century prince and his wife, Sadbh, who was the High King Brian Boru's daughter. They were of the Eoghanacht, a regal dynasty of Munster.

Their Munster possessions were vast. They sprinkled their 14 castles all around the Cork coast, west to Mizen Head. Many of their descendants are still there, many more scattered into new septs or emigrated.

In the courts of Europe they held distinguished military and diplomatic appointments and married into the nobility. Their chief representative in France to-day is the Vicomte Yves O Mahony of Orleans.

Colonel John O Mahony was a scholar whose nationalism forced him to emigrate to America, where he promoted the revolutionary Fenian cause. During the Civil War his Fenians served in the 99th Regiment of New York, of which he was colonel.

The celebrated 'Father Prout' who wrote the poem 'The Bells of Shandon' was in fact Francis Mahony, son of a woollen manufacturing family in Blarney. Dave Allen, the television comedian, was born David Tynan O Mahony, son of a Dublin journalist. 'The Pope' O Mahony, one of Dublin's best loved characters and a Cork barrister, raised genealogy to an art, weaving it into his speeches and broadcasts.

The very numerous O Mahonys are well served by a professional genealogical association which has held a rally in a different O Mahony castle every year for 30 years.

O Leary, see page 82
O Loghlen, see page 82

O Malley *Ó Máille*

Melia

The O Malleys are a very old Mayo family whose name is said to derive from the Celtic word for chief (maglios). For many centuries they were chieftains of the baronies of Burrishoole and Murrisk, where the sea was their chief occupation.

One of the most remarkable women in Irish history, Grace O Malley, (known as Granuaile) was the daughter of the O Malley chieftain Owen. As a mere 15-year-old she was married to an O Flaherty. When he was killed in battle she married a Burke. She frequently contended with the marauding English, both by land and by the sea from which she got her living. She was captured several times and was rescued from the gallows. In her old age, 'as a princess and equal', she visited Queen Elizabeth in London.

With the breakdown of the ancient chieftaincies the O Malleys disappeared abroad. Charles O Malley and his five brothers gave their lives to a diversity of armies. It was said, 'none of his family were ever known to follow any trade or profession but arms, earning no fortune to replace what had been taken from them'.

The O Malleys produced many high churchmen and one unorthodox priest, Thaddeus O Malley, who was returned from America because of his progressive religious and political views.

Ernest O Malley, a veteran of the Civil War, wrote a vivid autobiography entitled *On Another Man's Wound*.

Melia is sometimes found as a variant of O Malley.

O Neill

The name is the same in Irish as in English and for 1,000 years O Neill has been one of the most prestigious of Irish families. Niall means 'champion' and was first used by Domhnall, grandson of Nial Glun Dubh (black knee), King of Ireland, killed in 890 by the Norsemen. The O Neills go further back, claiming descent from the legendary Niall of the Nine Hostages.

They were very strong in Ulster, and to curb their power Queen Elizabeth had their Tullahogue inauguration stone broken up. In the 14th century they separated into two main branches; the senior branch were Princes of Tyrone while the junior branch were the Clanaboys of Antrim and Down.

Shane's Castle in Antrim is now a splendid show place, managed by Raymond, 4th Lord O Neill, a descendant of the Chichesters who adopted their maternal O Neill name.

Terence O Neill was Prime Minister of Northern Ireland from 1963-9. The O Neill pedigree is well looked after by the Irish Genealogical Association in Belfast which, in 1983, organised a big clan gathering. Jorge O Neill—his family have long been resident in Portugal—is the present representative of the Clanaboys. The Tyrone branch is extinct — or missing.

Eugene O Neill, the New York dramatist, and the politician 'Tip' O Neill are just two of the celebrated representatives of this great family in the USA.

O Meara, see page 82
O Moore, see Moore, page 65

O Reagan, see Regan, page 78
O Riordan, see page 82

O Reilly *Ó Raghailligh*

The O Reillys are thought to be kinsmen of the O Conor kings of Connacht through Maolmordha (Myles), whose great grandson was Ragheallach (gregarious race), from whom the O Reillys took their name. Their territory was around Lough Oughter in Cavan and as they increased they extended their families and their territory, particularly to Westmeath.

Cathal O Reilly, Prince of Breffny, founded the monastery on Lough Oughter in 1237 and, later, Cavan's Franciscan Abbey was founded by Giolla Iosa O Reilly. There were 39 O Reilly abbots and five held the primacy of Armagh as well as several bishoprics. They were also kinsmen of St Oliver Plunkett.

The celebrated Count Alexander O Reilly from Meath distinguished himself first in the Austrian service and then in the Spanish army. He put down a rebellion in Louisiana where he became governor. O Reilly pedigrees are found in Havana, as are many of their titled descendants. The O Reilly papers and portraits in Trinity College Dublin were donated by a descendant of Colonel Myles O Reilly, an officer in the Irish cavalry in 1641 who fled to Spain.

The O Reillys have a reputation as astute financiers. In the 15th century they devised their own coinage. A 'Reilly' has come to signify a coin of useful value. In the 20th century an O Reilly continues to head the family industry now amalgamated with the Irish Distillers Group (formerly John Power and Sons). Tony O Reilly, one time Irish rugby international, is chief executive of the American Heinz company as well as a number of companies in Ireland.

O Rourke *Ó Ruairc*

O Rourke is thought to have come from the Norse name Hrothrekr. These Norsemen stayed to integrate thoroughly and to produce three Kings of Connacht. Styled Lords of Breffny, their chieftains ruled territory in Cavan and Leitrim, where their stronghold was at Dromahair on Lough Gill. In the O Rourke pedigree there are 19 chieftains, all named Tiernan. Of these, the most notorious was the Tiernan who ravaged Meath and invaded Connacht where Dermot MacMurrough (see Kavanagh), the King of Leinster, was also foraging. Dermot MacMurrough abducted Tiernan's wife, Dervorgilla, earning his undying hatred. When Tiernan allied himself with the O Conor King of Connacht they deposed Dermot, who went to England to seek help. Thus began the Anglo-Norman invasion. Tiernan was slain by the Norman Hugo de Lacy.

Following the confiscation of their land by the Crown, the O Rourkes headed for Europe, where they distinguished themselves in a variety of exalted positions. There were many O Rourke bishops of Killala, including one who became chaplain to the Austrian court. The Empress Maria Theresa had two Owen O Rourkes in her service, one of whom was her ambassador to the exiled Stuarts at Vienna.

Count John O Rourke, Prince of Breffny, served the Russian Tsar and then the French, who made him a count. His nephew was the famous General Count Iosif Kornilievich O Rourke, who took part in the defeat of Napoleon. His portrait is in the Hermitage in Leningrad, where there are many O Rourke records. O Rourke descendants still live in Russia and Poland.

O Ryan, see **Ryan**, page 79
O Shaughnessy, see page 82
O Shea, see page 82

O Sullivan *Ó Súileabháin*

O Toole *Ó Tuathail*

In Irish Súileabháin means 'one' or maybe, 'hawk-eyed'. Their ancestry is from Olioll Olum, the 3rd-century King of Munster who was progenitor of the great Eoganacht clan. Tipperary was the first O Sullivan territory, and as they multiplied they spread to Cork and Kerry. The senior chieftain, O Sullivan Mór, had his stronghold at Kenmare Bay in Kerry. O Sullivan Beare occupied Dunboy on Bantry Bay.

The O Sullivans fought at Kinsale and defended Dunboy to the last stone. Then began O Sullivan Beare's epic march. In January 1602, with 400 soldiers and 600 civilians, they walked 200 miles north in two weeks of bitter cold and savage attacks to reach Brian O Rourke's Leitrim Castle. Only 35 had survived, including one woman. Although Elizabeth was dead, James I was no friend of the Irish. O Sullivan Beare and his family left for the hospitality of Philip III of Spain, where many of his family gave distinguished service in the army and navy.

In the 18th and 19th centuries there was a remarkable flowering of literary talent. Owen Roe O Sullivan, teacher, sailor and womanizer, is now acknowledged to be a great lyric poet.

In France, during the Revolution, an O Sullivan was one of the chief tyrants, sinking barges full of priests and aristocrats to bypass the slowness of the guillotine!

Sir Arthur O Sullivan was the musical half of the Gilbert and Sullivan operas.

O Toole comes from Tuathal, a 10th-century King of Leinster, of which province they were one of the great septs. Some scholars say tuathal means 'mighty people', while others think it means 'prosperous'. Although they originated from Kildare, the O Tooles are universally associated with Wicklow, where they built their castles and from which they set out to attack their neighbours and, later, the English.

When he was a young boy Laurence O Toole was captured by Dermot MacMurrough (*see* Kavanagh) who had killed his grandfather. When released, Laurence found his vocation in the monastic settlement at Glendalough. In 1161 he was appointed first Irish Archbishop of Dublin. A great church reformer and an intermediary between the Anglo-Normans and the Irish, he died at Eu on his way to plead with King Henry in Normany. In 1220 he was canonised and is patron saint of Dublin.

Laurence O Toole, one of the many O Tooles who fled abroad to join the Irish Brigades, had eight sons in the French army. His son, Colonel John O Toole, is the progenitor of the present Count of Limoges in France. Luke of Toole helped Princess Clementina to escape from Innsbruck to marry Prince Charles Stuart.

There were several O Toole septs in Ulster and Connacht. In Monaghan and Dundalk Toal and Toole are easily recognisable as stemming from O Toole.

Phalen, see page 82

Plunkett

Power
de Paor

The Plunketts—the name comes from a French word for blonde — are an aristocratic family who came to Ireland via Denmark before the Normans, and integrated well by marrying. They held spacious territories in Meath and Louth. In the early 1600s they were accorded a variety of titles. Randal Plunkett, 19th Baron Dunsany, farms his big estate in Meath. His nearby Kinsman, Oliver Plunkett, 19th Earl of Fingall, the last of his line, died in 1984. The 17th Lord Louth lives in the Channel Islands.

The Plunketts fought for the doomed Catholic Stuarts, fleeing with them to France to join the Irish regiments. In the 18th century, to save their lands, they conformed to the established religion. When religious persecution eased most returned to their original faith.

Their younger sons spread abroad to become British diplomats, admirals and soldiers. They were one of only two Irish families distinguished by a canonisation—Oliver Plunkett (1625-81). Ordained in Rome, he was Archbishop of Armagh and was martyred at Tyburn. In 1975 he was canonised in Rome, with his kinsman, Lord Dunsany, attending. He preserves the saint's crozier and ring in Dunsany Castle.

William Conyngham Plunket of Enniskillen, one of the finest speakers in the London House of Commons, was the 1st Baron Plunket. His grandson, also William Conyngham, 4th Baron Plunket, was Church of Ireland Archbishop of Dublin.

When the Powers came to Ireland with the Normans they were known as le Poer, meaning 'poor'. Maybe this had something to do with a vow of poverty they had taken at one time. They were certainly not poor, for they owned estates in Wicklow and in Waterford, where, as Marquesses of Waterford, they continue to maintain Curraghmore House (once described as the 'Versailles of Ireland').

Margaret Power, who married the Earl of Blessington, was known as 'the most beautiful Countess of Blessington'. When the Earl died, she and Count D'Orsay, the great dandy and painter, hosted a salon for the intellectuals of London — men only. The Earl had left no fortune. Soon she had to sell her London house and provide for herself and her improvident Limerick family. She wrote for ten hours a day, churning out books and articles until her death in Paris, where she had fled to escape her creditors.

William Grattan Tyrone Power of Waterford became a leading Irish actor on the English stage. Tyrone Power, the film star and romantic hero, was his great grandson. Another great grandson was Sir Tyrone Guthrie, theatre and television producer, and director of the Old Vic and Sadler's Wells theatres.

Sir James Power founded Powers Distillery in Dublin in 1791. His firm invented the famous 'Baby Power' miniature liquor bottle.

See page 82 for:
Quigley
Quinlan
Rafferty
Redmond

Regan *Ó Reagáin*

Roche *de Róiste*

Regan is a widespread name which came, not from one ancestor, but from several. There were Ó Riagáins in Meath and Dublin. They were important because they were of the 'Four Tribes of Tara'. They were very active against the Scandinavian invaders but lost their importance with the arrival of the Normans who drove them away to Leix.

The other and in no way related sept were descended from one of Brian Boru's brothers, Donnchadh. They were all of the powerful Dalcassian sept which ruled in counties Clare, Leinster and Tipperary.

Maurice O Regan, who was born about 1125, wrote a history concerning the arrival of the Normans. As a kind of diplomatic secretary to Dermot MacMurrough (see Kavanagh), King of Leinster, he was well positioned to give a first-hand account.

Reagans emigrated to the USA before the Famine. There was a Reagan Surgeon with Corcoran's Irish Legion. Another Reagan, a progressive jurist in Texas, was, at one time, Confederate Post Master. A Democrat, he lost popularity at the end of the Civil War because he advocated civil rights for negroes.

Ronald Reagan is one of the many distinguished descendants of Brian Boru. His grandfather emigrated from Ballyporeen, Tipperary, to London and later to Illinois. In Ireland Regan is pronounced Reegan, but genealogists agree that 'Raygan', as pronounced by Ronald Reagan, is correct for the sept from which he sprang.

It is thought the Roches originated in Flanders. They certainly arrived in Ireland with the Normans from Roch Castle, their Pembrokeshire fortress. Their name comes from this castle. They multiplied to become five different branches.

David Roche, who was created 1st Viscount Fermoy in 1570, was an ancestor of Princess Diana of Wales. The 8th Viscount Roche was one of the leaders in the rebellion of 1641. His wife, Lady Roche (née Power), was hanged for trying to defend Castletownroche. Her husband fled to join the Flemish army.

Maurice Roche, Mayor of Cork in the reign of Elizabeth I, was given his gold chain by her for his help in suppressing the rebel Earl of Desmond (*see* FitzGerald).

The Roches had many good churchmen, including a bishop of Ferns. They also had 'characters' such as the ferocious 'Tiger' Roche, a dandy who tricked innocent heiresses out of their fortunes and was too quick with his fists. His brother, the politician Boyle Roche, was notorious for his Irish 'bulls', particularly one that is still quoted: 'Why should we do anything for posterity — what has posterity ever done for us?'

In Ireland, Liam de Roiste, an Irish scholar and a member of the Gaelic League, took part in the fight for independence and sat in Daíl Éireann.

From the 1960s until comparatively recently the Roches used to hold an annual rally in one of their surviving castles. Perhaps this will be revived?

Reilly, see **O Reilly**, page 75
Rice, see page 82
Riordan, see **O Riordan**, page 82

Rooney, see page 82

Ryan *Ó Maoilriain*
Mulryan

The Ryans formed their name from an old personal name which could mean either 'administrator' or 'water'. Descending from a 2nd-century King of Leinster, Cathaoir Mór, the clan became very numerous and separated into two main branches. The Ó Riains of Idrone in Carlow and the Ó Maoilriains, who were chiefs in Owney around Tipperary and Limerick.

Following the Treaty of Limerick the Ryans went abroad. A Captain Luke Ryan commanded a French privateer during the American War of Independence. Juan Francesco O Ryan was an admiral and a minister in Chile. Descendants of Field Marshal Tomás O Ryan are still in Spain.

A family of Thady Ryans of Knocklong, Limerick, have been famous for centuries for their horses and their Scarteen Hounds. The present Thady Ryan has been chef d'équipe of the Irish Olympic team several times.

Journalists, editors and novelists have enhanced the Ryan name, among them Desmond Ryan, biographer and novelist, A.P. Ryan, editor of the London *Times* and Cornelius Ryan, who wrote the best-seller *The Longest Day*.

Many Ryans distinguished themselves in Australia and the USA, where Thomas Fortune Ryan, a penniless orphan, fulfilled the American dream by becoming a multi-millionaire known as the 'noiseless man of American finance'.

Sheridan *Ó Sirideáin*

The origins of the Sheridans is obscure. Their name was, at first, a personal name, and Cavan was their territory. Literature was their abiding talent, but they were also good churchmen, including one who helped the Provost of Trinity College Dublin to translate the Bible into Irish.

Thomas predominates in the Sheridan pedigree. There was the Thomas who was a close friend of James II, with whom he fled into exile. Thomas, his son, was one of the famous 'Seven Men of Moidart' and took part in the decisive battle of Culloden. Many were graduates of Trinity College Dublin, such as Thomas, a notable scholar and friend of Dean Swift of St Patrick's Cathedral. His son, Thomas, was manager of the Theatre Royal Dublin and was also a very good actor.

Thomas's second son, Richard Brinsley Sheridan, became the most successful dramatist of his day; *The Rivals* and *School for Scandal* are among his best known plays. His son Thomas was a short-lived poet whose wife was a novelist.

Joseph Sheridan Le Fanu (his mother was a Sheridan, his father a Huguenot) wrote enthralling tales of the supernatural.

Margaret Burke Sheridan broke the literary mould. She was an opera singer who lived in Italy and was a leading member of Milan's La Scala Theatre.

General Philip Sheridan's roots were in Cavan. He distinguished himself during the American Civil War at the battle for the Shenandoah Valley. His famous 20-mile ride is part of American folk history.

See page 82 for:
   Scanlon
   Scully
   Shannon
   Shea, see **O Shea**, page 82
   Sheehan, see page 82
   Sheehy, see page 82

Sullivan, see **O Sullivan**, page 76

Taaffe

Walsh *Breathnach*

David is the Welsh equivalent of Taaffe, and the family came from Wales in 1196 to settle in Louth.

Smarmore Castle, near Ardee, is still in Taffe possession. There were a number of Taaffes in the church, and a few eccentrics, including a priest who forged a Papal Bull giving him leave to do what he thought fit with the church in Ireland!

From earliest days the Taaffes were statesmen and soldiers. A Taaffe of Ballymote Castle in Sligo fought against the Irish at Kinsale and was duly rewarded with a knighthood.

Theobald, 2nd Viscount Taaffe, differing from his grandfather, joined the Catholic Confederacy at Kilkenny and commanded the Connacht forces against Cromwell.

Nicholas, 6th Viscount Taaffe, was a Lieutenant General in the Austrian army and chancellor to the king. He introduced the Irish potato to Silesia. He lived to be 92 in his Bohemian castle Elischau, today a Czechoslovakian military school.

Edward, 11th Viscount Taaffe, Baron of Ballymote, was Prime Minister of Austria for 14 years. Following the mysterious suicide of the Hapsburg heir, Prince Rudolph, Count Taaffe and his heirs were entrusted with the documents relating to the investigation.

Count Eduard Taaffe came to Ireland in the 1930s and was offered enormous sums to sell the Hapsburg papers. He declined and placed them in the Vatican archives.

The Taaffes are numerous in Ireland, on the land, in the professions and especially in horsebreeding.

Walsh was the name used to designate the hundreds of Welshmen who accompanied the Normans to Ireland. Consequently there is no common Walsh ancestor for this family.

Philip and his brother, David, who arrived in the 12th century, are supposed to be progenitors of the Walshes of Dublin, Kilkenny, Leix, Waterford and Wicklow. They are recorded plentifully in Burke's and other genealogical sources, sometimes with a final 'e' to the name. Others altered their name to Breathnach, the Irish for Welshman.

They were prominent in the church, both Catholic and Protestant. Nicholas, Bishop of Ossory about 1567, had his church services printed in Irish to help convert the 'papists'.

Peter Walsh, a Franciscan and a very contentious religious, suffered excommunication — he opposed the papal nuncio and repudiated papal infallability.

When Cromwell's soldiers planted Clonmel, Tipperary, the only Walsh left in the town was John, who had acted as Cromwell's loyal adviser.

Antoine Vincent Walshe, son of a Waterford shipbuilder, commanded the ship which landed Prince Charles Stuart in Scotland in 1745. His eldest son was the founder of the Counts Walsh de Serrant, who are still in France. A kinsman was Superior of the Irish College in Paris.

Maurice Walsh of Kerry, who spent many years in the customs service in Scotland, wrote a host of bestsellers, one of which, *The Quiet Man*, was made into a popular film.

A Short List of Other Prominent Names

Unless otherwise stated, all these names are derived from family personal names. Their meaning is given wherever it is possible to discover it.

Barrett, *Báróid:* Norman, Cork, Mayo, Galway.

Brady, *MacBrádaigh:* 'spirited', Ulster, Leinster, Cavan.

Breen, *O Braoin:* 'sadness', 'sorrow', Kilkenny, Wexford, Westmeath.

Brennan, *O Braonáin:* 'little drop', Kilkenny, Kerry, Westmeath.

Buckley, *O Buachalla:* 'boy', Cork, Kerry.

Carey, *O Ciardha:* Kildare, Kerry.

Cassidy, *O Caiside:* Fermanagh originally, now widespread.

Clancy, *MacFhlannchaidh:* 'ruddy warrior', Clare, Leitrim.

Coghlan, Coughlan, *MacCochlain* or *O Cochlain:* 'cape' or 'hood', Offaly, Cork.

Connolly, *O Conghaile:* 'Valorous', Connacht, Ulster, Monaghan, Cork.

Conroy, Mulconry, *O Conratha:* 'hound of prosperity', Roscommon, Clare.

Conway, *MacConnmhaigh:* Clare, Kerry, County Dublin.

Cooney, *O Cuanaic:* 'handsome', 'elegant', Galway, Clare, West Cork.

Corcoran, *O Corcrain:* 'ruddy', Fermanagh, Offaly, Mayo, Kerry.

Costello, Nangle, de Angulos, *MacOisdealbh:* 'son of Oistealb', Norman, Connacht, but widespread.

Crowley, *O Cruadhlaoich:* 'hunch-backed', Roscommon, Cork.

Cummins, *O Comáin:* 'a hurley', Mayo, Kerry, Limerick.

Curran, *O Corráin:* Ulster, Galway, Waterford, Kerry.

Delany, Delaney, *O Dubhshlaine;* 'of the river Slaney', Leix, Dublin.

Dempsey, *O Diomasaigh:* 'proud', Leix, Offaly.

Devine, *O Daimhin:* 'bard', 'poet', Fermanagh, Tyrone, Dublin, Cavan, Louth.

Devlin, *O Doibhlin:* Sligo, Tyrone.

Dolan, *O Dobhailen:* 'black defiance', 'challenge', Galway, Roscommon.

Doran, *O Deoradháin:* 'exile' or 'stranger', Down, Armagh, Leix, Wexford, Kerry.

Dowling, *O Dunlaing:* Leix, Kilkenny, Carlow, Wicklow, Dublin.

Duggan, *O Dubhagain:* 'black', Cork, Galway, Donegal, Tipperary.

Fagan, O Hagan, *O Faodhagain:* 'little Hugh', Kerry, Dublin.

Fahy, Fahey, *O Fathaigh:* 'field green', Galway, Tipperary.

Fallon, *O Fallamhain:* 'ruler', Galway, Donegal, Cork, Kerry, Wexford.

Fitzpatrick, *MacGiolla Padraig:* 'servant of St Patrick', Leix, widespread.

Flanagan, *O Flannagain:* 'red', Roscommon, Offaly, Fermanagh.

Flynn, *O Floinn;* 'red', 'ruddy', Cork, Roscommon, Antrim.

Fogarty, (cognate with Gogarty), *O Fogartaigh:* 'exiled', 'banished', Tipperary.

Foley, *O Foghladha:* 'plunderer', Waterford, mostly Munster.

Gaffney, *O Gamhna:* 'calf', Connacht.

Galvin, Gallivan, *O Gealbháin:* Kerry, Roscommon.

Garvey, *O Gairbith:* 'rough peace', Armagh, Down, Donegal.

Geraghty, *Mag Oireachtaigh:* 'court' or 'assembly', Roscommon, Galway.

Hickey, *O hIcidhe:* 'healer', Clare, Limerick, Tipperary.

Jennings, *MacSheóinín:* 'John' (originally Burkes), Connacht.

Kelleher, *O Céileachair:* 'loving spouse', Clare, Cork, Kerry.

Kinsella, *O Cinnsealach:* (originally Mac Murrough), Wexford, Wicklow.

Lalor, Lawlor, *O Leathlobhair:* 'half-leper', Leix.

Lee, *O Laoidhigh:* 'poetic', Tipperary, Galway, Cork, Limerick.

Lyons, Lehane, Lane, *O Laighin:* Galway.

MacAuley, *MacAmhlaoibh:* Fermanagh, Westmeath, Cork.

MacAuliffe, *MacAmhlaoibh:* Norse, 'Olaf', Cork.

MacBride, *MacGiolla Brighde:* 'son of the servant of St Brigid', Donegal.

MacCann, *MacAnnadh:* Armagh.

MacCormack, *MacCormaic:* all over Ireland.

MacElroy, *MacGiolla Rua:* 'red-haired youth', Fermanagh, Leitrim.

MacEvoy, *MacGuiollabhuidhe:* 'yellow lad', Louth, Leix.

MacGee, Magee, MacKee, *Mag Aodha:* Antrim, Down, Armagh.

MacGovern, Magauran, *Mag Samhrain:* 'summer', Cavan, Leitrim, Fermanagh.

MacHugh, *MacAoda:* Galway, Mayo, Leitrim, Donegal, Fermanagh.

MacInerney, *Mac an Airchinnigh:* 'steward of church lands', Connacht.

MacLoughlin, O Loghlen, *O Maoilsheachlainn:* Donegal, Meath, Clare.

MacManus, *MacMaghnuis:* Norse, 'Magnus', Fermanagh, Connacht.

MacNally, *Mac an Fhailghigh:* 'poor man', Mayo, Armagh, Monaghan.

MacNulty, *Mac an Ultaigh:* 'ulidian', 'of Ulster', also Mayo.

MacQuaid, *Mac Uaid:* 'Wat' or 'Walter', Ulster.

MacQuillan, *MacCoilin:* Norman, Ulster.

MacSweeney, *MacSuibhne:* 'Scottish mercenaries', Donegal, Cork.

Madden, *O Madáin:* 'small dog', Limerick, Longford, Galway, Offaly.

Maher, *O Meachair:* 'hospitable', Tipperary, Kilkenny.

Molloy, *O Maolmhudaidh:* 'noble chief', Offaly, widespread.

Moloney, *O Maoldhomhnaigh:* Clare, Tipperary.

Monahan, *O Manacháin:* 'monk', Roscommon.

Mooney, *O Maonaigh:* 'wealthy', Ulster, Offaly, Sligo.

Moran, *O Móráin:* 'great', Connacht.

Moriarty, *O Muircheartaigh:* 'expert navigator', Kerry.

Morrissey, *O Muirgheasa:* 'sea choice', Sligo, Waterford, Limerick, Cork.

Mulcahy, *O Maol Cataigh:* 'battle chief', Munster.

Mulligan, *O Maolagáin:* Donegal, Monaghan, Mayo.

Nolan, *O Nuaillain:* 'noble', 'famous', Carlow, West Cork.

O Casey, *O Cathasaigh:* 'vigilant', 'watchful', Munster.

O Dea, *O Deaghaidh:* Clare, Limerick, Tipperary, Cork, Dublin.

O Dowd, *O Dubhda:* 'black', Mayo, Sligo, Galway.

O Driscoll, *O hEidersceoil:* 'intermediary', Cork predominantly.

O Dwyer, *O Dubhuidir:* 'black odar', Sligo, Mayo.

O Flanagan, *O Flannagain:* 'red', Connacht.

O Gara, *O Gadhra:* 'a mastiff', Sligo, Mayo.

O Gorman, MacGorman, *O Gormain:* 'blue', Leix, Monaghan, Clare.

O Hagan, *O hAodhagain:* 'young', Tyrone.

O Halloran, *O hAllmhurain:* 'stranger beyond the sea', Clare, Galway.

O Hara, *O hEaghra:* Sligo, Antrim.

O Hegarty, *O hEigceartaigh:* 'unjust', Donegal, Derry, Cork.

O Higgins, *O hUigin:* 'knowledge', ingenuity', Sligo, Leinster, Munster.

O Leary, *O Laoghaire:* 'calf keeper', Cork.

O Meara, *O Meadhra:* 'mirth', Tipperary.

O Riordan, *O Riordáin:* 'royal bard', Tipperary, Cork.

O Shaughnessy, *O Seachnsaigh:* Galway, Clare, Limerick.

O Shea, *O Seaghada:* 'majestic', 'courteous', Kerry, Kilkenny.

Phelan, Whelan, *O Faoláin:* 'joyful', Waterford, Kilkenny, Wexford, Carlow.

Quigley, *O Coigligh:* 'untidy hair', Mayo, Donegal, Derry, Sligo, Galway.

Quinlan, *O Caoindealbháin:* 'gracefully shaped', Munster.

Quinn, *O Cuinn:* 'intelligent', Antrim, Longford, Clare.

Rafferty, *O Reachtaire:* Connacht.

Redmond, *Réamonn:* Norman, Wexford, Wicklow.

Rice, Welsh, *Rhys:* Kerry, Louth, Dublin, Ulster.

Rooney, *O Ruanaidh:* 'hero', Down, widespread.

Scanlan, *O Scannláin:* Kerry, Limerick, Cork, also Connacht.

Scully, *O Scolaidhe:* 'crier', Tipperary, Leinster.

Shannon, *O Seanacháin:* 'old', 'wise', Clare, Ulster.

Sheehan, *O Siodhacáin:* 'peaceful', Munster.

Sheehy, *Mas Sitigh:* Munster.

Tierney, *O Tighearnaigh:* 'lordly', Mayo, Donegal, Tipperary.

Tobin, de St Aubyn, *Tóibín:* Norman, Brittany, Munster.

Treacy, *O Treasigh:* 'fighter', Galway, Cork, Leix.

Tully, *O Taicligh:* 'peaceful', Connacht, Cavan, Longford, Westmeath.

Twomey, *O Tuama:* Cork, Kerry, Limerick.

Wall, de Valle, *du Val:* Norman, Carlow, Kilkenny, Waterford, Limerick, Cork.

Ward, *Mac an Bháird:* 'bard', Ulster, Connacht.

Woulfe, *de Bhulbh:* Norman, Kildare, Limerick, Cork.

BOOK III

IRISH PLACE NAMES

❧

by P.W. Joyce

About the Author

The author, Patrick Weston Joyce, was born in Glenosheen, County Limerick, in 1827. A teacher by profession,
he published a number of collections of Irish songs,
several histories of Ireland, and a collection of Gaelic
folk-tales, as well as the popular work, *English as we
Speak it in Ireland* (1910), a study of dialect variations.
Perhaps his best known work, however, is *The Origin and
History of Irish Names of Places* (three volumes). He died
in Dublin in 1914.

This book was originally published in 1870 under the
title *Irish Local Names Explained*.

Note that King's County and Queen's County are now
known as Offaly and Laois respectively.

Introduction

THE PROCESS OF ANGLICISING

1. Systematic Changes.

Irish pronunciation preserved: In anglicising Irish names, the leading general rule is, that the present forms are derived from the ancient Irish, as they were spoken, not as they were written. Those who first committed them to writing, aimed at preserving the original pronunciation, by representing it as nearly as they were able in English letters.

Generally speaking, this principle explains the alterations that were made in the spelling of names, in the process of reducing them from ancient to modern forms. Allowing for the difficulty of representing Irish words by English letters, it will be found that, on the whole, the ancient pronunciation is fairly preserved.

Aspiration: The most common causes of change in the reduction of Irish names, are aspiration and eclipsis. Some of the Irish consonants are, in certain situations, subject to what is called aspiration; it is indicated by the letter *h*, and it always changes the sound of the consonants.

B and *m* aspirated (*bh, mh*) are both sounded like *v* or *w*, and, consequently, where we find *bh* or *mh* in an Irish name, we generally have *v* or *w* in the English form: examples, Ardvally in Donegal and Sligo, in Irish *Ard-bhaile*, high town; Ballinwully in Roscommon, *Baile-an-mhulluigh*, the town of the summit (*mullach*). Sometimes they are represented by *f* in English, as in Boherduff, *Bothar-dubh*, black road, and often they are suppressed, especially in the end of words, or between two vowels, as in Knockdoo, *Cnoc-dubh*, black hill, the same as Knockduff in other places.

For *c* aspirated see p 86.

D and *g* aspirated (*dh, gh*), have a faint guttural sound, not existing in English, and they are consequently generally unrepresented in anglicised names, as in Lisnalee, *Lios-na-laegh*, the fort of the calves.

F aspirated (*fh*) totally loses its sound in Irish, and of course is omitted in English, as in Knockanree in Wicklow, *Cnoc-an-fhraeigh*, the hill of the heath.

P aspirated is represented by *f*, as in Ballinfoyle, *Baile-an-phoill*, the town of the hole, the same as Ballinphuill and Ballinphull elsewhere.

S and *t* aspirated (*sh, th*) both sound the same as English *h*, as in Drumhillagh in Cavan and Monaghan, *Druim-shaileach*, the ridge of the sallows, the same name as Drumsillagh in other counties, in which the original *s* sound is retained.

Eclipsis: An eclipsed consonant has its sound altogether suppressed, the sound of another consonant which is prefixed being heard instead. Thus when *d* is eclipsed by *n*, it is written *n-d*, but the *n* alone is pronounced. The eclipsed letter is of course always omitted in English.

When a noun is used in the genitive plural, with the article prefixed, its initial consonant is eclipsed. Each consonant has a special eclipsing letter of its own.

B is eclipsed by *m*. Knocknamoe, the name of a place in Queen's County, represents the Irish *Cnoc-na-mbo*, the hill of the cows.

C is eclipsed by *g*, as in Cloonnagashel near Ballinrobe, which ought to have been anglicised Coolnagashel, for the Four Masters write the name *Cuil-na-gcaiseal*, the corner of the *cashels* or stone forts.

D and *g* are both eclipsed by *n*, as in Mullananallog in Monaghan, *Mullach-na-ndealg*, the summit of the thorns or thorn bushes.

F is eclipsed by *bh*, which is represented by *v* in English, as in Carrignavar in Cork, which is in Irish *Carraig-na-bhfear*, the rock of the men.

P is eclipsed by *b*, as in Gortnaboul in Kerry and Clare, *Gort-na-bpoll*, the field of the holes.

S is eclipsed by *t*, in the genitive singular with the article, as in Ballintaggart, *Baile-an tsagairt*, the town of the priest.

T is eclipsed by *d*, as in Lisnadurk in Fermanagh *Lios-na-dtorc*, the fort of the boars.

2. Corruptions

While the majority of names have been modernized in accordance with the principle of preserving the pronunciation, great numbers on the other hand have been contracted and corrupted in a variety of ways. Some of these corruptions took place in the Irish language, but far the greatest number were introduced by the English-speaking people in transferring the words from the Irish to the English language. The following are some of the principal corruptions.

Interchange of l, m, n, r. The interchange of these letters is common in Irish and English, as well as in other languages. We find *l* very often substituted for *r*, as in Shrule, Shruel, Struell, Sroohill, in all of which the final consonant sound should be that of *r*, for they are derived from *Sruthair* (sruher), a stream.

N is sometimes, but not often, changed to l, as in Castleconnell near Limerick, which is the castle of the O'Connings, not of the O'Connells, as the present form of the name would indicate.

The change of *n* to *r* is of frequent occurrence, as in Kilmacrenan in Donegal, which should have been called Kilmacnenan, for the Irish authorities write it *Cill-mac-nEnain*, which Colgan translates the church of the sons of Enan, who were contemporaries and relatives of St. Columba.

The change of l to *r* is not very common, but we find it in Ballysakeery in Mayo, which is written by Mac-Firbis,

Baile-easa-caoile (Ballysakeely), the town of the narrow cataract.

M and *n* are occasionally interchanged. For example, the barony of Glenquin in Limerick, should have been called Glenquim, for the Irish is *Gleann-a'-chuim*, the glen of the *cum* or hollow. Kilmainham near Dublin is called Kilmannan by Boate, which is more correct than the present form. The name signifies the church of St. Mainen (Irish *Maighnenn*), who was bishop and abbot there in the seventh century.

Change of ch *and* th, *to* f. The guttural sound of *c* aspirated (*ch*) does not exist in English, and in anglicised names it is occasionally changed to *f*: for example, Knocktopher in Kilkenny, is from the Irish *Cnoc-a'-tochair*, the hill of the *togher* or causeway. *F* is also sometimes substituted for *th*: thus, Tiscoffin in Kilkenny

took its name from an old church called *Tigh-scoithin* (Tee-Scoheen), the house of St. Scoithin, who erected his primitive church here towards the close of the sixth century.

Substitution of g *for* d. *D* aspirated is often changed to *g*, as in Drumgonnelly in Louth, which should have been anglicised Drumdonnelly, for the Irish is *Druim-Dhonghaile*, the ridge or long hill of the Donnellys.

Addition of d *after* n, *and of* b *after* m. The letter *d* is often corruptly placed after *n*—as we find in case of Rathfryland in Down, which is called in Irish *Rath-Fraeileann*, Freelan's fort. *B* is also often placed after *m*, as in Cumber or Comber, the names of several places in the northern counties. The Irish word is *Comar*, which signifies the confluence of two waters, and it is correctly anglicised Cummer and Comer in many other names.

Note:

The following abbreviations have been used in quoting authorities for the Irish forms:

'F.M.,' The Annals of the Four Masters.
'Book of R.,' The Book of Rights (*Leabhar-na-gCeart*).
'Hy F.,' The Tribes and Customs of Hy Fiachrach.
'O'Dugan,' The topographical Poems of O'Dugan and O'Heeren.
'O'C. Cal.,' O'Clery's Calendar of Irish Saints, or, The Martyrology of Donegal.
'Wars of GG.,' The Wars of the *Gaedhil* with the *Gaill* (of the Irish with the Danes).
'Mart. Tam.,' The Martyrology of Tallaght.

The Irish forms are always in italics. The Irish root words are fully explained in the following section.

The pronunciation of the principal Irish words is given in brackets, as nearly as can be represented by English letters.

Irish Place Names

Abbeyfeale, in Limerick: *Mainister-na-Feile*, the monastery or abbey of the river Feale.

Abbeygormican, in Galway: the abbey of the O'Cormacans.

Abbeylara (also Lara), in Longford: *Leath-rath*, F. M. (Lah-rah), half rath or fort.

Abbeyleix, the abbey of the old principality of Leix, so called from a monastery founded there in 1183 by Conor O'Moore. In the reign of Felimy the Law-giver (AD 111 to 119), this territory was given by the king of Leinster to *Lughaidh Laeighseach* (Lewy Leeshagh), Conall Carnach's grandson, for helping to expel the Munstermen who had seized on Ossory. Lewy's descendants, the O'Moores, took from him the tribe name, *Laeighis* (Leesh), and their territory was called by the same name, now modernized to Leix.

Abbeyshrule, in Longford: from a monastery founded there by one of the O'Farrells. It was anciently called *Sruthair* (Sruher), F. M., i.e. the stream, of which Shrule is a corruption.

Abbeystrowry, in Cork: the same name as the last. The *sruthair* or stream from which it was called, gave name also to Bealnashrura (the *beal* or ford-mouth of the stream) a village situated at an ancient ford.

Achonry, in Sligo: *Achadh-Chonaire* (Aha-Conary), F. M., Conary's field.

Adare, in Limerick; *Ath-dara* (Ah-dara), F. M., the ford of the oak tree. A large oak must have anciently overshadowed the old ford on the Maigue.

Addergoole (also Addragool, Adrigole, Adrigoole), *Eadar-dha-ghabhal* (Adragoul), i.e. (a place) between two (river) forks.

Aderrig, *Ath-dearg*, red ford. *See* Aghaderg.

Affane, on the Blackwater below Cappoquin: *Atha-mheadhon*, (Ah-vane), F. M., middle ford.

Agha, in several counties: *Achadh* (Aha), a field.

Aghaboe, in Queen's County, where St. Canice of Kilkenny had his principal church. Adamnan in his Life of St. Columkille, written in the seventh century, has the following passage, which settles the meaning: 'St. Canice being in the monastery which is called in Latin *Campulus bovis* (i.e. the field of the cow), but in Irish *Ached-bou*.'

Aghaboy, *Achadh-buidhe* (Aha-boy), yellow field.

Aghacross, near Kildorrery in Cork: the ford of the cross; probably from a cross erected in connexion with St. Molaga's adjacent establishment, to mark a ford on the Funcheon. *See* Templemolaga.

Aghada, near Cork: *Ath-fhada* (Ahada), long ford.

Aghaderg, *Ath-dearg*, red ford. *See* Aderrig.

Aghadoe, near Killarney: *Achadh-dá-eó* (Aha-daw-o), F. M., the field of the two yew trees.

Aghadowey, in Derry: *Achadh-Dubhthaigh* (Ahaduffy), O'C. Cal., Duffy's field.

Achadown (also Aghadoon), the field of the *dun* or fort.

Aghadreen (also Aghadreenagh, Aghadreenan, Aghadrinagh), the field of the *dreens* or sloe bushes *(draeighean)*.

Aghafad (also Aghafadda), long field.

Aghagallon, the field of the *gallan* or standing stone.

Aghagower, in Mayo: the correct name would be Aghafower, for the ancient form, as found in the old Lives of St Patrick, is *Achadh-fobhair*, the field of the spring, from a celebrated well, now called St. Patrick's well. The present form is written in Hy F., *Achadh-gabhair*, which means the field of the goat.

Aghamore, *Achadh-mór*, great field.

Aghanloo, *Athan-Lugha*, Lugh's or Lewy's little ford.

Aghavea, in Fermanagh: *Achaah-beithe* (Ahabehy), F. M., the field of the birch trees.

Achaveagh, in Donegal and Tyrone: same as last.

Aghavilla (also Aghaville, Aghavilly), *Achadh-bhile*, the field of the *bile* or old tree.

Aghaviller, in Kilkenny: *Achadh-biorair* (Ahabirrer), F. M., the field of the watercresses (*r* changed to *l*).

Aghindarragh, in Tyrone: the field of the oak.

Aghintamy, near Monaghan: *Achadh-an-tsamhaidh*, the field of the sorrel.

Aghmacart, in Queen's County: the field of Art's son.

Aghnamullen, in Monaghan: the field of the mills.

Aghnaskea (also Aghnaskeagh, Aghnaskew), *Achadh-na-sceach*, the field of the white-thorn bushes.

Aghowle, in Wicklow: *Achadh-abhla*, field of apple trees.

Aglish, *Eaglais* (aglish), a church.

Aglisheloghane, in Tipperary: the church of the *clogh-aun* or row of stepping stones.

Aglishcormick, in Limerick: St. Cormac's church.

Aglishdrinagh, in Cork: *Eaglais-draeighneach*, the church of the *dreens* or sloe bushes.

Agolagh, in Antrim: *Ath-gobhlach*, forked ford.

Ahane (also Ahaun), *Athán*, little ford.

Ahaphuca, the ford of the *pooka* or spright.

Ahascragh, in Galway: *Ath-eascrach*, F. M., the ford of the *esker* or sand-hill.

Aille, *Aill*, a cliff.

Allen, *Aillín*, a little cliff.

Alt, *Alt*, a height, the side of a glen.

Altan, little cliff or glen side.

Altaturk, the glen side of the boar (*torc*).

Altavilla, the glen side of the *bile* or old tree.

Altinure, *Alt-an-iubhair* (yure), the glen side of the yew tree.

Altnaveagh (also Altnaveigh), *Alt-na-bhfiach*, the cliff or glen side of the *fiachs* or ravens.

Anna, *see* Annagh.

Annabella, near Mallow: *Eanach-bile*, the marsh of the *bile* or old tree.

Annaclone, the marsh of the meadow (*cluain*).

Annacotty, near Limerick: *Ath-na-coite*, the ford of the *cot* or little boat.

Annacramph, in Armagh and Monaghan: *Eanach-creamha*, the marsh of the wild garlick.

Annaduff, *Eanach-dubh*, F. M., black marsh.

Annagh, *Eanach*, a marsh.

Annaghaskin, in Dublin, near Bray: *Eanach-easgann*, the marsh of the eels.

Annaghbeg (also Annaghmore), little marsh, great marsh.

Annahagh (also Annahaia), in Monaghan and Armagh: *Ath-na-haithe*, the ford of the kiln (*aith*).

Annahavil, *Eanach-abhaill*, the marsh of the orchard (*abhall*).

Annahilt, in Down: *Eanach-eilte*, the marsh of the doe (*eilit*).

Annakisha, the ford of the *kish* or wickerwork causeway.

Annalong, in Down: *Ath-na-long*, the ford of the ships (*long*). The ford was near the place where vessels used to be moored or anchored.

Annamoe, in Wicklow: *Ath-na-mbo*, the ford of the cows (*bo*).

Anny, *see* Annagh.

Arboe, in Tyrone: *Ard-bo*, the cow's height.

Ard, high; a height.

Ardagh, *Ard-achadh* (Ard-aha), high field.

Ardaghy, *see* Ardagh.

Ardan (also Ardane, Ardaun), little *ard* or height.

Ardara, in Donegal: *Ard-a'-raith*, the height of the rath, from a hill near the village, on which stands a conspicuous fort.

Ardataggle (also Ardateggle), *Ard-a'-tseagail*, the height of the rye (*seagal*).

Arbane (also Ardbaun), white height.

Ardbeg, little height.

Ardbraccan, in Meath: St. Brecan's height. St. Brecan erected a church here in the sixth century, some time previous to his removal to the great island of Aran, where he had his chief establishment.

Ardcarn, the height of the *carn* or monumental heap.

Ardcath, the height of the battle (*cath*).

Ardee, in Louth: Old English form Atherdee, which represents the Irish *Ath-Fhirdia* (Ahirdee), as it is written in Irish authorities, the ford of Ferdia, a chieftain who was slain there in battle by Cuchullin in the first century.

Ardeen, in Cork and Kerry: little height.

Ardeevin, *Ard-aeibhinn*, beautiful height.

Arderin, the height of Erin or Ireland.

Ardfert, in Kerry: *Ard-ferta*, F. M., the height of the grave. Sometimes called Ardfert-Brendan, from St. Brendan the navigator, who founded a monastery there in the sixth century.

Ardfinnan, in Tipperary: the height of St. Finan, who founded a monastery there in the seventh century.

Ardgeeha, *Ard-gaeithe*, height of the wind.

Ardglass, *Ard-glas*, green height.

Ardgoul, *Ard-gabhal*, high fork.

Ardkeen, *Ardcaein*, beautiful height.

Ardkill, high church or wood (*cill* or *coill*).

Ardlougher, *Ard-luachra*, rushy height.

Ardmayle, *Ard-Maille*, F. M., Malley's height.

Ardmeen, smooth height.

Ardmore, in various counties: great height.

Ardmulchan, in Meath: *Ard-Maelchon*, F. M., Maelchon's height.

Ardnacrusha (also Ardnacrushy), the height of the cross.

Ardnageeha (also Ardnageehy), the height of the wind (*gaeth*).

Ardnanean, the height of the birds (*en*).

Ardnapreaghaun, the height of the *prehauns* or crows.

Ardnarea, near Ballina: *Ard-na-riaghadh* (reea), Hy F., the hill of the executions. Four persons were executed here in the seventh century, for the murder of Kellach, bishop of Kilmore-Moy.

Ardnurcher, in Westmeath: a corruption of Athnurcher, from *Ath-an-urchair*, F. M., the ford of the cast or throw. According to a very ancient legend, a battle was fought here in the first century, between the Connaught and Ulster forces. Keth Mac Magach, a Connaught chief, threw a hard round ball at Conor mac Nessa, king of Ulster, and struck him on the head, from the effects of which the king died seven years afterwards.

Ardpatrick, St. Patrick's height.

Ardrahan, *Ard-rathain*, the height of the ferns.

Ardskeagh, the height of the *skeaghs* or bushes.

Ardstraw, in Tyrone: *Ard-sratha* (Ard-srawha), F. M., the height of (or near) the river holm.

Ardvally, in Donegal and Sligo. *See* p 85.

Ardvarna (also Ardvarness, Ardvarney, Ardvarnish), *Ard-bhearna* and *Ard-bhearnas*, high gap.

Arless, in Queen's County: *Ard-lios*, high fort.

Armagh, written in all Irish authorities *Ard-Macha*, which, in the Book of Armagh, is translated *Altitudo Machæ*, Macha's height. From Queen Macha of the golden hair, who founded the palace of Emania, 300 years BC.

Armoy, in Antrim: *Airthir-Maighe* (Arhir-moy), F. M., eastern plain.

Artimacormack, in Antrim: *Ard-tighe-Mic-Cormaic*, the height of Mac Cormack's house.

Artrea, in Derry: *Ard-Trea* (Mart. Taml.), Trea's height. The virgin St. Trea flourished in the fifth century.

Askeaton took its name from the cataract on the Deel near the town, which the F. M. call *Eas-Gephtine* (Ass-Geftine), Gephtine's cataract.

Assan (also Assaun), small *ass* or waterfall.

Assaroe, at Ballyshannon. The Book of Leinster states that *Aedh-Ruadh* (Ay-roo), queen Macha's father (*see* Armagh), was drowned in this cataract, which was thence called from him *Eas-Aedha-Ruaidh* (Assayroo), *Aedh-Ruadh's* waterfall.

Assey, on the Boyne in Meath. The F. M. record that in AD 524 'the battle of *Ath-Sithe* (Ah-Shee) was gained by *Muircheartach* (king of Ireland) against the Leinstermen, where *Sithe* (Shee) the son of *Dian* was slain, from whom *Ath-Sithe* (*Sithe's* ford) is called.'

Athenry, *Ath-na-riogh* (ree), F. M., the ford of the kings.

Athgoe, in Dublin: the ford of the *gow* or smith.

Athlacca, in Limerick: from a ford on the Morning Star river, called *Ath-leacach*, stony ford.

Athleague, in Roscommon: *Ath-liag*, F. M., the ford of the stones.

Athlone, from the ancient ford over the Shannon, called in Irish authorities *Ath-Luain*, the ford of *Luan*, a man's name.

Athneasy, in Limerick: called in the F. M., *Ath-na-nDiese* (Athnaneasy), the ford of (the tribe of) the *Desii*, who inhabited the old territory of *Deisbeag*, round Knockany.

Athnid, in Tipperary: the ford of the *nead* or bird's nest.

Athnowen, a parish near Ballincollig in Cork: from a ford on the river Bride, called *Ath-'n-uamhainn* (Athnooan), the ford of the cave (*uaimh*), from the great limestone cave at 'The Ovens,' near the ford.

Athy: One of the battles between Lewy and the Munstermen (*see* Abbeyleix), was fought at a ford on the Barrow, where a Munster chief, *Ae*, was slain; and from him the place was called *Ath-I* (Wars of GG), the ford of *Ae*.

Attavally, *Ait-a'-bhaile*, the site of the *bally* or town.

Atti or Atty in the beginning of a name, is the anglicised form of *áit-tighe* (aut-tee), the place or site of a house (*ait* and *teach*).

Attidermot, the site of Dermot's house.

Attiduff, the site of the black house.

Attykit, the site of *Ceat's* or Keth's house.

Aughall, in Tipperary (also Aughil, in Derry): *Eochaill*, the yew wood (*eo* and *coill*). *See* Youghal and Oghill.

Aughinish, *Each-inis*, F. M., the island of horses.

Aughnacloy, *Achadh-na-cloiche* (Ahanacloha), the field of the stone.

Aughnahoy, *Achadh-na-haithe*, the field of the kiln (*aith*).

Aughnanure, near Oughterard, in Galway: *Achadh-na-niúbhar* (Ahananure), the field of the yew trees. One of the old yews still remains.

Aughnish, *see* Aughinish.

Aughrim, the name is written in Irish document, *Each-dhruim* (Agh-rim: *dh* silent), which Colgan translates *Equi-mons*, the hill, *druim*, or ridge, of the horse (*each*).

Aughris (also Aughrus), *Each-ros*, F. M., the peninsula of the horses.

Avalbane (also Avalreagh), white orchard, grey orchard (*abhall*).

Avonmore (also Avonbeg), great river, little river (*abhainn*).

Aubeg, *Abh-bheag*, little river.

Ayle, *see* Aille.

Bahana, *see* Behanagh.

Bailey lighthouse, at Howth, from the old *bally* or fortress of Criffan, king of Ireland in the first century, on the site of which it was built.

Balbriggan, in Dublin: *Baile-Breacain*, Brecan's town.

Baldoyle, in Dublin: *Baile-Dubhghoill*, *Dubhgall's* or Doyle's town.

Balfeddock, the town of the *feadogs* or plovers.

Balgeeth, in Meath: the town of the wind (*gaeth*).

Balla, in Mayo. In the Life of St. Mochua, we are told that before the saint founded his monastery there in the seventh century, the place was called *Ros-dairbh-reach* (Ros-dar'aragh), i.e. oak grove. He enclosed the wells of his establishment with a *balla* or wall, and hence the place received the new name of Balla.

Ballagh, *Bealach*, a road or pass.

Ballaghaderreen, in Mayo: the road of the *derreen* or little oak wood.

Ballaghbehy, the road of the birch (*beith*).

Ballaghboy, yellow road (*buidhe*).

Ballaghkeen, in Wexford: beautiful road (*caein*).

Ballaghkeeran, the road of the *keerans* or quicken trees.

Ballaghmore, great road.

Ballard, *Baile-ard*, high town.

Ballee, in Down: written in the Taxation of 1306, *Baliath*, from the Irish *Baile-atha*, the town of the ford.

Balleen, little *bally* or town.

Ballina, the name of many places: *Bel-an-atha* (Bellanaha), the mouth of the ford.

Ballinabarny, the town of the *bearna* or gap.

Ballinaboy, in Cork, Galway, and Roscommon: *Bel-an-atha-buidhe*, the mouth of the yellow ford.

Ballinaclogh, the town of the stones (*cloch*).

Ballinacor (also Ballinacur, Ballinacurra), *Baile-na-corra*, the town of the weir.

Ballinafad, *Bel-an-atha-fada* (Bellanafadda), the mouth of the long ford.

Bellinagar, *Bel-atha-na-gcarr* (Bellanagar), the ford-mouth of the cars.

Ballinahinch, the town of the *inis* or island.

Ballinakill, the town of the church or wood.

Ballinalack, in Westmeath: *Bel-atha-na-leac* (Bellanalack) the mouth of the ford of the flag-stones.

Ballinalee (also Ballinalea), *Bel-atha-na-laegh*, the ford-mouth of the calves.

Ballinamona, *Bail-na-mona*, the town of the bog.

Ballinamore, *Bel-1-atha-moir*, the mouth of the great ford.

Ballinamought, near Cork: *Baile-na-mbocht*, the town of the poor people (*bocht*).

Ballinard, the town of the *ard* or height.

Ballinascarty, the town of the *scart* or thicket.

Ballinasloe, *Bel-atha-na-sluaigheadh* (Bellanaslooa), F. M., the ford-mouth of the hosts or gatherings.

Ballinaspick (also Ballinaspig), *Baile-an-easpuig*, the town of the bishop.

Ballinastraw, the town of the *srath* or river-holm.

Ballinchalla, on Lough Mask in Mayo: *Baile-an-chala*, the town of the *callow* or landing place.

Ballinclare, the town of the *clar* or plain.

Ballincloghan, *see* Ballycloghan.

Ballincollig, *Baile-an-chullaigh*, the town of the boar.

Ballincurra (also Ballincurrig, Ballincurry), *Baile-an-chur-raigh*, the town of the *curragh* or marsh.

Ballinderry, the town of the *derry* or oak wood.

Ballindrait (also Ballindrehid), *Baile-an-droichid*, the town of the bridge.

Ballineddan, in Wicklow: *Baile-an-fheadáin,* the town of the *feadan* or streamlet.

Ballinfoyle, in Galway and Wicklow,

Ballingaddy, the town of the thief (*gadaighe*), i.e. the black thief O'Dwane.

Ballingarrane, the town of the *garran* or shrubbery.

Ballingarry, *Baile-an-gharrdha,* the town of the garden.

Ballinglanna (also Ballinglen), the town of the glen.

Ballingowan, the town of the smith (*gobha*).

Ballinlass (also Ballinlassa, Ballinlassy, Ballinliss), the town of the *lios* or fort.

Ballinlough, the town of the lake.

Ballinloughan (also Ballinloughaun), the town of the little lake.

Ballinlug (also Ballinluig), the town of the *lug* or hollow.

Ballinphuill (also Ballinphull), *see* p 85.

Ballinree, sometimes *Baile-an-fhraeigh,* the town of the heath (*fraech*); sometimes *Baile-an-righ,* the town of the king.

Ballinrobe, the town of the river Robe.

Ballinrostig, Roche's town.

Ballinspittle, the town of the *spital* or hospital.

Ballintaggart, *see* p 85.

Ballinteer, *Baile-an-tsaeir,* the town of the carpenter.

Ballintemple, the town of the *temple* or church.

Ballinteskin, *Baile-an-tsescenn,* the town of the morass.

Ballintlea (also Ballintleva, Ballintlevy, Ballintlieve), *Baile-an-tsleibhe,* the town of the mountain (*sliabh*).

Ballintober, the town of the well.

Ballintogher, the town of the *togher* or causeway.

Ballintubbert (also Ballintubbrid), *see* Ballintober.

Ballinure, the town of the yew tree (*iubhar*).

Ballinvally, *Baile-an-bhealaigh,* the town of the road.

Ballinvarrig (also Ballinvarry), Barry's town.

Ballinvella (also Ballinvilla), *Baile-an-bhile,* the town of the *bile* or ancient tree.

Ballinvoher, *Baile-an-bhothair,* the town of the road.

Ballinvreena, in Limerick and Tipperary: the town of the *bruighean* (breen) or fairy mansion.

Ballinwillin, *Baile-an-mhuilinn,* the town of the mill.

Ballinwully, in Roscommon: *see* p 85.

Ballytore, in Kildare, took its name from a ford on the river Greece: *Bel-atha-a'-tuair* (Bellatoor), the ford mouth of the *tuar* or bleach green.

Ballyard, high town.

Bailybaan (also Ballybane, Ballybaun), white town.

Ballybay, in Monaghan: *Bel-atha-beithe* (Bellabehy), the ford mouth of the birch.

Ballybeg, small town.

Ballyboe, i.e. 'cow-land,' a measure of land.

Ballybofey, in Donegal. The correct old name is *Srath-bofey.* Some occupier named *Fiach* or Fay must have in past times kept his cows on the holm along the Finn: *Srath-bo-Fiaich,* F. M., the river holm of Fiach's cows.

Ballyboghil, in county Dublin: the town of the *bachal* or crozier; from St. Patrick's crozier.

Ballyboley, the town of the *booley* or dairy place.

Ballybough, near Dublin: *Baile-bocht,* poor town. The same as Ballybought in other places.

Ballyboy, in King's County: written in Irish authorities *Baile-atha-buidhe* (Ballyboy) the town of the yellow ford. The name is common in other counties and sometimes means yellow town (*Baile-buidhe*).

Ballybrack, speckled town.

Ballybrannagh, Walsh's town. The proper name Walsh is in Irish *Breathnach* (Branagh), i.e. Briton.

Ballybunnion, in Kerry: Bunnion's town.

Ballycahan (also Ballycahane), O'Cahan's town.

Ballycahill, Cahill's or O'Cahill's town.

Ballycastle, in Antrim: the town of the castle.

Ballycastle, in Mayo: the town of the *cashel* or circular stone fort.

Ballyclare, *see* Ballinclare.

Ballyclerahan, in Tipperary: O'Clerahan's town.

Ballyclogh (also Ballyclohy), the town of the stones.

Ballycloghan, the town of the *cloghan* or row of stepping stones across a river.

Ballyclug, in Antrim: the town of the bell (*clog*).

Ballycolla, the town of Colla, a man's name.

Ballyconnell, in Cavan. According to tradition, Conall Carnagh, one of the most renowned of the Red Branch knights of Ulster, was slain here in the first century; hence it was called *Bel-atha-Chonaill,* the mouth of the ford of Conall.

Ballycormick, Cormac's or O'Cormac's town.

Ballycullane, O'Cullane's or O'Collins's town.

Ballydehob, in Cork: *Bel-atha-da-chab,* the ford of the two *cabs* or mouths, from some local feature.

Ballyduff, black town.

Ballyea, O'Hea's or Hayes's town.

Ballyeighter, *Baile-iochtar,* lower town.

Ballyfoyle, the town of the hole (*poll*).

Ballygarran (also Ballygarraun), the town of the *garran* or shrubbery.

Ballyglass, green town.

Ballygowan, the town of the smith (*gobha*).

Ballyheige, in Kerry: *Baile-ui-Thadg,* the town of O'Teige.

Ballyhooly, near Mallow: took its name from an ancient ford on the blackwater, called in the Book of Lismore *Ath-ubhla* (Ahoola), the ford of the apples. The people now call it in Irish *Baile-atha-ubhla* (which they pronounce *Blaa-hoola*), the town of the apple ford.

Ballykeel, *Baile-cael,* narrow town.

Ballyknock, the town of the hill.

Ballyknockan (also Ballyknockane), the town of the little hill.

Ballylanders, in Limerick: Landers's town, from an English family of that name.

Ballylig, the town of the *lug* or hollow.

Ballylongford, in Kerry: *Bel-atha-longphuirt,* the ford-mouth of the *longphort* or fortress, because it led to Carrigafoyle castle, two miles off.

Ballylough (also Ballyloughan, Ballyloughaun), the town of the lake.

Ballylusk (also Ballylusky), *Baile-loisgthe,* burnt town, from the practice of burning the surface in tillage.

Ballymena (also Ballymenagh), *Baile-meadhonach,* middle town.

Ballymoney, the town of the shrubbery (*muine*).

Ballymore, great town. Sometimes when the place is on a river it is *Bel-atha-moir* (Bellamore), the mouth of the great ford.

Ballymote, *Baile-an-mhota*, F. M., the town of the moat or mound.

Ballynabarna (also Ballynabarny, Ballynabearna), the town of the gap. *See* Ballinabarny.

Ballynaboley (also Ballynaboola, Ballynabearna), the town of the *booley* or dairy place (*buaile*). *See* Ballyboley.

Ballynacally, the town of the *calliagh* or hag.

Ballynacarrick (also Ballynacarrig, Ballynacarriga, Ballynacarrigy), the town of the rock (*carraig*).

Ballynaclogh (also Ballynacloghy), *Baile-na-cloiche*, the town of the *cloch* or stone.

Ballynacor (also Ballynacorra), the town of the weir (*cora*).

Ballynacourty, the town of the *court* or mansion.

Ballynagall (also Ballynagaul), the town of the *Galls* or foreigners.

Ballynagard, the town of the *ceards* or artificers.

Ballynagee (also Ballynageeha), town of the wind (*gaeth*).

Ballynageeragh, the town of the sheep (*caera*).

Ballynaglogh, *Baile-na-gcloch*, the town of the stones.

Ballynagore, the town of the goats (*gabhar*).

Ballynagowan, the town of the smiths (*gobha*).

Ballynagran, *Baile-na-gcrann*, the town of the trees.

Ballynahaglish, the town of the church (*eaglais*).

Ballynahinch, the town of the *inis* or island.

Ballynahone (also Ballynahown, Ballynahowna), the town of the river (*abhainn*).

Ballynahow, the town of the river (*abh*).

Ballynakill (also Ballynakilla, Ballynakilly), the town of the church or wood (*cill* or *coill*).

Ballynalacken, the town of the *leacan* or hill side.

Ballynamona, the town of the bog (*móin*).

Ballynamuck, the town of the pigs (*muc*).

Ballynamuddagh, *Baile-na-mbodach*, the town of the *bodachs* or churls.

Ballynaraha, the town of the rath or fort.

Ballynatona (also Ballynatone), the town of the *backside* or hill (*tóin*).

Ballynatray, the town of the strand (*traigh*).

Ballyneety, *Baile-an-Fhaeite*, the town of White, a family name of English origin.

Ballyness, the town of the waterfall (*eas*).

Ballynew (also Ballynoe), *Baile-nua*, new town.

Ballynure, *Baile-an-iubhair*, the town of the yew.

Ballyorgan, in Limerick: Organ's or Horgan's town.

Ballyragget, in Kilkenny: *Bel-atha-Raghat*, F. M., Ragat's ford-mouth.

Ballyroe, *Baile-ruadh*, red town.

Ballyroosky, the town of the *rusk* or marsh.

Ballysadare, in Sligo: originally *Eas-dara* (Assdara), the cataract of the oak, from the beautiful fall on the Owenmore river. It was afterwards called *Baile-easa-dara* (Ballyassadara) F. M., the town of Assdara, which has been shortened to the present name.

Ballysaggart, the town of the *sagart* or priest.

Ballysakeery, in Mayo. *See* p 85.

Ballysallagh, dirty town.

Ballyshane, Shane's or John's town.

Ballyshannon: the old ford on the Erne is called by the annalists *Ath-seanaigh* and *Bel-atha-seanaigh* (Bellashanny). From the latter, the present name is derived, and it means the mouth of *Seanach's* or *Shannagh's* ford, a man's name in common use. The *on* is a modern corruption. The peasantry call the town *Ballyshanny*, which is nearer the original. Ballyshannon in Kildare is similarly derived.

Ballytarsna (also Ballytarsney), cross-town; i.e. the village or townland had a *cross* or transverse position.

Ballyteige, O'Teige's town.

Ballytrasna, *see* Ballytarsna.

Ballyvaghan, in Clare: *Baile-ui-Bheachain*, O'Behan's town.

Ballywater, *Baile-uachtar*, upper town.

Ballywillin, the town of the mill (*muileann*)

Balrath, *Baile-ratha*, the town of the fort.

Balrathboyne, in Meath: St. *Baeithin* (Bweeheen, but often pron. Boyne), the son of *Cuana*, built a church here near an ancient rath, and the rath remains, though the church is gone. Hence it was called *Rath-Baeithin*, and in recent times, Balrathboyne, the town of *Baeithin's* rath.

Balrothery, *Baile-a'-ridire* (Ballyariddery), the town of the knight.

Baltinglass, written *Bealach-Chonglais* (Ballaconglas) in Irish authorities, the road or pass of *Cuglas*, a person about whom there is a very ancient legend.

Baltrasna, *see* Ballytarsna.

Baltray, the town of the strand (*traigh*).

Banagh, barony of, in Donegal. It is called in the annals *Baghaineach* (Bawnagh), i.e. the territory of *Boghaine* (Boana) or *Enna Boghaine*, the son of Conall Gulban, son of the great king Niall of the Nine Hostages, who reigned from AD 379 to 405.

Banagher (also Bangor), *Beannchor* (Banaher), F. M., (from the root *beann*), signifies horns, or pointed hills or rocks, and sometimes simply a pointed hill.

Bannow, in Wexford: the harbour was called *Cuan-an-bhainbh* (Coon-an-wonniv), the harbour of the *bonniv* or sucking pig, and the village has preserved the latter part of the name changed to Bannow.

Bansha, *Bainseach* (Bawnsha), a level place.

Bantry, *Beantraighe* (Bantry), Book of R., i. e. the descendants of *Beann* (Ban), one of the sons of Conor Mac Nessa, king of Ulster in the first century. A part of the tribe settled in Wexford, and another part in Cork, and the barony of Bantry in the former county, and the town of Bantry in the latter, retain their name.

Barna, *Bearna*, a gap.

Barnaboy, yellow gap.

Barnageeha (also Barnageehy), windy gap (*gaoth*).

Barnane Ely, in Tipperary: from the remarkable gap in the Devil's Bit mountain, *Bearnán-Eile*, the little gap of Ely, the ancient territory in which it was situated.

Barnes (also Barnish), *Bearnas*, a gap.

Barnismore, great gap.

Barr, the top of anything.

Baslick, *Baisleac*, F. M., a *basilica* or church.

Batterstown, the town of the *batter* (*bóthar*) or road.

Bawnmore, great green field.

Bawnoge, little green field.

Bawnreagh, greyish green field.

Baunskeha, the green field of the bush (*sceach*).

Bawnboy, yellow field.

Bawnfune, *Bán-fionn*, white field.

Bawnmore, great green field.

Beagh, *Beitheach* (Beha), a place of birches.

Bear, barony, island, and haven, in Cork. Owen More, king of Munster in the second century, spent nine years in Spain, and, according to an old legend, he married *Beara*, daughter of the king of that country. On his return to Ireland to make war against Conn of the hundred battles, he landed on the north side of Bantry bay, and called the place *Beara* in honour of his wife.

Beheenagh (also Behernagh), a place of birches (*beith*).

Behy, birch land.

Belfarsad, *see* Belfast.

Belfast. In old times the Lagan used to be crossed here by a *farset* or sandbank, and hence the place was called *Belfeirste*, F. M., the *bel* or ford of the *farset*.

Bellaghy, the mouth or entrance of the *lahagh* or slough.

Bellanacargy, in Cavan: *Bel-atha-na-cairrge*, the mouth of the ford of the rock (*carraig*).

Bellanagher, in Roscommon: *Bel-atha-na-gcarr*, the mouth of the ford of the cars.

Bellananagh, in Cavan: *Bel-atha-na-neach*, the mouth of the ford of the horses (*each*).

Bellaugh, in Roscommon: *see* Bellaghy.

Belleek, near Ballyshannon: *Bel-leice* (Bellecka), F. M., the ford-mouth of the flag stone, from the flat surfaced rock in the bed of the river. Belleek in other places is similarly derived.

Beltany, from *Bealtaine* or *Beltaine*, the first of May, because the May day sports used to be celebrated there.

Ben, a peak, a pointed hill (*beann*).

Benbo mountain near Manorhamilton, is called in Irish *Beanna-bo*, F. M., the peaks or horns of the cow, from its curious double peak.

Benburb, in Tyrone: from a cliff over the Blackwater, called in the annals *Beann-borb*, the proud peak.

Bengore head, the peak of the goats (*gabhar*).

Bengorm, blue peak.

Benmore, great peak.

Bignion (also Binnion), small *ben* or peak.

Billy, in Antrim: Bile, an ancient tree.

Binbulbin, correct name, *Binn-Gulbain*, Gulban's peak.

Bogagh (also Boggagh, Boggan, Boggaun), a boggy place.

Boher, *Bothar* (boher), a road.

Boherard, high road.

Boherboy, yellow road.

Boherduff, *see* p 85.

Bohereen, little road.

Bohermeen, smooth road.

Boherroe, red road.

Boho, in Fermanagh: *Botha* (boha), tents or huts.

Bohola, *Both-Thola*, Hy. F., *St. Tola's* hut.

Boley, *buaile*, a milking place for cattle.

Boleybeg, little *boley* or dairy place.

Boola, booley, *see* Boley.

Boolyglass, green *booley*.

Booterstown, near Dublin: the town of the *bothar*, *batter*, or road. In a roll of the fifteenth century it is called *Ballybothyr*, which shows that the Irish name was *Baile-an-bhothair*, the town of the road, of which the present name is a kind of half translation.

Borheen, *see* Bohereen.

Borris, *Buirghes* (burris), a *burgage* or borough.

Borris-in-Ossory, from the old territory of Ossory.

Borrisokane, O'Keane's borough town.

Borrisoleigh, from the ancient territory *Ui Luighdheach* (Hy Leea), in which it was situated.

Bourney, in Tipperary: *Boirne* (bourny), rocky lands, the plural of *Burren*.

Bovevagh, *Both-Mheidhbhe* (Boh-veva), the hut or tent of Maev or Mabel, a woman's name.

Boylagh, barony of, in Donegal: i. e. the territory of the O'Boyles.

Boyounagh, yellow *ounagh* or marsh (*abhnach*).

Braade, *see* Braid.

Brackagh (also Brackenagh, Brackernagh, Bracklagh), a speckled place, from *breac*, speckled.

Bracklin (also Brackloon), *Breac-cluain*, speckled meadow.

Braid, the, in Antrim: applied to the deep glen through which the river flows. *Braghad* (braud), a gullet or gorge.

Brandon hill in Kerry, and also in Kilkenny: both called from St Brendan the Navigator, who flourished in the sixth century.

Bray, in Wicklow: it is called Bree in old documents, and it took name from the rocky head near it: *Bri* (bree), a hill. The name of Bray head in Valentia Island in Kerry, is similarly derived.

Breaghva (also Breaghwy, Breaghy), *Breach-mhagh* (Brea-vah), the plain of the wolves (*breach*, a wolf; *magh*, a plain).

Breandrum, stinking *drum* or ridge.

Brigown, near Mitchelstown, in Cork: written *Bri-gobh-unn* (Breegown) in the Book of Lismore, the *bree* or hill of the smith (*gobha*).

Brittas, speckled land.

Britway, in Cork: *see* Breaghva.

Brockagh, a place of *brocs* or badgers.

Bruff, in Limerick: a corrupt form of *Brugh* (bru), a fort or mansion. The *brugh* is the old fort near the town.

Bruis, another form of *Brugh* (bru), a mansion.

Bruree, in Limerick: called in Irish documents *Brugh-righ* (Bruree), the fort or palace of the king, for it was the chief seat of Olioll Olum, king of Munster in the second century, and afterwards of the O'Donovans. Several of the old forts still remain.

Bullaun, *Bullán*, a well in a rock.

Bun, the bottom or end of anything; the mouth of a river.

Buncrana, the mouth of the river Crana.

Bunlahy, the end of the *lahagh* or slough.

Bunratty, in Clare: the mouth of the river Ratty, now called the Owen O'Garney.

Burren, *Boireann,* a rock, a rocky district.

Burriscara, the *burris* or borough of Carra.

Burrishoole, derived like Burriscarra, from the territory of *Umhall* (ool) or 'The Owles.'

Burrisnafarney, in Tipperary: the *burris* or borough of the alder-plain (*see* Farney).

Buttevant, in Cork: from the French motto of the Barrys, *Boutez-en-avant,* push forward. The Irish name is Kilnamullagh, the *cell* or church of the summits (*mullach*).

Cabragh, bad land.

Caher, *cathair* (caher) a circular stone fort.

Caherbarnagh, gapped *caher* or fort: (*bearnach,* gapped).

Caherconlish, in Limerick: *Cathair-chinn-lis,* the *caher* at the head of the *lis* or fort.

Caherduggan, Duggan's *caher* or stone fort.

Cahergal, white *caher* or stone fort.

Caherkeen, in Cork: beautiful *caher* or fort.

Cahersiveen, in Kerry: it exactly preserves the pronunciation of the Irish name *Cathair-Saidhbhín,* the stone fort of *Saidhbhín,* or Sabina, a woman's name.

Cahirconree mountain, near Tralee: *Curoi's* caher, i.e. the celebrated chief, *Curoi Mac Daire,* who flourished in the first century. His caher still remains on a shoulder of the mountain.

Caldragh, *Cealdrach,* an old burying ground.

Callow, *Cala,* a marshy meadow along a river.

Callowhill, *Callchoill,* hazel wood (*coll* and *coill*).

Caltragh, *see* Caldragh.

Calluragh, *Ceallurach,* an old burial ground.

Camas (also Camus), anything that winds, a winding stream: from *cam,* crooked.

Camlin, crooked line. Often applied to a river.

Camlough, crooked lake (*cam* and *loch*).

Cappa (also Cappagh), *ceapach,* a plot of land laid down for tillage.

Cappaghbeg, little tillage-plot.

Cappaghmore (also Cappamore), great tillage-plot.

Cappaghwhite, in Tipperary: White's tillage-plot.

Capparoe, red plot.

Cappog (also Cappoge), little *cappagh* or plot.

Cappoquin, *Ceapach-Chuinn,* Conn's tillage-plot.

Caran (also Caraun), a rocky place (from *carr*).

Carbury baronies, in Longford and Sligo: so called because they were inhabited by the descendants of Carbery, one of the sons of Niall of the Nine Hostages, king of Ireland from AD 379 to 405.

Cargagh, a rock place (from *carraig*).

Cargan (also Cargin), a little rock, a rocky place.

Carha, *Cairthe* (carha), a pillar stone.

Carhoo, *ceathramhadh* (carhoo) a quarter (of land).

Carlingford, *ford* is the Danish *fiord,* a sea inlet. The old Irish name is *Cairlinn*: Carlingford, the *fiord* of *Cairlinn.*

Carlow, called in Irish documents *Cetherloch* (Caherlough), quadruple lake (*cether,* four); the Barrow anciently formed four lakes there.

Carn, a monumental heap of stones.

Carnacally, the carn of the hag (*cailleach*).

Carnalbanagh, the carn of the *Albanach* or Scotchman.

Carnaun, little carn or monumental heap.

Carnbane, white carn (*ban* (bawn), white).

Carndonagh, in Innishowen: so called because the carn was situated in the parish of Donagh.

Carnew, *Carn-Naoi* (Nee), Naoi's carn.

Carnglass, green carn.

Carnmore, great carn.

Carnsore Point. The old Irish name is *carn,* a monumental heap; the termination *ore* is Danish, and signifies the sandy point of a promontory: Carnsore is merely Carn's *ore,* the *ore* or sandy point of the carn.

Carnteel, in Tyrone: *Carn-tSiadhail* (Carn-teel), F M , *Siadhal's* or Shiel's carn (*s* eclipsed).

Carn Tierna, near Fermoy. *Tighernach* (Tierna) *Tetbannach,* king of Munster in the first century, was buried under the great carn which still remains on the top of the hill; and hence the name, signifying Tierna's carn.

Carntogher hills, in Londonderry: the carn of the *togher* or causeway.

Carrantuohill, the highest mountain in Ireland. It descends on the Killarney side by a curved edge, which the spectator catches in profile, all jagged and serrated with great masses of rock projecting like teeth. *Tuathail* (thoohil) means left-handed, and is applied to anything reversed from its proper direction; *carrán* is a reaping hook; and Carrantuohill is "the reversed reaping hook," because the teeth are on a convex instead of a concave edge.

Carrick, a rock, Irish *carraig* (carrig).

Carrickbeg, little rock.

Carrickduff, black rock.

Carrickfergus, Fergus's rock.

Carrickmore, great rock.

Carrick-on-Shannon. Carrick is here a corruption of *carra,* a weir; and the place took its name from an ancient weir across the Shannon. Its old anglicised name was Carrickdrumrusk, properly Carra-Drumrusk, the weir of Drumrusk.

Carrick-on-Suir, the rock of the Suir; from a large rock in the bed of the river.

Carrig, a rock, *see* Carrick.

Carrigafoyle, on the Shannon, near Ballylongford: *Carraig-a'-phoill,* the rock of the hole; from a deep hole in the river, near the castle.

Carrigaholt, in Clare: written by the F. M., *Carraig-an-chobhlaigh* (Carrigahowly), the rock of the fleet; and it took its name from the rock which rises over the bay where the fleets anchored. The local pronunciation of the Irish name is Carrigaholty, from which the present name is derived. Another place of the same name which preserves the correct pronunciation, is Carrigahowly on Newport bay in Mayo, the castle of the celebrated Grace O'Malley.

The Carrick-a-Rede Rope Bridge, Co Antrim

Carrigaline, in Cork: the rock of O'Lehane.
Carrigallen, in Leitrim: *Carraig-áluinn,* beautiful rock; from the rock on which the original church was built.
Carrigan (also Carrigane), little rock.
Carrigans, little rocks.
Carrigdownane, Downan's or Downing's rock.
Carrigeen, little rock: **Carrigeens,** little rocks.
Carrignavar, in Cork: *see p 85.*
Carrigogunnell, near the Shannon in Limerick: *Carraig-O-gCoinneli,* F. M., the rock of the O'Connells.
Carrigroe, red rock.
Carrow, a quarter (of land). *see* Carhoo.
Carroward, high quarter-land.
Carrowbane (also Carrowbaun), white quarter-land.
Carrowbeg, little quarter-land.
Carrowcrin, the quarter-land of the tree (*crann*).
Carrowduff, black quarter-land.
Carrowgarriff (also Carrowgarve), rough quarter (*garbh,* rough).
Carrowkeel, narrow quarter (*cael,* narrow).
Carrowmanagh, middle quarter-land.
Carrowmore, great quarter-land.
Carrownaglogh, the quarter of the stones (*cloch*).
Carrownamaddoo (also Carrownamaddra, Carrowna-namaddy), the quarter of the dogs (*madadh,* and *madradh*).

Carrowntober, the quarter-land of the well (*tobar*).
Carrowreagh (also Carrowrevagh), grey quarter (*riabhach*).
Carrowroe, red quarter-land.
Cartron, an Anglo-Norman word, meaning a quarter of land.
Cashel: all the places of this name, including Cashel in Tipperary, were so called from a *caiseal* (cashel) or circular stone fort.
Cashen river, *casán* a path: for this river was, as it were, the high road into Kerry.
Cashlan, *Caislen,* a castle.
Castlebane (also Castlebaun), white castle.
Castlebar, in Mayo: shortened from Castle-Barry; for it belonged to the Barrys after the English invasion.
Castlecomer, the castle of the river-confluence (*comar*).
Castleconnell, near Limerick: *see p 85.*
Castledermot, in Kildare: The old name was Disert-dermot, Diarmad's *desert* or hermitage, from Diarmad son of the King of Ulidia, who founded a monastery there about AD 800. The present form of the name is derived from a castle built there by Walter de Riddles-ford in the time of Strongbow.
Castledillon, in Kildare: Irish name *Disert-Iolladhan* (Disertillan), *Iolladhan'* or Illan's hermitage; and the word Castle was substituted for Disert.
Castlelyons, in Cork: the castle of O'Lehane or Lyons.
Castlemoyle, bald or dilapidated castle (*mael*).
Castlepook, the castle of the *pooka* or spright.
Castlerahan, the castle of the little rath or fort.
Castlereagh, grey castle (*riabhach*).
Castleterra, in Cavan: a corruption from the Irish *Cosa'-tsiorraigh* (Cussatirry), the foot (*cos*) of the *searrach* or foal. The name is accounted for by a legend about a stone with the print of a colt's foot on it.
Castleventry, in Cork: the Irish name is *Caislean-na-gaeithe* (Cashlaunnageeha), the castle of the wind, of which the present name is a kind of translation.
Cavan, *Cabhan,* a hollow place. In some parts of Ulster it is understood to mean a hard round hill.
Cavanacaw, the round hill of the chaff (*cáth*); from the practice of winnowing.
Cavanaleck, the hill of the flag-stone.
Cavanreagh, grey hill (*riabhach* (reagh) grey).
Celbridge, in Kildare: the *cell, kill,* or church, of the bridge; a kind of half translation from the original Irish Irish name *Cill-droichid* (Kildrohed), the church of the *drohed* or bridge, which is still retained as the name of the parish, but shortened to Kildrought.
Cheek Point, on the Suir below Waterford: a corruption of *Sheega* Point, the Irish name being *Pointe-na-síge,* the point of the *sheegas* or fairies.
Claggan, *Claigeann,* the skull, a round hill.
Clankee, barony of, in Cavan: *Clann-an-chaoich* (Clann-an-kee), the *clan* or descendants of the one-eyed man. They derived this cognomen from Niall O'Reilly, slain in 1256, who was called *caech* (kee), i. e. one-eyed.
Clanmaurice, barony of, in Kerry: the *clan* or descendants of Maurice Fitzgerald.

Clanwilliam, baronies of, in Limerick and Tipperary: the *clan* or descendants of William Burke.

Clara (also Claragh), a level place; from *clar*.

Clare, a level piece of land (*clar*).

Clareen, little *clar* or level plain.

Clare-Galway. Irish name *Baile-an-chlair* (Ballinclare), F. M., the town of the plain; of which only the latter part is retained: called Clare-Galway to distinguish it from other Clares.

Clash, *Clais,* a trench or furrow.

Clashduff, black trench.

Clashganniff (Clashganniv, Clashganny), the trench of the sand, i. e. a sandpit (*gainimh* (ganniv), sand).

Clashmore, great trench.

Cleenish, *Claen-inis* (Cleeninish), sloping *inis* or island.

Cleggan, *see* Claggan.

Clifden, in Galway: a modern corruption of the Irish name *Clochán,* a beehive-shaped stone house.

Cliffs of Moher. The term *Mothar* (Moher) is applied in the south of Ireland to the ruin of a *caher, rath,* or fort: and on a cliff near Hag's Head there stands an old stone fort, called Moher O'Ruan, O'Ruan's ruined fort, from which the cliffs of Moher received their name.

Clogh, a stone; often applied also to a stone castle.

Cloghan (also Cloghane, Cloghaun), a row of stepping stones across a river (from *cloch*).

Cloghbally, stony *bally* or townland.

Cloghboley (also Cloghboola), stony *booley* or dairy.

Cloghbrack, speckled stone.

Cloghcor, rough stone.

Clogheen, little stone or stone castle.

Clogher, generally applied to stony land—a place full of stones; but occasionally it means a rock.

Clogherbrien, in Kerry: *Braen's* stony place.

Cloghereen, a place full of stones (*cloch*).

Cloghermore, great stony place.

Cloghernagh (also Clogherny), a stony place.

Cloghfin, *Cloch-finn,* white stone.

Cloghineely, in Donegal: *Cloch-Chinnfhaelaidh* (Clogh-Kineely), F.M., Kineely's or Mac Kineely's stone. Name accounted for by a long legend. The stone which gave name to the district is still preserved.

Cloghoge, a stony place.

Cloghpook, the *pooka's* or spright's stone.

Cloghran, *Cloichreán,* a stony place.

Cloghvoley (also Cloghvoola, Cloghvoolia, Cloghvoula), *Cloch-bhuaile,* stony *booley* or dairy place.

Cloghy, a stony place.

Clogrennan, *Cloch-grianáin,* the stone castle of the *grianan* or summer residence.

Clomantagh, in Kilkenny: Mantagh's stone castle.

Clon, a meadow. *See* Cloon.

Clonad, *Cluain-fhada* (Cloonada), long meadow.

Clonagh, *Cluain-each,* horse meadow.

Clonallan, in Down: called by Colgan and others *Cluain-Dallain,* Dallan's meadow; from Dallan Forgall, a celebrated poet of the sixth century.

Clonalvy, *Cluain-Ailbhe, Ailbhe's* or Alvy's meadow.

Clonamery, the meadow of the *iomaire* or ridge.

Clonard, in Meath: written in Irish authorities *Cluain-Eraird,* Erard's meadow. There are several other places called Clonard and Cloonard; but in these the Irish form is probably *Cluain-ard,* high meadow.

Clonarney, *Cluain-airne,* the meadow of sloes.

Clonaslee, the meadow of the *slighe* (slee) or road.

Clonbeg, little meadow.

Clonbrock, the meadow of the *brocs* or badgers.

Cloncrew, in Limerick: *Cluain-creamha* (crawa), the meadow of wild garlic.

Cloncullen, holly meadow.

Cloncurry, shortened from *Cluain-Conaire* (Cloon-Conary), F. M.,Conary's meadow.

Clondalkin, near Dublin: *Cluain-Dolcain,* Dolcan's meadow.

Clonduff, in Down: *Cluain-daimh* (dav), O'C. Cal., the meadow of the ox.

Clone, a meadow: *see* Clon and Cloon.

Large round tower and crosses, Clonmacnois

Cloneen, little meadow.

Clonegall, in Carlow: *Cluain-na-nGall* (Cloon-nung-aul), the meadow of the *Galls* or foreigners.

Clonenagh, in Queen's County: *Cluain-eidhnech* (enagh), O'C. Cal., the meadow of ivy (*see eidhneán* in vocab.). It was so called before the sixth century, and to this day it abounds in ivy.

Clones (pronounced in two syllables), *Cluain-Eois* (Cloonoce), F. M., the meadow of *Eos* (Oce), a man's name.

Clonfad (also Clonfadda, and Cloonfad), *Cluain-fada,* long meadow.

Clonfeacle, in Tyrone: called *Cluain-fiacla* (feckla) in the Book of Leinster; the meadow of the tooth.

Clonfert: the Book of Leinster writes the name *Cluain-ferta*, the meadow of the grave.

Clongill, *Cluain-Gaill*, the meadow of the foreigner.

Clongowes, the meadow of the smith (*gobha*).

Clonkeen, *Cluain-caein* (keen), beautiful meadow.

Clonlea (also Clonleigh, and Cloonlee), *Cluain-laegh* (lee), the meadow of the calves.

Clonliff, the meadow of herbs (*lubh*, an herb).

Clonmacnoise, written in Irish documents of the eighth century *Cluain-maccu-Nois*, which was the old pagan name: it signifies the meadow of the sons of *Nos*. This *Nos* was the son of *Fiadhach* (Feeagh), a chief of the tribe of *Dealbhna* or Delvin, in whose territory Clonmacnoise was situated.

Clonmeen, *Cluain-mín* (meen), smooth meadow.

Clonmel, *Cluain-meala* (malla), the meadow of honey (*mil*).

Butler tomb, Clonmel

Clonmellon, *Cluain-milain*, F. M., Milan's meadow.

Clonmelsh, *Cluain-milis*, sweet meadow (from honey).

Clonmore, great meadow.

Clonmult, the meadow of the wethers (*molt*).

Clonoghil, the meadow of the yew-wood (*eóchaill*).

Clonoulty, *Cluain-Ultaigh* (ulty), the Ulsterman's meadow.

Clonshire, *Cluain-siar*, western meadow.

Clonsillá, *Cluain-saileach*, the meadow of sallows.

Clonskeagh, *Cluain-sceach*, the meadow of the white thorns.

Clontarf, *Cluain-tarbh* (tarriv), F. M., the meadow of the bulls.

Clontibret, written by the annalists *Cluain-tiobrat*, the meadow of the spring (*tipra*, same as *tobar*).

Clonturk (also Cloonturk), the boar's meadow (*torc*).

Clonty, *see* Cloonty.

Clonygowan, *Cluain-na-ngamhan* (*Cloon-nung-own*), F. M., the meadow of the calves.

Clonyhurk, *Cluain-da-thorc* (Cloonahork), F. M., the meadow of the two boars.

Cloon (also Cloone), a meadow. *See Cluain* in vocabulary.

Cloonagh, the meadow of horses (*each*).

Cloonard, *See* Clonard.

Cloonawillin, *Cluain-a'-mhuilinn*, the meadow of the mill.

Cloonbeg, little meadow.

Clooncah, the meadow of the battle (*cath*).

Clooncoose (also Clooncose), *Cluain-cuas*, F. M., the meadow of the caves.

Clooncraff, *see* Cloncrew.

Clooncunna (Clooncunnig, Clooncunny), the meadow of the firewood (*conadh*).

Cloondara, *Cluain-da-rath*, F. M., the meadow of the two raths or forts.

Cloonee (also Clooney), meadow land.

Clooneen, little meadow.

Cloonfinlough, the meadow of the clear lake.

Cloonkeen, *Cluain-caein*, beautiful meadow.

Cloonlara, the meadow of the mare (*lárach*).

Cloonlougher, the meadow of the rushes (*luachra*).

Cloonmore, great meadow.

Cloonnagashel, in Mayo. *See* p 85.

Cloonshannagh (also Cloonshinnagh), fox meadow (*sionnach*).

Cloonshee, the meadow of the fairies (*sidh*).

Cloonsillagh, the meadow of sallows.

Cloonteen, little meadow.

Cloonties, *Cluainte*, meadows (English plural form).

Cloontubbrid, *see* Clontibret.

Cloontuskert, *Cluain-tuaisceirt* (tooskert), F. M., northern meadow.

Cloonty, *Cluainte*, meadows, plural of *cluain*.

Cloran (also Clorane, Clorhane), a stony place (*cloch*).

Clough, a stone or stone castle.

Cloyne, in Cork: shortened from *Cluain-uamha* (Cloon-ooa), as it is written in the Book of Leinster. The name signifies the meadow of the cave (*uaimh*); and the cave is still to be seen.

Druid altar, or cromlech, Castle Mary, near Cloyne

Clyduff, black dyke or mound (*cladh*).

Colehill, *Coll-choill,* hazel wood.

Coleraine. We are told in the Tripartite Life of St. Patrick, that a chieftain named Nadslua presented the saint with a piece of land on the bank of the river Bann, on which to build a church. It was a spot overgrown with ferns, and it happened at the moment that some boys were amusing themselves by setting them on fire. Hence the place was called *Cuil-rathain* (Coolrahen) which Colgan translates *Secessus filicis,* the corner (*cuil*) of the ferns. Coolrain, Coolrainey and Coolrahnee, are similarly derived.

Collon, a place of hazels (*coll*).

Colp, near Drogheda. According to an ancient legend, when the Milesian brothers invaded Ireland, one of them, Colpa the swordsman, was drowned at the mouth of the Boyne; hence it was called Inver-Colpa, Colpa's river mouth; and the parish of Colp, on its southern bank, retains part of the name.

Comber (also Comer), *see* p 86.

Commaun, a little *cum* or hollow.

Conicar (also Conicker, Conigar, Coneykeare), *Cuinicer* (cunnikere) a rabbit warren.

Conlig, the *liag* or stone of the hounds (*cu*).

Connello, baronies of, in Limerick. This was the ancient territory of the tribe of Hy Conall or *Hy Conaill Gabra* (Goura) (so written in the Book of Leinster), who were descended and named from Conall, the ninth in descent from Olioll Olum, king of Munster in the second century.

Connemara. Maev, queen of Connaught in the time of Conor mac Nessa, had three sons by Fergus mac Roy, ex-king of Ulster, namely, *Ciar* (Keer), *Con-mac,* and *Modhruadh* (Moroo). The descendants of *Conmac* were called *Conmacne* (*ne,* a progeny), and they were settled in Connaught, where they gave name to several territories. One of these, viz., the district lying west of Lough Corrib and Lough Mask, from its situation near the sea, was called, to distinguish it from the others, *Conmacne-mara* (O'Dugan: *muir,* the sea, gen. *mara*), or the sea-side *Conmacne,* which has been shortened to the present name Connemara.

Connor, in Antrim: written *Condeire* or *Condaire* in various authorities; the *derry* or oak wood of the dogs (*cu*), or as it is explained in a gloss in the Martyrology of Aengus, 'The oak wood in which were wild dogs formerly, and she wolves used to dwell therein.'

Convoy (also Conva), *Con-mhagh,* hound plain (*cu* and *magh*).

Conwal, *Congbhail* (Congwal), F. M., a habitation.

Cooga (also Coogue), *Coigeadh* (Coga), a fifth part.

Cool (also Coole), *cuil,* a corner, or *cul,* a back.

Coolattin, the corner of the furze (*aiteann*).

Coolavin, a barony in Sligo: *Cuil-O'bhFinn* (Coolovin): F. M., the corner or angle of the O'Finns.

Coolbanagher, the angle of the pinnacles. (*see* Banagher.)

Coolbane (also Coolbaun), white corner or back.

Coolcashin, Cashin's corner or angle.

Coolderry, back *derry* or oak word.

Cooleen, little corner; **Cooleeny,** little corners.

Cooleeshal (also Coolishal), low corner (*íseal*).

Cooley hills, near Carlingford. After the defeat of the Tuatha De Dananns by the Milesians, at Teltown in Meath, the Milesian chief *Cuailgne* (Cooley), following up the pursuit, was slain here; and the district was called from him, *Cuailgne,* which name is still applied to the range of hills.

Coolgreany, sunny corner or back (*grian* the sun).

Coolhill (also Coolkill), *cúl-choill,* back wood.

Coolnahinch, the corner of the *inis,* island, or river meadow.

Coolock (also Coologe), little corner or angle.

Coolroe, red corner or back.

Coom (also Coombe), *cúm,* a hollow or mountain valley.

Coomnagoppul, at Killarney: *Cum-na-gcapall,* the hollow or valley of the horses; from the practice of sending horses to graze in it.

Coomyduff, near Killarney: *Cum-ui-Dhuibh* (Coomywiv), O'Duff's valley; usually but erroneously translated Black valley.

Coos (also Coose), *cuas,* a cave.

Coosan (also Coosane, Coosaun), little cave.

Cor (also Corr). This word has several meanings, but it generally signifies a round hill.

Corballis (also Corbally), odd town: *cor* here means odd.

Corbeagh, round hill of the birch (*beith*).

Corcomohide, in Limerick: *Corca-Muichet* (Book of Lismore), the race (*corca*) of *Muichet,* one of the disciples of the druid, *Mogh Ruith.*

Corcomroe, barony of, in Clare: *Corca-Modhruadh* or *Corcomruadh* (Corcomrua: Book of Leinster), the race (*corca*) of *Modhruadh,* son of queen Maev. (*See* Connemara.)

Corcreevy, branchy hill. *Craebh* (creeve), a branch.

Cordangan, fortified *cor* or round hill.

Cordarragh, round hill of the oak (*dair*).

Corduff, black round hill.

Corgarve, rough round hill (*garbh*).

Corglass, green round hill (*glas*).

Corick, the meeting of two rivers.

Cork, *Corcach,* a marsh. The city grew round a monastery founded in the sixth century on the edge of a marsh, by St. Finbar.

Corkagh, *see* Cork.

Corkaguiny, barony of, in Kerry: *Corca-Duibhne* (divny: O'Dugan), the race (*corca*) of *Duibhne,* son of Carbery Musc, who was son of Conary II., king of Ireland from AD 158 to 165. D changed to g: *see* p 86.

Corkaree, barony of, in Westmeath: *Corca Raeidhe* (Ree: O'Dugan), the race (*corca*) of *Fiacha Raidhe* (Feeha Ree), grandson of Felimy the Lawgiver, king of Ireland from AD 111 to 119.

Corkeeran (also Corakeeran), the round hill of the *keerans* or quicken trees (*caerthainn*).

Corkey, *see* Cork.

Corlat, the round hill of the sepulchres (*leacht*).

Corlea, grey round hill.

Corlough, the lake of the *corrs* or herons.

Cormeen, smooth round hill.

Cornacreeve, the round hill of the branchy tree (*craebh*).

Cornagee (also **Cornageeha**), the round hill of the wind (*gaeth*).

Cornahoe, the round hill of the cave (*uaimh*).

Cornamucklagh, the round hill of the piggeries. *See* Mucklagh.

Cornaveagh, the round hills of the ravens (*fiach*).

Corratober, the round hill of the well (*tobar*).

Corrinshigo (also **Corrinshigagh**), the round hill of the ash trees. *See* Fuinnse in vocabulary.

Corrofin, in Clare: *Coradh-Finne* (Corrafinna), F. M., the weir of Finna, a woman's name.

Corskeagh, the round hill of the white thorns.

Coshbride (also **Coshlea, Coshma**), baronies, the first in Waterford, the others in Limerick. Cosh (Irish *cois*, from *cos* a foot), means at the foot of, near, beside. Coshbride, the barony along the river Bride. Cosh-lea, *cois-shleibhe* (cushleva), at the foot of the *sliabh* or mountain, i. e. the Galties. Coshma, *Cois-Maighe* (ma), the barony along the river Maigue.

Craan (also **Craane**), a stony place (from *carr*).

Crag (also **Craig**), other forms of *carraig*, a rock.

Cran, *Crann*, a tree.

Cranfield, a corruption of *Creamh-choill* (Cravwhill), the wood (*coill*) of wild garlic (*creamh*).

Crannagh, a place abounding in *cranns* or trees.

Crannoge, a habitation on an artificial island in a lake.

Cranny, *see* Crannagh.

Cratloe (also **Crataloe**), sallow wood.

Craughwell, *Creamh-choill*, wild garlic wood.

Crecora, in Limerick: *Craebh-cumhraidhe* (Crave-coory) O'Dugan, sweet scented *creeve* or branchy tree.

Creevagh, a branchy place (*craebh*).

Creeve, *Craebh* (creeve), a branch, a branchy tree.

Creevelea, grey branch or branchy tree.

Creevy, *see* Creevagh.

Creg (also **Cregg**), *Creag*, a rock.

Creggan (also **Creggane, Creggaun**), little rock, rocky ground.

Cremorne barony, in Monaghan: *Crioch-Mughdhorn* (Cree-Mourne), the country (*crioch*) of the tribe of *Mughdhorna* (Mourna), who were descended and named from *Mughdhorn* (Mourne), the son of Colla Meann, one of the three brothers who conquered Ulster, and destroyed the palace of Emania in AD 332.

Crew, *see* Creeve.

Croagh, *Cruach*, a rick or stacked up hill.

Croaghan (also **Croaghaun**), a round or piled up hill.

Croaghpatrick, St. Patrick's rick or hill.

Crock is very generally used in the northern half of Ireland instead of Knock, a hill.

Crockanure, *Cnoc-an-iúbhair*, the hill of the yew.

Crogh, *see* Croagh.

Croghan (also **Crohane**), *see* Croaghan.

Crossakeel, slender crosses.

Crossan (also **Crossane, Crossaun**), little cross.

Crossboyne, *Cros-Baeithin*, Hy F., *Baeithin's* or Boyne's cross.

Crosserlough, the cross on (*air*) or near the lake.

Crossgar, short cross.

Crossmaglen, in Armagh: *Cros-meg-Fhloinn* (Cros-meg-lin: *fh* silent), the cross of Flann's son.

Crossmolina, in Mayo: *Cros-ui-Mhaelfhina*, F. M., O'Mulleeny's or Mullany's cross.

Crossoge, little cross.

Crossreagh, grey cross (*reabhach*).

Crott, *Cruit*, a hump, a humpy backed hill.

Cruagh, *see* Croagh.

Cruit, *see* Crott.

Crumlin (also **Cromlin**), *Cruim-ghlinn*, (Crumlin), F. M., curved glen.

Crusheen, *Croisin*, little cross.

Cuilbeg (also **Cuilmore**), little wood, great wood (*coill*).

Culdaff, *Cul-dabhach* (Culdava), the back (*cul*) of the flax-dam or pool.

Culfeightrin, in Antrim: *Cuil-eachtrann* (Coolaghtran), the corner (*cuil*) of the strangers.

Cullan (also **Cullane, Cullaun**), a place of hazels (*coll*)

Culleen, *Coillín*, little wood.

Cullen, *Cuillionn* (Cullen), holly, holly land.

Cullenagh, a place producing holly.

Cullentra (also **Cullentragh**), *see* Cullenagh.

Cullenwaine, in King's County: *Cuil-O-nDubhain* (Cool-onuan), F. M., the corner or angle of the O'Duanes.

Cullion, *see* Cullen.

Cully, woodland; from *coill.*

Culmullen, in Meath: the angle of the mill.

Cumber (also **Cummer**). *see* p 86.

Curra (also **Curragh**), *currach*, generally a marsh; sometimes a race course.

Currabaha (also **Currabeha**), the marsh of the birch.

Curraghbeg, little marsh.

Curraghboy, yellow marsh.

Curraghduff, black marsh.

Curraghlahan (also **Curraghlane**), broad marsh.

Curraghmore, great marsh.

Curragh of Kildare. The word here means a race course: the Curragh of Kildare has been used as a race course from the earliest ages.

Curraheen, little *currach* or marsh.

Curry, another form of Curragh, a marsh.

Cush. *See* Coshbride.

Cushendall, in Antrim: *Cois-abhann-Dhalla* (Cush-oun-dalla), the foot or termination of the river Dall.

Cushendun, in Antrim: called by the F. M., *Bun-abhann-Duine*, the end, i. e. the mouth of the river Dun; this was afterwards changed to *Cois-abhann-Duine* (Cush-oun-Dunny) by the substitution of *Cois*, the end for *Bun.*

Cutteen, *Coitchionn* (cutteen), common, a commonage.

Dalkey Island near Dublin. The Irish name is *Delg-inis* (O'C. Cal.), thorn island; which the Danes, who had a fortress on it in the tenth, translated to the present name, by changing *Delg* into their word *Dalk*, a thorn; and substituting the northern word *ey*, an island, for *inis.*

Dangan, *Daingean* (dangan), a fortress.

Dangandargan, in Tipperary: Dargan's fortress.

Darragh, a place producing oaks (*dair*).

Darraragh (also Darrery), an oak forest, a place abounding in oaks (*Dairbhreach*).

Dawros, *Damhros,* the peninsula of oxen (*damh* and *ros*).

Deelis (also Deelish), *Duibh-lios* (Divlis), black *lis* or fort.

Delvin. There were formerly seven tribes called *Dealbh-na* (Dalvana), descended and named from *Lughaidh Dealbhaeth* (Lewy Dalway), who was the son of *Cas mac Tail* (seventh in descent from Olioll Olum: see Connello), the ancestor of the Dalcassians of Thomond: *Dealbhna,* i. e. *Dealbhaeth's* descendants. None of these have perpetuated their name except one, viz., *Dealbhna mor,* or the great *Dealbhna,* from whom the barony of Delvin in Westmeath received its name.

Dernish (also Derinch, Derinish), oak island (*dair*).

Derrada (also Derradd), *Doire-fhada,* long oak grove.

Derragh, *see* Darragh.

Derroon, little *derry* or oak grove or wood.

Derreens (also Derries), oak groves.

Derry, *Doire* (Derry), an oak grove or wood.

Derryad (also Derryadda), *Doire-fhada,* long oak wood.

Derrybane (also Derrybawn), whitish oak wood.

Derrybeg, little oak wood.

Derrycreevy, the oak wood of the branchy tree.

Derrydorragh (also Derrydorraghy), dark oak wood (*dorcha*)

Derryduff, black oak wood.

Derryfadda, long oak wood.

Derrygarriff (also Derrygarve), rough oak wood (*garbh*).

Derrylahan (also Derrylane), broad oak wood (*leathan*).

Derrylea, grey oak wood.

Derrylough (also Derryloughan), oak wood of the lake.

Derrymore, great oak wood.

Derrynahinch, the oak wood of the island or river meadow (*inis*).

Derrynane, in Kerry: *Doire-Fhionain* (Derry-Eenane: *Fh* silent), the oak grove of St. Finan Cam, a native of Corkaguiny, who flourished in the sixth century.

Derrynaseer, the oak grove of the *saers* or carpenters.

Derryvullan, in Fermanagh: *Doire-Maelain* (Derry-Velan: *M* aspirated), F. M., Maelan's oak grove.

Desert, *Disert,* a desert or hermitage.

Desertcreat, corrupted from *Disert-da-Chrioch* (Disert-a-cree), F.M., the hermitage of the two territories.

Desertegny, Egnagh's hermitage.

Desertmartin, Martin's hermitage.

Desertmore, great desert or hermitage.

Desertserges, in Cork: Saerghus's hermitage.

Devenish Island, in Lough Erne: *Daimhinis* (Davinish) F. M., the island of the oxen (*damh*).

Diamor, written in the Dinnseanchus, *Diamar,* i. e., a solitude.

Dingle, from Dingin, another form of *Daingean,* a fortress, by a change to *n* to *l* (p 85). Called in the annals, *Daingean-ui-Chuis,* now usually written Dingle-I-Coush, the fortress of O'Cush, the ancient proprietor.

Dinish (also Deenish), *Duibh-inis* (Divinish), black island.

Disert, *see* Desert.

Stone detail, Devenish Island

Donabate, *Domhnach-a'-bhaid,* the church of the boat.

Donagh, *Domhnach* (Downagh), a church.

Donagheloney, in Down: the church of the *cluain* or meadow.

Donaghcumper, in Kildare: the church of the *cummer* or confluence.

Donaghedy, in Tyrone: *Domhnach-Chaeide* (Donaheedy), the church of St. Caidoc, a companion of St. Columbanus.

Donaghmore, great church.

Donaghmoyne, in Monaghan: *Domhnach-Maighin,* the church of the little plain.

Donard, high *dun* or fort.

Donegal. The Danes had a settlement there before the Anglo-Norman invasion; and hence it was called *Dunna-nGall* (Doonagall), the fortress of the *Galls* or foreigners.

Doneraile, in Cork: written in the Book of Lismore *Dun-air-aill,* the fortress on the cliff.

Donnybrook, *Domhnach-Broc,* St. Broc's church.

Donnycarney, *Cearnach's* or Carney's church.

Donohill, the fortress of the yew wood (*eóchaill*).

Donore, *Dun-uabhair* (Dunoor), F. M. the fort of pride.

Doogary, *Dubhdhoire* (Dooary), black derry or oak wood.

Doon, *Dún,* a fortress.

Doonan (also Doonane), little *dun* or fort.

Doonard, high fort.

Doonass, near Killaloe: *Dun-easa,* the fortress of the cataract, i. e. the great rapid on the Shannon.

Doonbeg, little fortress.

Doondonnell, Donall's fortress.

Dooneen, little fort.

Doonfeeny, the fort of Finna (a woman).

Doonisky (also Dunisky), the fort of the water (*uisge*).

Doonooney, Una's fort.

Douglas, *Dubh-ghlaise,* black stream.

Down, a form of *Dun,* a fortress.

Downings, *Dooneens* or little forts.

Downpatrick takes its name from the large entrenched *dun* near the cathedral. In the first century this fortress was the residence of a warrior of the Red Branch

Knights, called *Celtchair*, or Keltar of the battles, from whom it is called in Irish authorities, Dunkeltar. By ecclesiastical writers it is commonly called *Dun-da-leth-glas*, the fortress of the two broken locks (*glas*) or fetters. This long name was afterwards shortened to *Dun* or Down, which was extended to the county. The name of St. Patrick was added, to commemorate his connexion with the place.

Downs, *duns* or forts.

Dreen, *Draeighean* (dreen), the blackthorn.

Dreenagh, a place producing blackthorns.

Dreenan, blackthorn, a place of blackthorns.

Drehidtarsna, in Limerick: cross bridge.

Dressoge (also Dressogagh), a briery or bushy place.

Dresternagh (also Dresternan, Dristernan), *see* Dressoge.

Drim, a form of *druim*, a ridge.

Drimeen (also Drimmeen), little ridge.

Drimna (also Drimnagh), ridges, a place full of ridges or hills.

Drinagh (also Drinaghan), a place producing *dreens* or blackthorns.

Drinan (also Drinaun), *see* Dreenan.

Drishaghaun (also Drishane, Drishoge), *see* Dressoge.

Droghed, *Droichead*, a bridge.

Drogheda, *Droiched-atha* (Drohedaha), F. M., the bridge of the ford; from the ford across the Boyne, used before the erection of a bridge.

Drom, *Druim*, a ridge or long hill.

Dromada (also Dromadda), long *drum* or ridge.

Drombeg (also Drumbeg), small ridge.

Dromcolliher, in Limerick: a corruption of *Druim-Coll-choille* (Drum-Collohill), the ridge of the hazel wood.

Dromdaleague, in Cork: the ridge of the two *liags* or pillar stones.

Dromgarriff, rough ridge.

Dromin, *see* Drom.

Dromineer, in Tipperary: *Druim-inbhir* (Druminver), the ridge of the *inver* or river mouth: because it is situated near where the Nenagh river enters Lough Derg.

Dromkeen, beautiful ridge.

Dromore, great ridge or long hill.

Dromtrasna, cross ridge.

Drum, *Druim*, a ridge or long hill.

Drumad, *Druim-fhada*, long ridge.

Dromadoon, the ridge of the *dun* or fort.

Drumahaire, in Leitrim: *Druim-da-ethiar* (Drum-a-ehir), F. M., the ridge of the two air-demons.

Drumanure, the ridge of the yew tree.

Drumany (also Drummany), ridges, ridged land.

Drumard, high ridge or long hill.

Drumatemple, the ridge of the temple or church.

Drumavaddy, the ridge of the dog (*madadh*).

Drumballyroney, the ridge of O'Roney's town.

Drumbane (also Drumbaun), white ridge.

Drumbarnet, the ridge of the gap (*bearna*).

Drumbo (also Drumboe), *Druimbo*, F. M., the cow's ridge.

Drumbrughas, the ridge of the farm-house.

Drumcanon, the ridge of the white-faced cow: *ceann-fhionn* (canon), whitehead

Drumcar, in Louth: *Druim-caradh* (Drumcara) F. M., the ridge of the weir.

Drumcliff, in Sligo: *Drium-chliabh* (Drumcleev), F. M., the ridge of the baskets.

Drumcolumb, St. Columba's ridge.

Drumcondra, Conra's ridge.

Drumcrin, the ridge of the tree (*crann*).

Drumcrow, the ridge of the cattle sheds (*cro*).

Drumcullen (also Drumcullion), the ridge of holly.

Drumderg, *Druim-dearg*, red ridge.

Drumduff, *Druim-dubh*, black ridge.

Drumfad, *Druim-fada*, long ridge.

Drumgill, the ridge of the *Gall* or foreigner.

Drumgoose (also Drumgose), the ridge of the caves (*cuas*).

Drumgowna (also Drumgownagh), *Druim-gamhnach*, the ridge of the heifers.

Drumharrif (Drumherriff), *Druim-thairbh* (Drum-har-riv), the ridge of the bull.

Drumhillagh, *see* p 85.

Drumhirk, *Druim-thuirc*, the ridge of the boar.

Drumhome, in Donegal. In O'C. Cal. the name is written *Druim-Thuama* (Drumhooma), and Adam-nan translates it *Dorsum Tommae*, the ridge of Tomma, a pagan woman's name.

Drumillard (also Drummillar), the eagle's ridge (*iolar*).

Drumkeen, beautiful ridge.

Drumkeeran, the ridge of the quicken trees.

Drumlane, *Druim-leathan* (lahan), F. M., broad ridge.

Drumlease, *Druim-lias*, the ridge of the huts.

Drumlish, the ridge of the *lis* or fort.

Drumlougher, the ridge of the rushes (*luachra*).

Drumman, *see* Drum.

Drummeen, little ridge.

Drummin, *see* Drum.

Drummond, a corrupt form of Drumman. See p 86.

Drummuck, the ridge of the pigs (*muc*).

Drummully, the ridge of the summit (*mullach*).

Drumnacross, the ridge of the cross.

Drumneen, little ridge.

Drumquin, *Druim-Chuinn*, Conn's ridge.

Drumraine (also Drumrainy), ferny ridge (*ráthain*).

Drumreagh, *Druim-riabbach*, grey ridge.

Drumroe, *Druim-ruadh*, red ridge.

Drumroosk, the ridge of the *roosk* or marsh.

Drumshallon, the ridge of the gallows (*sealan*).

Drumshanbo, the ridge of the old *both* or tent (*sean*, old).

Drumsillagh, *see* p 85.

Drumsna (also Drumsnauv), *Druim-snamha* (snawa), the ridge of the swimming. See Lixnaw.

Drumsurn, the ridge of the furnace or kiln (*sorn*).

Duagh, in Kerry: *Dubh-ath* (Dooah), black ford, from a ford on the river Feale.

Dublin. The name is written in the annals *Duibh-linn* (Duvlin), which, in some of the Latin Lives of the saints, is translated *Nigra therma*, black pool; it was originally the name of that part of the Liffey on which the city is built, and is sufficiently descriptive at the present day. In very early ages an artificial ford of hurdles was constructed across the Liffey, where the main road from Tara to Wicklow crossed the river; and the city that subsequently sprung up around it was called from this circumstance *Ath-cliath* (Ah-clee), F. M., the ford of hurdles, which was the ancient name of Dublin. This name is still used by speakers of Irish in every part of Ireland; but they join it to Bally—*Baile-atha-cliath* (which they pronounce *Blaa-clee*), the town of the hurdle ford.

Dufferin, barony of, in Down: *Dubh-thrian* (Duv-reen), F. M., the black·*treen* or third part.

Duhallow, in Cork: *Duthaigh-Ealla* (Doohy-alla), F. M., the district of the Allo, from the Blackwater river, a portion of which was anciently called the Allo.

Dulane, in Meath: *Tuilen,* F. M., little *tulach* or hill.

Duleek, in Meath: *Daimhliag* (Davleeg), O'C. Cal., stone house or church *(daimh,* a house, and *liag).*

Dunamase, in Queen's County: should have been called Dunmask, for the Irish name is *Dun-Masg,* F. M., the fortress of *Masg,* who was one of the ancestors of the Leinster people.

Dunamon, in Galway: so called from a castle of the same name on the Suck; but the name, which the annalists write *Dun-Iomgain,* Imgan's fort, was anciently applied to a *dun,* which is still partly preserved.

Dunboe, in Derry: the fortress of the cow.

Dunboyne, *Dun-Baeithin, Baeithin's* or Boyne's fort.

Duncannon, Conan's fortress.

Duncormick, Cormac's fortress.

Dundalk. The name was originally applied to the great fortress now called the moat of Castletown, a mile inland, which was the residence of *Cuchullin,* chief of the Red Branch knights in the first century. *Dun-Deal-gan* (Dalgan), F. M., the fortress of *Delga,* a Firbolg chief, who built it.

Dunderrow, in Cork: written *Dun-dermaigi* (Dundarwah) in the Book of Leinster, the fortress of the oak-plain (see Durrow); and the large dun from which it received the name is still in existence, half a mile south of the village.

Dundonald, in Down, Donall's fortress: so called from a fort that stands not far from the church.

Dundrum, *Dun-droma,* F.M., fortress on ridge or hill.

Duneane, in Antrim: written in the Felire of Aengus, *Dun-da-én* (Dun-a-ain), the fortress of the two birds.

Dunfanaghy, *Dun-Fionnchon* (Finahan), *Finchu's* fort.

Dungannon, in Tyrone: *Dun-Geanainn* (Gannin), F. M., *Geanan's* or Gannon's fortress.

Dungarvan, *Dun-Garbhain,* F. M., Garvan's fortress.

Dunhill, *Dun-aille,* the fortress of the cliff.

Dunkineely, in Donegal: *Dun-mhic-Chionnfhaelaidh* (Dunvickaneely), Mackineely's fort.

Dunkit, *Ceat's* or Keth's fortress.

Dunleer, in Louth. Old name *Land-léri* (Book of Leinster), the church *(land* or *lann)* of austerity. Present name formed by substituting *dun* a fort for *lann.*

Dunluce castle, near the Giant's Causeway: *Dunlios,* F. M., strong *lios* or fort. *Dun* is here an adjective, meaning strong.

Dunmanway, in Cork. Old name *Dun-na-mbeann* (Dunaman), F. M., the fortress of the gables or pinnacles. The last syllable *way* is from *buidhe* yellow (bwee, or with the *b* aspirated, wee):—Dunmanway, the fortress of the yellow pinnacles.

Dunmore, great fort.

Dunmurry, *Dun-Muireadhaigh,* Murray's fort.

Dunquin, in Kerry: *Dun-caein* (Dunkeen), F. M., beautiful fort.

Dunshaughlin, in Meath. A church was founded here for bishop *Sechnall* or Secundinus, St. Patrick's nephew; and hence it was called *Domhnach-Seachnaill* (Donna-Shaughnill), F. M., the church of St. *Sechnall,* which has been shortened to the present name.

Duntryleague, in Limerick. According to a passage in the Book of Lismore, a *dun* or palace was built here for Cormac Cas, son of Olioll Olum (see Connello); and his bed was supported by three *liagáns* or pillar stones, from which the place was called *Dun-tri-liag,* the fortress of the three *liags* or pillar stones.

Durrow, in King's County, a favourite residence of St. Columbkille. Venerable Bede has a short passage in his Eccl. Hist. (lib. iii., cap. iv.), in which the original form and translation of this name are given:—"Before he (Columba) passed over into Britain, he had built a noble monastery in Ireland, which, from the great number of oaks, is in the Scotic (Irish) language called *Dearmhagh* (Darwah), the field of the oaks" (*dair* and *magh*).

Dysart (also Dysert), see Desert.

Dysartenos, in Queen's County. St. Aengus the Culdee, who died in the year 824, built a cell for himself here; and hence the place was called *Disert-Aenghusa,* Aengus's hermitage.

Easky, in Sligo: from the river:*Iascach* (Eeska), fishy (from *iasg,* a fish).

Eden, *Eudan* (edan), the brow; a hill brow.

Edenderry, the hill brow of the oak wood.

Edenmore, great hill brow.

Edergole (also Edergoole), see Addergoole.

Eglish, a church: see Aglish.

Eighter, *Iochtar* (eeter), lower.

Eliogarty, in Tipperary: a shortened form of Ely O'Fogarty (shortened by having the *f* aspirated and omitted: see p85), O'Fogarty's *Ely,* so called from its ancient possessors the O'Fogartys. See Ely.

Elphin, in Roscommon. St. Patrick founded a church here near a spring, over which stood a large stone; and hence the place was called *Aill-finn,* which Colgan interprets the rock (*aill*) of the clear spring (*finn* white, clear).

Ely. The different tribes called *Eile* or Ely were so named from their ancestor *Eile,* the seventh in descent from Cian, son of Olioll Olum (see Connello).

Emlagh, *Imleach* (Imlagh), land bordering on a lake; and hence a marshy or swampy place.

Emly, in Tipperary. St. *Ailbhe* founded his establishment here in the fifth century, on the margin of a lake, which has been only lately drained. The place is called in the

Irish authorities *Imleach-iobhair* (yure), the lake-marsh of the yew tree.

Emlygrennan, in Limerick: a corruption of the Irish name *Bile-Ghroidhnín* (Billa-Gryneen), Grynan's ancient tree.

Enagh, the name of twenty townlands. Sometimes *Aenach*, a fair; sometimes *Eanach*, a marsh.

Ennereilly, in Wicklow: *Inbher-Daeile* (Invereela), F. M., the *inver* or mouth of the river formerly called the Deel, now the Pennycomequick.

Ennis, *inis*, an island; a meadow along a river.

Enniskeen, *Inis-caein* (keen), F. M., beautiful island or river meadow.

Enniskerry, *Ath-na-scairbhe* (Annascarvy), the ford of the *scarriff* or rough river-crossing; from an ancient stony ford where the old road crosses the river.

Enniskillen, *Inis-Cethlenn* (Kehlen), F. M., the island of *Kethlenn*, wife of Balor, the Fomorian king of Tory Island.

Ennistimon, *Inis-Diomain*, F. M., *Diaman's* river meadow.

Errigal, *Aireagal*, a habitation, a small church.

Errigal Keeroge, in Tyrone: *Aireagal Dachiarog* (Dakeeroge), F. M., the church of St. *Dachiarog.*

Errigal Trough, in Monaghan: the church of (the barony of) Trough.

Esker, *Eiscir*, a sandhill.

Eskeragh (also Eskragh), a place full of *eskers.*

Ess (also Essan, Essaun), a waterfall.

Estersnow, in Roscommon: a strange corruption from the Irish *Disert-Nuadhan* (Nooan), F. M., the hermitage of St. *Nuadha* (Nooa). Disert is often corrupted to *ister, ester, tirs, tristle,* etc.

Faddan, *Feadan*, a small brook.

Faha (also Fahy), an exercise green. *See* Faithche, p 126.

Farnagh (also Farnane, Farnoge), a place of *Fearns* (Farns), or alders.

Farney, in Monaghan: *Fearnmhagh* (Farnvah), Book of R., the alder plain (*fearn* and *magh*).

Farran, *Fearann*, land.

Farset (also Farsid), *Fearsad*, a sandbank in a river.

Fartagh (also Fertagh), a place of graves (*feart*).

Fasagh (also Fassagh), a wilderness (*Fásach*).

Fassadinin, in Kilkenny: the *fasagh* or wilderness of, or near, the river Dinin.

Feagh, *Fiodhach* (Feeagh), a woody place (*fidh*).

Fearmore, great grass (*féur*) or grassy place.

Feddan, *see* Faddan.

Feenagh, *Fiodhnach* (Feenagh), woody (*fidh*); a woody place.

Feighcullen, in Kildare: *Fiodh-Chuilinn*, F. M., Cullen's wood.

Fenagh, *see* Feenagh.

Fennor, *Fionnabhair* (Finner), F. M., white field.

Fermanagh, so called from the tribe of *Fir-monach*, O'Dugan), the men of *Monach*, who were originally a Leinster tribe, so named from their ancestor, *Monach*, fifth in descent from Cahirmore, monarch of Ireland from AD 120 to 123.

Fermoy, in Cork: *Feara-muighe* (Farra-moy), O'Dugan, the men of the plain.

Fermoyle, *Formaeil*, a round hill.

Fernagh (also Ferney), *see* Farnagh.

Ferns, *Fearna* (Farna), F. M., alders, a place abounding in alders: English plural termination added.

Ferrard, barony of, in Louth: *Feara-arda* (Farra-arda), F. M., the men of the height, i. e. of Slieve Bregh.

Fethard, *Fiodh-ard* (Fecard), F. M., high wood.

Fews, baronies of, in Armagh: *Feadha* (Fa), F. M., woods; with the English plural termination added. Fews in Waterford has the same origin.

Fiddan, (also Fiddane, Fiddaun), *see* Faddan.

Fiddown, in Kilkenny: *Fidh-duin* (Feedoon), F. M., the wood of the *dun* or fort.

Fingall, a district lying north of Dublin, in which the Danes settled; and hence it was called *Fine-Gall* (O'C. Cal.), the territory or tribe (*fine*) of the *Galls* or foreigners.

Finglas, clear stream (*fionn*, white, clear; and *glaise*).

Finn river and lake in Donegal: *Loch-Finne*, the lake of *Finna*, a woman, about whom there is an interesting legend. The river took its name from the lake.

Finnea, in Westmeath: *Fidh-an-atha* (Fee-an-aha) F. M., the wood of the ford.

Fintona, *Fionn-tamhnach* (Fintowna), F. M., fair coloured field.

Foil, *Faill*, a cliff.

Foilduff, black cliff.

Forenaght (also Forenaghts, Fornaght, Farnaght), *Fornocht*, a bare, naked, or exposed hill.

Formil (also Formoyle, Formweel), *see* Fermoyle.

Forth. The descendants of Ohy Finn *Fothart* (Fohart), brother of Conn of the hundred battles (king of Ireland from AD 123 to 158) were called *Fotharta* (Foharta), Book of R. Some of them settled in the present counties of Wexford and Carlow, where the two baronies of Forth still retain their name.

Foy (Foygh), forms of *Faithche. See* Faha.

Foybeg (also Foymore), little and great exercise green.

Foyduff, black exercise green.

Foyle, *see* Foil.

Freagh (also Freugh), *Fraech*, heath, a heathy place.

Freaghduff (also Freeduff), black heath.

Freaghillan (also Freaghillaun), heathy island (*oileán*).

Freshford, Irish name *Achadh-úr* (Book of Leinster), which should have been translated *Freshfield: Achadh* was mistaken for *ath.*

Freughmore (also Freaghmore), great heath.

Funcheon, *Fuinnseann* (Funshin), the ash tree: the ash-producing river.

Funshin (also Funshinagh, Funshog, Funshoge), a place producing ash trees (*fuinnse*).

Galbally (also Gallavally, Galvally, Galwally), English town; *Gall* here means an Englishman.

Galboley (also Galboola, Galbooley, Galwolie), a *booley* or dairy place belonging to *Galls* or English people.

Gallagh, a place full of rocks or standing stones. *See* Gall.

Gallan (also Gallane), *Gallan*, a standing stone.

Gallen. The descendants of *Cormac Gaileng*, great grandson of Olioll Olum (*see* Connello), were called *Gailenga* (O'Dugan), the race of Gaileng, and they gave name to the barony of Gallen in Mayo.

Gallon is used in Cavan to signify a measure of land.

Gallow, *see* Gallagh.

Gardrum (also Gargrim), *Gearr-dhruim*, short ridge or hill: *d* changed to *g* in Gargrim (*see* p.86).

Garnavilla, in Tipperary: *Garran-a'-bhile* (Garranavilla), the shrubbery of the *bile* or old tree.

Garracloon, *Garbh-chluain*, rough meadow.

Garran (also Garrane, Garraun), *Garrán*, a shrubbery.

Garranamanagh, the shrubbery of the monks (*manach*).

Garranbane (also Garranbaun), white shrubbery.

Garranekinnefeake, Kinnefeake's shrubbery.

Garry, a garden (*garradha*).

Garryard, high garden.

Garrycastle. The Mac Coghlans' castle, near Banagher in King's County, is called in the annals *Garrdha-an-chaislein* (Garrancashlane), the garden of the castle; and from this the modern name Garrycastle has been formed, and extended to the barony.

Garryduff, black garden (*dubh*).

Garrymore, great garden.

Garryowen, near Limerick: Owen's garden.

Garrysallagh, dirty garden (*salach*).

Garryspellane, Spellane's garden.

Gartan, a little garden. *See* Gort, p.126.

Garvagh, *Garbhach*, rough land (from *garbh*, rough).

Garvaghy, rough *achadh* or field.

Garvary, *Garbhaire*, rough land.

Gay island in Fermanagh, goose island (*gedh*).

Geara (also Gearagh, Gairha), *Gaertha* (gairha) a bush place along a river.

Gearhameen river, at Killarney: *min* smooth, small; a *gearha* composed of small delicate bushes.

Giants' Causeway. Irish name *Clochán-na-bhFomhuraigh* (Clohanavowry), the *cloghan* or stepping stones of the Fomorians. These sea rovers were magnified into giants in popular legend, and the name came to be translated 'Giants' Causeway.'

Girley, in Meath: *Greallach* (Grallagh), a miry place.

Glack, *Glaic*, a hollow.

Glanbehy, birchy glen (*beith*).

Glantane (also Glantaun), little glen.

Glanworth, in Cork: recently corrupted from its Irish name, *Gleann-amhnach* (Glenounagh), as it is written in the Book of Rights, the watery or marshy glen.

Glascloon, green *cloon* or meadow.

Glasdrummon (also Glasdrummond), green ridge.

Glashaboy (also Glashawee), yellow streamlet (*glaise* and *buidhe*).

Glasheen, a little stream.

Glasmullagh, green *mullach* or summit.

Glasnevin, near Dublin: takes name from a streamlet flowing through Delville into the Tolka at the bridge. In remote ages some pagan chief named *Naeidhe* (Nee), must have resided on its banks; from him it was called

Glas-Naeidhen (Neean), F. M., *Naeidhe's* streamlet; and the name extended to the village, while its original application is quite forgotten.

Glassan, a green place.

Glasthule, *Glas-Tuathail* (thoohil), *Tuathal's* or Toole's streamlet.

Glenagarey, *Gleann-na-gcaerach* (Glenagaira), the glen of the sheep (*caera*).

Glenanair, the glen of slaughter (*ár*).

Glenavy, in Antrim. The G is a modern addition. The Irish name, as given in the Calendar, is *Lann-Abhaich* (Lanavy), the church of the dwarf. When St. Patrick had built the church there, he left it in charge of his disciple Daniel, who, from his low stature, was called *Abhac* (avak or ouk), i. e. dwarf.

Glenbane (also Glenbaun), white glen.

Glencar, on the borders of Leitrim and Sligo. *Gleann-a'-chairthe* (Glenacarha), the glen of the pillar stone (*cairthe*).

Glencullen (also Glencullin), holly glen (*cuillionn*).

Glendine (also Glandine), deep glen (*doimhin*).

Glendowan mountains, in Donegal: *see* Glendine.

Glenduff, black glen (*dubh*).

Glengarriff, rough or rugged glen (*garbh*).

Gleninagh, ivy glen (see *eidhneán* in vocabulary).

Glenkeen, beautiful glen.

Glenmore, great glen.

Glennamaddy, the valley of the dogs (*madadh*).

Glenogra, in Limerick: Ogra's glen.

Glenosheen, in Limerick: *Oisin's* or Osheen's glen.

Glenquin, barony of, in Limerick: *see* p 86.

Glenreagh (also Glenrevagh), grey glen.

Glenroe, red glen (*ruadh*).

Glentane (also Glentaun), little glen.

Glenties, in Donegal: *Gleanntaidhe* (glenty), glens; from two fine glens at the head of which it stands.

Glenwhirry, in Antrim: *Gleann-a'-choire* (Glenacurry: change of *ch* to *wh*), the glen of the river Curry or *Coire*. *Coire* means a caldron, and the river got this name from a deep pool formed under a cataract.

Glynn, a glen or valley.

Gneeve (also Gneeves), *Gniomh* (gneeve), a measure of land.

Gola, forks; the plural of *gabhal* (goul).

Golan, a little *goul* or fork.

Golden, in Tipperary: *Gabhailin* (Gouleen), a little fork: the Suir divides there for a short distance, forming a fork.

Gort, *Gort*, a tilled field.

Gortahork (also Gortahurk), the field of the oats (*coirce*).

Gortalassa, the field of the *lis* or fort.

Gortanure (also Gortinure), the field of the yew.

Gortavoher, the field of the *boher* or road.

Gortboy, yellow field (*buidhe*).

Gortbrack, speckled field (*breac*).

Gorteen, little field.

Gortfad (also Gortfadda), long field.

Gortgranagh, grain field.

Gortin, little field; *see* Gorteen.

Gortmore, great field.

Gortnaglogh, *Gort-na-gcloch*, the field of the stones.

Gortnagross, *Gort-na-gcros*, the field of the crosses.

Gortnahoo (also Gortnahoon), the field of the cave (*uaimh*).

Gortnamona, the field of the bog (*moin*).

Gortnamucklagh, the field of the piggeries. *See* Mucklagh.

Gortnasillagh, the field of the sallows.

Gortnaskea (also Gortnaskeagh, Gortnaskeha, Gortnaskey), the field of the *sceachs* or whitethorn bushes.

Gortreagh, grey field (*riabhach*).

Gortroe, red field (*ruadh*).

Gougane Barra, in Cork: St. Finbar's rock-cleft.

Goul (also Gowel), *Gabhal*, a fork.

Gowlan (also Gowlane, Gowlaun), little fork.

Graffa (also Graffin, Graffoge, Graffy), grubbed land, or land rooted up by a *grafaun* or grubbing axe.

Graigue, a village.

Graiguenamanagh, the village of the monks.

Grallagh, *Greallach* (Grallagh), a miry place.

Granagh (also Granaghan), a place producing grain.

Grangegeeth, windy grange (*gaeth*).

Gransha, a grange, a place for grain.

Greagh, a moory level spot among hills.

Great Connell, great *congbhail* or habitation (*see* Conwal).

Greenan (also Greenane, Greenaun, Grenan), *Grianan*, a summer residence, a royal palace. From *grian*, the sun.

Greenoge, a sunny little spot. From *grian*.

Grillagh (also Grellagh), *see* Grallagh.

Gurteen, little tilled field; *see* Gorteen.

Gurteenroe, red little field.

Guilcagh, a place producing broom (*giolcach*, broom).

Gyleen, near Trabolgan in Cork: little *gobhal* or fork.

Heagles, near Ballymoney: *Eaglais*, a church.

Howth, from the Danish *Hoved*, a head. Old Irish name *Ben Edar*, the peak of Edar, a legendary personage.

Idrone, baronies of, in Carlow. So called from the tribe of *Hy Drona* (Book of R.), the former occupants, who were named from their ancestor *Drona*, fourth in descent from Cahirmore, monarch of Ireland from AD 120 to 123.

Illan (also Illane, Illaun), *Oileán* (oilaun), an island.

Imaile, in Wicklow: *Hy Mail* (O'Dugan), the descendants of Mann *Mal*, brother of Cahirmore. *See* Idrone.

Inch, *Inis*, an island; a low meadow along a river.

Inchmore, great island or river meadow.

Inis (also Inish), an island.

Inishannon, in Cork: written in the Book of Leinster *Inis-Eoganain* (Inishowenan), Owenan's or little Owen's island or river meadow.

Inishargy, in Down: called in the Taxation of 1306, *Inyscargi*, showing that the Irish form is *Inis-carraige*, the island of the rock. The rising ground where the church stands was formerly surrounded by marshes.

Inishbofin, the island of the white cow (*bo*): name explained by a legend.

Inishkeen, beautiful island.

Inishkeeragh, the island of sheep (*caera*).

Inishlounaght, in Tipperary: *Inis-leamhnachta* (lounaghta), the island or river holm of the new milk, probably because it was good grazing land.

Inishmaan (also Inishmean), middle island (*meadhon*).

Inishmacsaint, a parish in Fermanagh, taking its name from an island in Lough Erne, which is called in the annals *Inis-muighe-samh* (moy-sauv), the island of the plain of sorrel, from which the present name has been formed by a corrupt pronunciation.

Inishmore, great island.

Inishowen, in Donegal: the island of Owen, son of Niall of the Nine Hostages (king from 379 to 405). *See* Tyrone.

Inishrush, the island of the peninsula (*ros*).

Inishturk, in Mayo: *Inis-tuirc*, Hy F., the boar's island (*torc*). Several islands of this name.

Inishtioge, in Kilkenny: written in the Book of Leinster *Inis-Teoc*, Teoc's island.

Innisfallen, in the lower Lake of Killarney: called in the Book of Leinster *Inis-Faithlenn* (Fahlen), the island of *Faithlenn*, a man's name.

Inver, *Inbhear* (inver), the mouth of a river.

Ireland's Eye. Original name *Inis-Ereann* (Eran) (the island of *Eire* or Eria, a woman), of which the present name is an attempted translation. *Eye* is the Danish *ey*, an island, and the translators understanding *Ereann* to mean Ireland, rendered the name Ireland's *Ey* (or island) instead of Eria's *Ey*.

Isertkelly, in Galway: corrupted (similarly to the next two names) from *Diseart-Cheallaigh* (Disertkelly), F. M., *Cellach's* or Kelly's hermitage.

Isertkieran, in Tipperary: the *desert* or hermitage of St. Kieran of Ossory. *See* Seirkieran.

Ishartmon, in Wexford: the *desert* or hermitage of St. Munna. *See* Taghmon.

Island Magee, the island or peninsula of the *Mac Aedhas* or Magees, its former possessors. Anciently called *Rinn-Seimhne* (Rinn-sevne), the point of *Seimhne*, the old territory in which it was situated.

Iverleary, in Cork: took its name from the O'Leary, its ancient proprietors. *See* next name.

Iverk, in Kilkenny: *Ui-Eirc* (Ee-erc), O'Dugan, a tribe name, signifying the descendants of *Erc. Ui* (ee) or *uibh* (iv), signifies descendants.

Iveruss, in Limerick: the old tribe of *Uibh-Rosa* the descendants of *Rosa*.

Kanturk, in Cork: *Ceann-tuirc* (Kanturk), F. M., the boar's head or hill; from the hill near the town.

Keadew (also Keady), *Ceide* (Keady), a hill level and smoth at top.

Keale (also Keel), *Caol*, narrow; a narrow place, valley, or river.

Keeloge (also Keeloges), *Caelóg*, a narrow stripe or ridge.

Keelty, *Coillte* (Coiltha), woods, from *coill*.

Keenagh (also Keenaghan), a mossy place (*caenach*, moss).

Keenaght barony in Londonderry. The descendants of *Cian* (Kean), son of Olioll Olum (*see* Connello), were called *Cianachta* (Keenaghta), i. e. the race of *Cian*. The O'Conors of Glengiven, who were a portion of this tribe, possessed the barony of Keenaght, and gave it its name.

Keimaneigh, pass of, in Cork: *Ceim-an-fhiaigh* (Kamean-ee), the pass of the deer (*fiadh*).

Kenmare, *Ceann-mara*, the head of the sea (*muir*), i.e. the highest point reached by the tide in a river. *See* Kinvarra and Kinsale.

Kerry. The descendants of *Ciar* (Keer: *see* Connemara) were called *Ciarraidhe* (Keery: Book of R.), i. e. the race of *Ciar*. They possessed the territory lying west of Abbeyfeale, which was called from them *Ciarraighe*, and ultimately gave name to the whole county.

Kesh, in Fermanagh: *Ceis* (Kesh), a wickerwork causeway.

Keshcarrigan, in Leitrim: the wickerwork causeway of the little rock.

Kilbaha, *Coill-beithe*, birch wood.

Kilbarron, in Donegal: St. Barron's church.

Kilbarry, in Waterford and Cork: from St. Finbar. *See* Cork and Gougane Barra.

Kilbeg, small church or wood.

Kilbeggan, Beccan's church.

Kilbeheny, *Coill-beithne* (Kilbehena), F. M., birch wood.

Kilbreedy, *Cill-Bhrighde*, St. Brigid's church.

Kilbride, *see* Kilbreedy.

Kilbroney, church of *Bronagh*, a virgin saint.

Kilcarragh, in Kerry and Waterford: the church of St. *Carthach* (Caurha) of Lismore.

Kilcavan, in Wexford: church dedicated to St. Kevin of Glendalough.

Kilcleagh (also Kilclay), *see* Kilclief.

Kilclief, in Down: *Cill-cleithe* (Kilcleha), the hurdle church (*cliath*). The original church was constructed of hurdles, after the early Irish fashion.

Kilcolman, St. Colman's church.

Kilcommon, St. Coman's church.

Kilcullen, *Cill-cuillinn*, the church of the holly.

Kildalkey, in Meath: written in an Irish charter in the Book of Kells, *Cill-Delga*, Delga's church.

Kildare. According to Animosus, St. Brigid built her little cell here under a very high oak tree, and hence it was called *Cill-dara*, which the same writer translates *Cella quercûs*, the cell or church of the oak.

Kildimo, in Limerick: St. Dima's church.

Kildorrery, in Cork: *Cill-dairbhre* (Kildarrery), the church of the oaks. *See* Darraragh.

Kildrought, in Kildare. *See* Celbridge.

Kilduff, black church or wood.

Kilfinnane, in Limerick: the church of St. Finan. *See* Ardfinnan.

Kilfithmone, in Tipperary: the church of the wood of the bog (*fidh* and *móin*).

Kilflyn, Flann's church.

Kilgarriff (also Kilgarve), rough wood.

Kilgarvan, *St. Garbhan's* or Garvan's church.

Kilkee, in Clare: St. *Caeidhe's* (Kee's) church.

Kilkeedy, in Clare and Limerick: St. *Caeide's* (Keedy's) church.

Kilkeel, narrow church.

Kilkenny, *Cill-Chainnigh* (Kilkenny), F.M., the church of St. *Cainneach*, or Canice, who died in the year 598. *See* Aghaboe.

Killadysart, the church of the *desert* or hermitage

Killaloe, in Clare and Kilkenny: *Cill-Dalua* (Killaloo. *d* aspirated–*see* p 85), the church of St. Dalua or Molua, who flourished in the sixth century.

Killanummery, in Leitrim: *Cill-an-iomaire* (ummera), F.M., the church of the ridge.

Killarney, *Cill-airne*, the church of the sloes.

Killashandra. The original church was built within the enclosure of a rath or fort which still partly exists, hence *Cill-a'-sean-ratha* (Killashanraha), the church of the old rath.

Killashee, in Kildare: *Cill-ausaille*, the church of St. *Ausaille* or Auxilius, a contemporary of St. Patrick. Killashee in Longford is probably the church of the *sidh* or fairy hill.

Doorway, round tower near Kildare

Killaspugbrone, near Sligo. In the Book of Armagh it is stated that St. Patrick built a church at *Cassel Irra* for his disciple *Brón* or Bronus, who became bishop of

Cuil Irra, the peninsula lying south-west of Sligo: hence the place was called *Cill-easpuig-Bróin*, F. M., the church of bishop Bronus (*easpug*, a bishop).

Killaspuglonane, in Clare: *Cill-easpuig-Fhlannáin*, F. M., the church of bishop Flannan.

Killawillin, in Cork: *Cill-a'-mhuilinn*, the church of the mill.

Killeany, in Clare and Galway: the church of St. Eany or Endeus of Aran, who flourished in the fifth century.

Killeedy, in Limerick: the church of the virgin saint Ita or *Ide*, who founded a nunnery here in the early part of the sixth century. *See* Kilmeedy.

Killeen, the name of more than 80 townlands, nearly all from *Cillín* a little church, but a few from *Coillín*, a little wood.

Killeentierna, in Kerry: *Tighernach's* (Tierna's) little church.

Killeigh, in King's County: *Cill-achaidh* (Killahy), F. M., the church of the field.

Killenaule, in Tipperary: the church of St. *Naile* (Nawly) or Natalis.

Killery harbour, in Connemara: corrupted by a change of *l* to *r* (p 85), from *Cael-shaile* (Keelhaly), narrow sea-inlet, but the full name is *Cael-shaile-ruadh*, F. M., the reddish (*ruadh*) narrow sea-inlet.

Killevy (also Killeavy), in Armagh: called from its proximity to Slieve Gullion, *Cill-shleibhe* (Killeva), F. M., the church of the *sliabh* or mountain.

Killiney, in Dublin: corrupted from *Cill-inghen* (Killineen); full name *Cill-inghen-Leinín*, the church of the daughters of *Leinin*.

Killiney, in Kerry: *see* Killeany.

Killisk (also Killiskey), the church of the water (*uisge*).

Killoe, *Cill-eó*, O'C. Cal., the church of the yews.

Killure, *Cill-iubhair*, the church of the yew.

Killursa, *Cili-Fhursa*, the church of St. Fursa, who flourished in the sixth century.

Killybegs, *Cealla-beaga*, F. M., little churches.

Killygorden, in Donegal: *Coill-na-gcuiridin* (Kilnagurridin), F. M., the wood of the parsnips.

Killyon, the church of St. *Liadhan* (Leean) or Liedania, mother of St. *Ciaran* of Ossory. *See* Seirkieran.

Kilmacanoge, in Wicklow: the church of St. *Mochonog*, one of the primitive Irish saints.

Kilmacrenan, in Donegal: *see* p 85.

Kilmainham, near Dublin: *see* p 86.

Kilmallock, in Limerick: *Cill-Mocheallog* (Kilmohelog), the church of St. *Mocheallog*, who flourished in the beginning of the seventh century.

Kilmanagh, near Kilkenny: *Cill-manach* (Mart. Taml.), the church of the monks.

Kilmeedy, the church of St. *Mide*, or Ité, for both are the same name. *See* Killeedy.

Kilmihil, the church of St. Michael the Archangel.

Kilmore, there are about 80 parishes and townlands of this name, most of them signifying great church, some great wood (*cill* and *coill*).

Kilmurry. There are more than fifty places of this name, which were all so called from places dedicated to the

Blessed Virgin: *Cill-Mhuire*, Mary's church.

Kilnaleck, the wood of the flag-surfaced land.

Kilnamanagh, in Tipperary: *Coill-na-manach*, F. M., the wood of the monks.

Kilnamona, the church of the bog (*moin*).

Kilpatrick, St. Patrick's church.

Kilquane, *Cill-Chuain*, St. Cuan's church.

Kilrook, in Antrim: *Cill-ruadh*, F. M., red church.

Kilrush, the church of the wood or peninsula.

Kilskeer, in Meath: the church of the virgin saint *Scire*, who flourished in the sixth century.

Kiltenanlea, in Clare: *Cill-tSenain-leith*, the church of St. Senan the hoary.

Kiltullagh, in Roscommon: *Cill-tulaigh*, the church of the hill.

Kiltybegs, *Coillte-beaga*, little woods.

Kilwatermoy, in Waterford: *water* is here a corruption of *uachtar*, upper: the church of the upper plain.

Kinalea, barony of, in Cork: *Cinel-Aedha* (Kinel-Ay), O'Dugan, the descendants of *Aedh* or Hugh, who was the father of *Failbhe-Flann*, king of Munster in A D 636.

Kinalmeaky, barony of, in Cork: *Cinel-mBece* (Kinel-mecka), O'Dugan, the descendants of *Bece*, the ancestor of the O'Mahonys.

Kinard, *Ceann-ard*, high head or hill.

Kinawley, in Fermanagh: *Cill-Naile* (Kilnawly, which would have been the correct anglicised form), O'C. Cal., the church of St. *Naile* or Natalis, who died in A D 564.

Kincon, the hound's head (*ceann* and *cu*).

Kincora, at Killaloe, the site of Brian Boru's palace, took its name from an ancient weir across the Shannon: *Ceann-coradh* (Kancora), F. M., the head or hill of the weir.

Kinneigh (also Kinnea), *Ceann-ech*, F. M., the horse's head or hill.

Kinnitty, in King's County: *Ceann-Eitigh* (Kan-Etty), *Etech's* head. So called, according to a gloss in the Felire of Aengus, because the head of *Etech*, an ancient Irish princess, was buried there.

Kinsale (also Kinsaley), *Ceann-saile*, the head of the brine, i. e. the highest point to which the tide rises in a river. *See* Kenmare.

Kinure, *Ceann-uibhair*, the head of the yew.

Kinvarra, in Galway: *Ceann-mhara*, F. M., the head of the sea. *See* Kenmare.

Knappagh, *Cnapach*, a place full of *cnaps* or round hillocks.

Knock, *Cnoc*, a hill.

Knockacullen, the hill of the holly.

Knockaderry, the hill of the oak wood.

Knockagh, *Cnocach*, a hilly place.

Knockainy, in Limerick: the hill of *Aine* or Ainy, a celebrated *banshee*.

Knockalisheen, the hill of the little *lis* or fort.

Knockalough, the hill of the lake.

Knockane (also Knockaun), little hill.

Knockanglass (also Knockaneglass), green little hill.

Knockanree, *see* p 85.

Knockanroe (Knockaneroe, Knockaunroe), red little hill.

Knockanure, *Cnoc-aniubhair*, yew hill.

Knockatemple, the hill of the temple or church.

Knockatirriv (also Knockatarry, Knockaterriff), *Cnoc-a'-tairbh*, the hill of the bull.

Knockatober, the hill of the well.

Knockatoor, the hill of the *tuar* or bleach green.

Knockatotaun, *Cnoc-a'-teotain*, the hill of the burning or conflagration.

Knockaunbaun, white little hill.

Knockavilla (also Knockaville), the hill of the *bile* or old tree.

Knockavoe, near Strabane: *Cnock-Buidhbh* (Knockboov), F. M., the hill of Bove Derg, a legendary Tuatha De Danann chief.

Knockbane (also Knockbaun), white hill.

Knockboy, *Cnoc-buidhe*, yellow hill.

Knockbrack, *Cnoc-breac*, speckled hill.

Knockcroghery, in Roscommon: the hill of the *crochaire* or hangman. It was a place of execution.

Knockdoo (also Knockduff), *see* p 85.

Knockeen, little hill.

Knockfierna, in Limerick: *Cnoc-fírinne*, the hill of truth, or of truthful prediction, for it serves as a *weather glass* to the people of the circumjacent plains, who can predict whether the day will be wet or dry by the apparance of the summit in the morning.

Knockglass, *Cnoc-glas*, green hill.

Knockgorm, *Cnoc-gorm*, blue hill.

Knocklayd, in Antrim: called from its shape *Cnoc-leithid* (lehid), the hill of breadth, i. e. broad hill.

Knocklofty, in Tipperary: *Cnoc-lochta*, the *lofted* or shelving hill.

Knocklong, in Limerick: *Cnoc-luinge*, the hill of the encampment, for Cormac mac Art encamped with his army, on this hill, when he invaded Munster in the third century.

Knockmanagh, middle hill.

Knockmealdown mountains, *Cnoc-Maeldomhnaigh*, Maeldowney's hill.

Knockmore, great hill.

Knockmoyle, *Cnoc-mael*, bald or bare hill.

Knockmullin, the hill of the mill.

Knocknaboley (also Knocknabooly), the hill of the *booley* or dairy place.

Knocknacrohy, *Cnoc-na-croiche*, the hill of the gallows; a place of execution.

Knocknagapple (also Knocknagappul), *Cnoc na-gcapall*, the hill of the horses.

Knocknagaul, in Limerick: the hill of the *Galls* or foreigners.

Knocknageeha, the hill of the wind (*gaeth*).

Knocknagin, *Cnoc-na-gceann* (na-gan), the hill of the heads; a place of execution.

Knocknaglogh, the hill of the stones (*cloch*).

Knocknagore, the hill of the goats (*gabhar*).

Knocknahorna, the hill of the barley (*eórna*).

Knocknamona, the hill of the bog.

Knocknamuck, the hill of the pigs.

Knocknarea, in Sligo: the hill of the executions. *See* Ardnarea.

Knocknaskagh (also Knocknaskeagh), the hill of the *sceachs* or white thorn bushes.

Knockninny, a hill in Fermanagh, which gives name to a barony, *Cnoc-Ninnidh* (Ninny), the hill of St. *Ninnidh*, who was a contemporary of St. Columba.

Knockpatrick, Patrick's hill.

Knockraha, (also Knockrath, Knocknaraha), the hill of the *rath* or fort.

Knockranny, *Cnoc-raithnigh* (rahnee), ferny hill.

Knockrawer (also Knockramer, Knockrower, Knockrour), *Cnoc-reamhar* (rawer or rower), *fat* or thick hill.

Knockreagh, grey hill.

Knockroe, red hill.

Knockshanbally, the hill of the old town.

Knocksouna, near Kilmallock in Limerick: written in the Book of Lismore, *Cnoc-Samhna* (Souna), the hill of *Samhuin* (Sowan or Savin), the first of November, which was kept as a festival by the pagan Irish. *See* Origin and History of Irish Names of Places, p 194.

Knocktemple, the hill of the temple or church.

Knocktopher, in Kilkenny: *see* p 86.

Knoppoge (also Knappoge), a little hill. *See* Knappagh.

Kyle, about half the names partly or wholly formed from Kyle, are from *Cill*, a church; the other half from *Coill*, a wood.

Kylebeg, small church or wood.

Kylemore, generally great wood (*coill*), sometimes great church (*cill*). Kylemore (lake) near the Twelve Pins in Connemara, is *Coill-mhor*, great wood.

Labby (also Labby), *Leaba* (labba), a bed, a grave.

Labbasheeda, in Clare: *Leaba-Sioda*, *Sioda's* or Sheedy's *labba*, bed, or grave.

Labbamolaga, St. Molaga's grave. *See* Templemolaga.

Lack, *leac* (lack), a stone, a flag stone.

Lacka, the side of a hill.

Lackabane (also Lackabaun), white hill side.

Lackagh, a place full of stones or flags.

Lackamore, great hill side.

Lackan, *see* Lacka.

Lackandarragh (also Lackendarragh), the hill side of the oaks.

Lackareagh, grey hill side (*riabhach*).

Lackaroe, red hill side (*ruadh*).

Lackeen, a little rock or flag.

Lacken, *see* Lacka.

Lag (also Legg), a hollow; a hollow in a hill.

Lagan, a little hollow. Sometimes it means a pillar stone (*liagan*). The river Lagan probably took its name from a little hollow on some part of its course.

Laghil (also Laghile), *Leamhchoill* (Lavwhill), elm wood.

Laght, *Leacht*, a sepulchre or monument.

Laghy, a slough, a miry place.

Laharan, *Leath-fhearann* (Laharan), half land.

Lahard, *Leath-ard*, half height; a gentle hill.

Lahardan (also Lahardane, Lahardaun), a gentle hill.

Lakyle, *Leath-choill*, half wood.

Lambay island near Dublin. The latter part is Danish: Lamb-ey, i. e. lamb island. Its ancient Irish name was

Rechru or *Reachra*; and the adjacent parish on the mainland was called from it, *Port-Reachrann* (Portrahern), the *port* or landing place of *Reachra*, which in the course of ages, has been softened down to the present name, Portraine.

Laragh (also Lauragh), *Lathrach*, the site of any thing.

Laraghbryan, in Kildare: Bryan's house site.

Largan, *Leargan*, the side or slope of a hill.

Largy, *Leargaidh, see* Largan.

Larne, in Antrim: *Latharna* (Laharna: Book of L.), the district of *Lathair* (Laher), son of Hugony the great, monarch of Ireland before the Christian era. Until recently it was the name of a district which extended northwards towards Glenarm, and the town was then called *Inver-an-Laharna*, the river mouth of (the territory of) Larne, from its situation at the mouth of the *Ollarbha* or Larne Water.

Latt, *see* Laght.

Latteragh, in Tipperary: *Leatracha* (Latraha), the plural of *Leitir*, a wet hill-side (*see* Letter). It is called in O'C. Cal., *Letracha-Odhrain* (Oran), *Odhran's* wet hill-slopes, from the patron, St. *Odhran*, who died in the year 548.

Laughil, *Leamhchoill* (Lavvhill), elm wood.

Laune river, at Killarney: *Leamhain*, F. M., elm; the elm-producing river.

Lavagh, *Leamhach* (Lavagh), a place producing elms.

Lavally, *Leath-bhaile*, half town or townland.

Lavey, in Cavan: *see* Lavagh.

Leagh, *Liath* (Leea), grey; a grey place.

Leam, *Leim*, a leap.

Leamlara, in Cork: the mare's leap.

Leamnamoyle, in Fermanagh: the leap of the *mael* or hornless cow.

Lear, *see* Lyre.

Lecale, barony of, in Down, *Leth-Chathail* (Lecahil), F. M., *Cathal's* half. *Cathal* was a chief who flourished about the year 700, and in a division of territory, this district was assigned to him, and took his name.

Lecarrow, *Leth-ceathramhadh* (Lecarhoo), half quarter (of land).

Leck, *see* Lack.

Leckan (also Leckaun), *see* Lacka.

Leckpatrick, Patrick's flag-stone.

Leeg (also Leek, Leeke), *see* Lack.

Legacurry (also Legaghory), *Lag-a-choire* (curry), the hollow (*lag*) of the caldron or pit.

Legan (also Legaun), *see* Lagan.

Legland, *see* Leighlin. D added: *see* p 86.

Lehinch, *Leith-innse*, F. M., half island, i. e. a peninsula.

Leighlin, in Carlow: *Leith-ghlionn* (Leh-lin), F. M., half glen; from some peculiarity of formation in the little river bed.

Leighmoney, grey *muine* or shrubbery.

Leinster. In the third century before the Christian era, *Labhradh Loingseach* (Lavra Linshagh, Lavra the mariner), brought an army of Gauls from France to assist him in recovering the kingdom from his uncle, the usurper, Coffagh Cael Bra. These foreign soldiers used a kind of broad pointed spear, called *laighen* (layen); and from this circumstance the province in which they settled, which had previously borne the name of *Galian*, was afterwards called *Laighen*, which is its present Irish name. The termination *ster*, which has been added to the names of three of the provinces, is the Scandinavian or Danish *stadr*, a place. *Laighen-ster* (the place or province of *Laighen*) would be pronounced *Laynster*, which is the very name given in a state paper of 1515, and which naturally settled into the present form, Leinster.

Leitrim, the name of more than 40 townlands and villages: *Laith-dhruim* (Lee-drum), F. M., grey *drum* or ridge.

Leixlip, a Danish name, meaning salmon leap (*lax*, a salmon), from the well-known cataract on the Liffey, still called Salmon leap, a little above the village. By Irish-Latin writers it is often called *Saltus-salmonis* (the leap of the salmon), and from this word *saltus*, a leap, the baronies of Salt in Kildare have taken their name.

Lemanaghan, in King's County: *Liath-Manchain*, F. M., St. Manchan's grey land.

Lena (also Leny), a wet meadow.

Lenamore, great wet meadow.

Lerrig, in Kerry: a hill side. *See* Largan.

Letter, *Leitir*, a wet hill side.

Lettera (also Letteragh, Lettery), wet hill-sides. *See* Latteragh.

Letterkenny, a shortened form of *Letter-Cannanan*, the O'Cannanans' hill-slope. The O'Cannanans, or as they now call themselves, Cannons, were anciently chiefs or kings of Tirconnell, till they ultimately sank under the power of the O'Donnells.

Lettermacaward, in Donegal: *Leitir-Mic-a'-bhaird*, the hill slope of Mac Ward, or the bard's son.

Lettermore, great wet hill-side.

Lettermullan, *Leitir-Meallain*, F. M., Meallan's hill-slope.

Levally, *see* Lavally.

Levny. The descendants of *Luigh* or Lewy, the son of *Cormac Gaileng* (*see* Gallen), were called *Luighne* (Leyny: O'Dugan), and they gave name to the barony of Leyny in Sligo (*ne*, descendants).

Lick, *see* Lack.

Lickbla, in Westmeath: shortened from *Liag-Bladhma* (Leeg-Blawma), F. M., the flag-stone of *Bladh* (Blaw), a man's name. *See* Slieve Bloom.

Lickeen, little flag-stone.

Lickfinn, in Tipperary: white flag-stone.

Lickmolassy, in Galway: St. *Molaise's* (Molasha's) flag-stone.

Lickoran, the flag of the cold spring (*uaran*).

Limerick, corrupted from the Irish form *Luimnech* (Liminagh), F. M., by a change of *n* to *r* (*see* p 85): the name signifies a bare spot of land, from *lom*, bare.

Lis (also Liss), *Lios*, a circular earthen fort.

Lisalbanagh, the *Albanagh's* or Scotchman's fort.

Lisanisk (also Lisanisky), the fort of the water (*uisge*).

Lisbane (also Lisbaun), white *lis* or fort.

Lisbellaw, *Lios-bel-atha,* the *lis* of the ford-mouth.

Lisboy, yellow fort; probably from furze blossoms.

Liscannor, in Clare: Canar's fort.

Liscarrol, in Cork: *Cearbhall's* or Carroll's fort.

Liscartan, the fort of the forge (*ceardcha*).

Lisdoonvarna, in Clare: takes its name from a large fort on the right of the road as you go from Ballyvaghan to Ennistymon. The proper name of this is *Dunbhearnach* (Doonvarna), gapped fort (*see* Barna), from its shape, and the word *Lis* was added, somewhat in the same manner as 'river' in the expression 'the river Liffey': Lisdoonvarna, i. e. the *lis* (of) Doonvarna.

Lisdowney, in Kilkenny: Downey's fort.

Lisduff (also Lidsoo), *Lios-dubh,* black fort.

Lisheen, little *lis* or fort.

Lislea, *Lios-liath* (lee), grey fort.

Lislevane, in Cork: *Lios-leamhain,* elm fort.

Lismore, great fort. Lismore in Waterford received its name from the *lis* or entrenchment built by St. *Carthach* (Caurhagh) round his religious establishment. It was previously called *Magh-sciath* (Maskee), the plain of the shield. *See* Origin and History of Irish Names of Places, p 261.

Lismoyle, *Lios-mael,* bald or dilapidated fort.

Lismullin, the fort of the mill.

Lisnagat, *Lios-na-gcat,* the fort of the (wild) cats.

Lisnageeragh, the fort of the sheep (*caera*).

Lisnalee, the fort of the calves (*laegh*). *See* p 85.

Lisnamuck, the *lis* or fort of the pigs.

Lisnaskea, in Fermanagh: the fort of the *sceach* or white-thorn tree. It took its name from the celebrated *Sceach-ghabhra* (Skagowra), under which the Maguire used to be inaugurated.

Lisnisk (also Lisnisky), the fort of the water.

Lissan (also Lissane), little *lis* or fort.

Lissaniska (also Lissanisky), the fort of the water.

Lissaphuca, the fort of the *pooka* or spright.

Lissard, high fort.

Listowel, *Lios-Tuathail* (Lis-Thoohil), *Tuathal's* fort.

Lissonuffy, in Roscommon: *Lios-O-nDubhthaigh* (Lisonuffy), F. M., the fort of the O'Duffys.

Lixnaw, in Kerry: *Lic-Snamha* (Snawa), F. M., the flag-stone of the swimming (*snamh*). *See* Drumsna.

Loughill (also Loughil), *Leamhchoill* (Lavwhill), elm wood.

Londonderry. Its most ancient name, according to all our authorities, was *Doire-Chalgaich* (Derry-Calgagh), the derry or oak wood of *Calgach* or *Galgacus*. In the tenth or eleventh century it began to be called *Derry-Columcille,* in honour of St. Columbkille, who founded his monastery there in 546, and this name continued to the time of James I, whose charter, granted to a company of London merchants, imposed the name of Londonderry.

Longfield, in almost all cases a corruption of *Leamhchoill* (Lavwhill), elm wood.

Longford, *Longphort* (Longfort), a fortress. The town of Longford is called in the Annals Longford O'Farrell, from a castle of the O'Farrells, the ancient proprietors.

Loop Head, in Clare: a Danish modification of Leap Head; Irish *Leim-Chonchuillinn* (Leam-Conhullin), F. M., *Cuchullin's* leap. For legend *see* Origin and History of Irish Names of Places, p 163.

Lorum, in Carlow: *Leamh-dhruim* (Lavrum), elm ridge.

Lough, a lake; an inlet of the sea.

Loughan (also Loughane, Loughaun), little lake.

Loughanreagh, grey little lake.

Loughbeg, little lake.

Lough Boderg, the lake of the red cow.

Lough Bofin, the lake of the white cow.

Loughbrickland, corrupted by changing *r* to *l,* and adding *d* (*see* p 86.) from *Loch-Bricrenn,* F. M., the lake of *Bricriu,* a chief of the first century.

Lough Conn, in Mayo: *Loch-Con,* F. M., the lake of the hound.

Lough Corrib, the correct Irish name is *Loch Orbsen,* F. M., which was corrupted by the attraction of the *c* sound in *Loch* to *Orbsen,* and by the omission of the syllable *sen. Orbsen* was another name for *Manannan Mac Lir,* a celebrated legendary personage.

Loughcrew, in Meath: *Loch-craeibhe* (creeve), the lake of the branchy tree.

Lough Derg, on the Shannon: contracted from *Loch-Dergdherc* (Dergerk), the lake of the red eye, which is explained by a legend.

Lough Derravara, in Westmeath: *Loch Dairbhreach* (Darravara), F. M., the lake of the oaks. See Darraragh.

Lough Erne, the lake of the *Ernai,* a tribe of people.

Lough Finn, see Finn river.

Lough Guitane, near Killarney: *Loch-coiteáin* (cut-thaun), the lake of the little *cot* or boat.

Lough Melvin, corrupted from *Loch-Meilghe* (Melye), the lake of *Meilghe,* an ancient king of Ireland.

Lough Neagh, written in the Book of Leinster *Loch-nEchach* (nehagh), the lake of *Eochy* (Ohy), a Munster chief, who was drowned in it at the time of its eruption in the first century. The *N* is a mere grammatical inflection, and the name is often used without it; for instance, we find it spelled *Lough Eaugh* in Camden, as well as in many of the maps of the 16th and 17th centuries.

Lough Oughter, in Cavan: *Loch-uachtar,* upper lake, i. e. upper as regards Lough Erne.

Loughrea, in Galway: *Loch-riabhach,* grey lake.

Lug, a hollow: *see* Lag.

Lugduff mountain, over Glendalough: black hollow, from a hollow at the base.

Luggelaw, the hollow of the *lagh* or hill.

Lugmore, great hollow.

Lugnaquillia, the highest mountain in Wicklow: *Lug-na-gcoilleach* (Lugnagulliagh), the hollow of the cocks, i. e. grouse.

Lumcloon, bare meadow (*lom,* bare).

Lurgan, the shin; a long hill.

Lurganboy, yellow long hill.

Lurraga, see Lurgan.

Lusk, in Dublin: *Lusca,* a cave.

Lusmagh, in King's County: the plain of herbs (*lus*, a herb).

Lynally. In the sixth century there was a forest here called the wood of Ela, and the church founded by St. Colman, about the year 590, was thence called *Lann-Ealla* (O'C. Cal.), the church of *Ela*, which has been anglicised to the present name.

Lynn, a form of *Lann*, a house or church.

Lyre, *Ladhar* (Lyre), a fork formed by rivers or glens. *See* Lear.

Mace, *Más* (Mauce), the thigh, a long low hill.

Mackan (also Mackanagh, Macknagh, Mackney), a place producing parsnips (*meacan*, a parsnip).

Macosquin, in Derry: corrupted from *Magh-Cosgrain* (Macosgran), F. M., *Cosgran's* plain.

Maghera, *Machaire*, a plain. Maghera in Down and Maghera in Derry are both contracted from *Machaire-ratha* (Maghera-raha), the plain of the fort.

Magherabeg, little plain.

Magheraboy, yellow plain.

Magheracloone, the plain of the *cloon* or meadow.

Magheraculmoney, the plain of the back (*cul*) of the shrubbery.

Magheradrool, in Down: *Machaire-eadarghabhal* (Maghera-addrool), the plain between the (river) forks (*eadar*, between, and *gabhal*). *See* Addergoole.

Magherahamlet, in Down: the plain of the *Tamlaght* or plague monument. *See* Tallaght.

Magheramenagh, middle plain (*meadhonach*).

Magheramore, great plain.

Magherareagh, grey plain (*riabhach*).

Maghery, a form of Maghera, a plain.

Magunihy, barony of, in Kerry: *Magh-gCoincinm* (Magunkinny), F. M., the plain of the O'Conkins.

Mahee island, in Strangford Lough: the island of St. *Mochaei* (Mohee), bishop, a disciple of St. Patrick, and the founder of Nendrum.

Maigue, a river in Limerick: called *Maigh* in the annals, i. e., the river of the plain.

Mallow, in Cork: called in the Annals *Magh-Ealla* (Moyalla), the plain of the river Allo, which was anciently the name of that part of the Blackwater flowing by the town. *See* Duhallow.

Manulla, in Mayo: *Magh-Fhionnalbha* (Mah-Innalva), Hy. F., Finalva's plain.

Massareene, in Antrim: *Más-a'-rioghna* (Massareena), the queen's hill.

Maul, *Meall*, a lump, a hillock.

Maum, *Madhm* (Maum), a high mountain pass.

Maumturk, the pass of the boars (*torc*).

Maw, *Magh*, a plain.

Maynooth, *Magh-Nuadhat* (Ma-nooat), F. M., *Nuadhat's* plain, from *Nuadhat*, king of Leinster, foster-father to Owen More king of Munster. *See* Bear.

Mayo, *Magh-eó* (Ma-ó), the plain of the yews. Full name *Magheó-na-Saxan*, F. M., Mayo of the Saxons, from a number of English monks settled there in the seventh century, by St. Colman, an Irish monk, after he had retired from the see of Lindisfarne.

Meelick, *Miliuc* (Meeluck), F. M., low marshy ground.

Meen, a mountain meadow.

Meenadreen, the mountain meadow of blackthorns.

Meenkeeragh, mountain meadow of the sheep.

Milleen, a little hillock. *See* Maul.

Moan, *Moin* (mone), a bog.

Moanduff, black bog.

Moanmore, great bog.

Moanroe, red bog.

Moanvane (also Moanvaun), *Moin-bhán*, white bog.

Moat, *Móta*, a high mound.

Moate, in Westmeath: from the great mound at the village; full name Moategranoge, the moat of *Graine-óg* or young Grace, who, according to tradition, was a Munster princess.

Mocollop, the plain (*magh*) of the *collops* or cattle.

Modeshill, *Magh-deisiol* (Ma-deshil), southern plain.

Mogeely, *Magh-Ile*, F. M., the plain of *Ile* or Ely.

Moher, *see* Cliffs of Moher.

Mohill, *Maethail* (Mwayhill), soft or spongy land; from *maeth*, soft.

Moig (also Moigh), forms of *Magh*, a plain.

Moira, *Magh-rath*, F. M., the plain of the forts.

Mon, *see* Moan.

Monabraher (also Monambraher, Monamraher), *Moin-na-mbrathar*, F. M., the bog of the friars.

Monagay, in Limerick: the bog of the goose (*gedh*); from wild geese.

Monaghan, *Muineachois*, F. M., a place full of little hills or brakes (*muine*).

Monamintra, in Waterford: *Moin-na-mbaintreabhaigh* (Monamointree), the bog of the widows.

Monard, high bog.

Monasteranenagh, in Limerick: *Mainister-an-aenaigh* (Monasteraneany), F. M., the monastery of the fair. Anciently called *Aenach-beag*, little fair.

Monasterboice, in Louth: the monastery of St. *Boethius* or *Buite*, who founded it in the sixth century.

Monasterevin, the monastery of St. Evin, the founder a contemporary of St. Patrick.

Monasteroris, in King's County: *Mainister-Fheorais*, (*orish: F* aspirated and omitted: *see* p 85.), the monastery of Mac *Feorais* or Bermingham, who founded it in A D 1325.

Monear, a meadow.

Moneen, a little bog (*moin*).

Money, *Muine* (munny), a shrubbery.

Moneydorragh, *Muine-dorcha*, dark or gloomy shrubbery.

Moneyduff, *Muine-dubh*, black shrubbery.

Moneygall, the shrubbery of the *Galls* or foreigners.

Moneygorm, *Muine-gorm*, blue shrubbery.

Moneymore, great shrubbery.

Monivea, in Galway: *Muine-an-mheadha* (Money-an-va), F. M., the shrubbery of the mead, a kind of drink.

Monroe, *Moin-ruadh*, red bog.

Montiagh (also Montiaghs), *Mointeach*, a boggy place.

Morgallion. A branch of the *Gailenga* (*see* Gallen), settled in Leinster, and a portion of them gave name to the territory of *Mor-Gailenga* or the great *Gailenga*, now the barony of Morgallion in Meath.

Mothel (also Mothell), *see* Mohill.

Mountmellick. The old anglicised name is *Montiagh-meelick*, the bogs or boggy land of the *meelick* or marsh. *See* Montiagh and Meelick.

Mourne mountains, in Down. The ancient name was *Beanna Boirche* (Banna-Borka), F. M., the peaks of the shepherd *Boirche*, who herded on these mountains the cattle of *Ross*, king of Ulster in the third century. About the middle of the twelfth century, a tribe of the Mac Mahons from Cremorne (*see* Cremorne), settled in the south of the present county of Down, and gave their tribe name of *Mughdhorna* (Mourna), to the barony of Mourne, and to the Mourne mountains.

Movilla, in Down: *Magh-bhile* (Ma-villa), O'C. Cal., the plain of the ancient tree.

Moville, in Donegal: *see* Movilla.

Moy, *Magh* (mah), a plain.

Moyacomb, in Wicklow: *Magh-da-chon* (Moy-a-con), F. M., the plain of the two hounds.

Moyaliff, in Tipperary: *Magh-Ailbhe* (Moyalva), F. M., *Ailbhe's* or Alva's plain.

Moyard, high plain.

Moyarget, *Magh-airgid*, the plain of silver.

Moyarta, in Clare: *Magh-fherta* (*fh* silent: see p 85), the plain of the grave.

Moycullen, in Galway: the plain of holly.

Moydow, in Longford. *Magh-dumha* (Moy-dooa), F. M., the plain of the burial mound.

Moygawnagh, in Mayo: written in the Book of Lecan, *Magh-gamhnach*, the plain of the milch cows.

Moyglass, green plain.

Moygoish. The descendants of *Colla Uais* (*see* Cremorne), were called *Ui mic Uais* (Ee-mic-Oosh), a portion of whom were settled in Westmeath, and gave their name to the barony of Moygoish.

Moyle, *Mael*, a bald or bare hill.

Moylough, the plain of the lake.

Moymore, great plain.

Moynalty, in Meath: *Magh-nealta* (Moynalta), the plain of the flocks (*ealta*).

Moyne, *Maighin* (Moin), a little plain.

Moynoe, in Clare: same as Mayo.

Moynure, the plain of the yew (*iubhar*).

Moyrus, the plain of the *ros* or peninsula.

Moys, i. e. plains; from *magh*.

Muckamore, in Antrim: *Magh-comair* (Ma-cummer), F. M., the plain of the *cummer* or confluence (of the Six mile Water with Lough Neagh).

Muckanagh (also Muckenagh), *Muiceannach*, a resort of pigs; a place where pigs used to feed or sleep (from *muc*).

Muckelty (also Mucker, Muckera, Muckery), *see* Muckanagh.

Mucklagh, *Muclach*, *see* Muckanagh.

Muckinish, pig island.

Muckloon (Mucklone, Mucklin), *Muc-chluain*, pig meadow.

Muckno, in Monaghan: *Mucshnamh* (Mucknauv), F. M., the swimming place (*snamh*) of the pigs; the place where pigs used to swim across the little lake.

Muckross, the peninsula of the pigs.

Muff, a corruption of *Magh*, a plain.

Muing, a sedgy place.

Mullacrew, in Louth: *Mullach-craeibhe* (Mullacreeva), the summit of the spreading tree.

Mullagh, *Mullach*, a summit.

Mullaghareirk mountains, near Abbeyfeale in Limerick: *Mullach-a'-radhairc* (rīrk), the summit of the prospect.

Mullaghbane, white summit.

Mullaghboy, yellow summit.

Mullaghbrack, speckled summit.

Mullaghdoo (also Mullaghduff), black summit.

Mullaghglass, green summit.

Mullaghmeen, *Mullach-mín*, smooth summit.

Mullaghmore, great summit.

Mullaghroe, *Mullach-ruadh*, red summit.

Mullan (also Mullaun), a little *mullach* or summit.

Mullans, little summits.

Mullen (also Mullin), *Muileann* (mullen), a mill.

Mullinahone, in Tipperary: *Muileann-na-huamhainn* (Mullinahooan), the mill of the cave (*uamha*); from a cave near the village through which the little river runs.

Mullinavat, in Kilkenny: *Muilenn-a'-bhata*, the mill of the stick.

Mully, *see* Mullagh.

Multyfarnham, in Westmeath: *Muilte-Farannain* (Multy-Farannan), Farannan's mills (*muilenn*, plural *muille*).

Munster. Old Irish name *Mumhan* (Mooan), which, with *ster* added (*see* Leinster), forms *Mughan-ster* (Moonster) or Munster.

Murragh (also Murreagh), *Murbhach* (Murvagh), a flat marshy piece of land by the sea.

Murrow of Wicklow: *see* Murragh.

Muskerry. The people descended from Carbery Musc, son of Conary II. (*see* Corkaguiny), were called *Muscraidhe* (Muskery: O'Dugan). Of these there were several tribes, one of which gave name to the two baronies of Muskerry in Cork.

Myshall, in Carlow: *Muigh-íseal* (Mweeshal), low plain.

Naas, in Kildare, the most ancient residence of the kings of Leinster, *Nás* (Nawee), a fair or meeting place.

Nantinan, in Limerick: *Neantanán*, a place of nettles (*neanta*).

Nappan, in Antrim: *Cnapán*, a little hill.

Naul, in the north of Dublin, *'n-aill* (naul), the cliff. The article incorporated: *see* Nenagh.

Ned, *Nead* (Nad), a bird's nest.

Nenagh, in Tipperary. Irish name *Aenach* (Enagh), a fair; the *N* is a contraction for the Irish definite article 'an', which has become incorporated with the word: *'n-Aenach* (Nenagh), the fair. The full name is *Aenach-Urmhumlan* (Enagh-uroon) the fair of Ormond or east Munster, and this name is still used by those speaking Irish.

Newrath, *'n-Iubhrach* (Nuragh), the yew land; by the incorporation of the article.

New Ross. Irish name *Ros-mic-Treoin* (Rosmictrone), the wood (*ros*) of the son of *Treun*.

Newry. Ancient name *Iubhar-cinn-tragha* (Yure-Kin-traw), the yew tree at the head of the strand. In after ages this was shortened to *Iubhar*, which, with the article prefixed (*see* Nenagh), and *y* added, became changed to the present form Newry.

Nicker, in Limerick: *Cuinicér* (Knickere), a rabbit warren (from *coinín*).

Nobber, *Obair* (obber), work, with the article incorporated (*see* Nenagh): Nobber, 'the work', a name applied, according to tradition, to the English castle erected there.

Nohoyal, in Cork and Kerry: shortened from *Nuachongbhail* (Nuhongval), new *congbhail* or habitation. *See* Conwal.

Nure, *see* Newry.

Nurney, in Kildare and Carlow: *Urnaidhe* (urny), F. M., a prayer house or oratory, with the article incorporated. *See* Nenagh and Urney.

Offaly, baronies of, in Kildare. The descendants of *Rosfailghe* (faly) or *Ros* of the rings, the eldest son of Cahirmore (king of Ireland from A D 120 to 123) were called *Hy Failghe* (O'Dugan), i. e. the descendants of *Failghe* (*see* Iverk), and a portion of their ancient inheritance still retains this name, in the modernized form Offaly.

Offerlane, in Queen's County: a tribe name; *Ui Foircheallláin* (Hy Forhellane), F. M., the descendants (*ui*) of *Foircheallán*.

Oghill, *Eóchaill* (Oghill), yew wood (*eó* and *coill*).

Oneilland. *Niallán*, the fourth in descent from *Colla Da Chrioch* (cree) brother of Colla Meann (*see* Cremorne), was the progenitor of the tribe called *Hy Niallain* (i. e. Niallan's race), F. M., and their ancient patrimony forms the two baronies of Oneilland in Armagh, which retain the name. D added; *see* p 86.

Oola, in Limerick and Waterford: *Ubhla* (Oola), a place of apples, an orchard (from *ubhall* or *abhall*).

Oran, *Uaran* (uran) a cold spring.

Oranmore, in Galway: great cold spring.

Oughterard, upper height (*uachdar*, upper).

Oulart, in Wexford: *abhall-ghort* (oulort), an orchard, compounded of *abhall* and *gort*.

Ounageeragh river, flowing into the Funcheon: *Abh-na-gcaerach*, the river of the sheep.

Ovens, The, near Ballincollig in Cork: called in Irish *Uamhanna* (Oovana) i. e. the caves, from the great limestone caves near the village. The people by a slight change of pronunciation have converted these *oovans* or caves into *ovens*. *See* Athnowen.

Owbeg river, *Abh-beag*, little river.

Owenass river, at Mountmellick: the river of the cataract (*eas*).

Owenboy, yellow river (*abhainn*).

Owenclogy, stony river (*abhainn* and *cloch*).

Owenduff, black river.

Owenmore, *Abhainn-mór*, great river.

Owenreagh, grey river (*riabhach*).

Oxmanstown (also Ostmantown), in Dublin: so called because the Danes or Ostmen had a fortified settlement there.

Ox mountains: called in Irish *Sliabh-ghamh* (Slievegauv), F. M., the mountain of the storms, which in the spoken language was mistaken for *Sliabh-dhamh*, the mountain of the oxen, and translated accordingly.

Park, Irish *Pairc*, a field.

Parkmore, great field.

Phoenix Park, in Dublin, took its name from a beautiful spring well near the Viceregal Lodge, called *Fionn-uisg'* feenisk), clear or limpid water.

Poll, a hole, pit, or pool.

Pollacappul, *Poll-a'-chapaill*, the hole of the horse.

Pollagh, a place full of holes or pits.

Pollanass, at Glendalough: the pool of the waterfall.

Pollans, holes, pools, or pits.

Pollaphuca, the *pooka's* or demon's hole.

Pollrone, in Kilkenny: *Poll-Ruadhain* (Ruan), *Ruadh-an's* hole.

Pollsallagh (also Pollsillagh), the hole of the sallows.

Portlaw, in Waterford: *Port-lagha*, the bank or landing place of the hill.

Portmarnock, St. Mernoc's bank or landing place.

Portnashangan, the *port*, bank, or landing place of the *seangans* or pismires.

Portraine, *see* Lambay island.

Portrush, in Antrim: *Port-ruis*, the landing place of the peninsula.

Portumna, in Galway: *Port-omna*, F. M., the landing place of the oak.

Pottle, in Cavan: a measure of land.

Preban (also Prebaun, Pribbaun), *Preabán*, a patch.

Pubble, *Pobul*, people, a congregation.

Pubblebrien, in Limerick: O'Brien's people; for it was the patrimony of the O'Briens.

Pullagh, a place full of holes.

Pullans (also Pullens), little holes or pits.

Quilcagh mountain at the source of the Shannon in Cavan, *Cailceach*, chalky; from its white face.

Quilly, *Coillidh* (cuilly), woodland.

Racavan, *Rath-cabhain*, the fort of the hollow.

Rahan, in King's County: *Raithin*, a ferny place.

Rahaniska (also Rahanisky), the rath of the water.

Rahard, *Rath-ard*, high fort.

Raharney, in Westmeath: *Rath-Athairne*, Aharny's fort.

Raheen, little rath or fort.

Raheenduff, black little fort.

Raheenroe, *Raithín-ruadh*, red little fort.

Rahelty, *Rath-eilte*, the fort of the doe (*eilit*).

Raheny, near Dublin: *Rath-Enna*, F. M., Enna's fort.

Rahugh, in Westmeath: the fort of St. *Aedh* or Hugh, the son of *Brec*, who built a church in the old rath in the sixth century.

Raigh, *see* Rath.

Rakeeragh, the fort of the sheep (*caera*).

Ramoan, in Antrim: *Rath-Modhain,* Modan's fort.

Ranaghan (also Rannagh), a ferny place (*raithne,* a fern).

Raphoe, in Donegal: *Rath-bhoth* (Ra-voh), F. M., the fort of the *boths,* tents, or huts.

Rasharkin, in Antrim: *Ros-Earcáin,* Erkan's promontory.

Rashee, in Antrim: *Rath-sithe* (Ra-shee) F. M., the fort of the fairies.

Ratass, in Kerry: *Rath-teas,* southern fort.

Rath, a circular fort.

Rathangan, in Kildare: *Rath-Iomghain* (Rath-Imgan), Imgan's fort.

Rathanny, *Rath-eanaighe,* the fort of the marsh.

Rathaspick, the fort of the bishop (*easpug*).

Rathbane (also Rathbaun), white rath.

Rathbeg, little fort.

Rathborney, in Clare: *Rath-boirne,* the fort of Burren, from its situation in the old district of Burren.

Rathcormack, Cormac's fort.

Rathdowney, in Queen's County: *Rath-tamhnaigh* (Rath-towney), F. M., the fort of the green field (*tamhnach*).

Rathdrum, the fort of the long hill.

Rathduff, black fort.

Rathfeigh, in Meath: the fort of the exercise green. *See* Faha.

Rathfryland, in Down: *see* p 86.

Rathglass, green fort.

Rathkeale, *Rath-Gaela,* Gaela's fort.

Rathkenny, *Rath-Cheannaigh* (Kanny), *Ceannach's* fort.

Rathkieran, in Kilkenny: Kieran's fort; from St. Kieran of Ossory. *See* Seirkieran.

Rathmore, great fort.

Rathmoyle, bald or dilapidated fort.

Rathmullan, *Rath-Maelain,* F. M., Maclan's rath.

Rathnew, in Wicklow, *Rath-Naoi,* F. M., *Naoi's* fort.

Rathreagh, *Rath-riabhach,* grey fort.

Rathroe, red fort.

Rathronan, Ronan's fort.

Rathsallagh, *Rath-salach,* dirty fort.

Rathvilly, in Carlow, *Rath-bile,* F. M., the fort of the old tree.

Rattoo, *Rath-tuaidh* (too), northern fort.

Raw, *Rath,* a fort.

Rea, *Reidh,* a coarse mountain flat.

Reask (also Reisk), *Riasg* (Reesk), a marsh.

Reen, *Rinn,* a point of land.

Relagh, *Reidhleach* (Relagh), *see* Rea.

Relickmurry, *Reilig,* a church: the church of the Blessed Virgin Mary.

Riesk, *see* Reask.

Rin (also Rine, Rinn), *Rinn,* a point of land.

Ring, *see* Rin.

Ringabella, near the mouth of Cork harbour: the point of the old tree (*bile*).

Ringagonagh, near Dungarvan: *Rinn-O' gCuana* (Ogoona), the point or peninsula of the O'Cooneys.

Ringbane (also Ringbaun), white point.

Ringcurran, near Kinsale: the point of the *corrán* or reaping hook; from its shape.

Ringrone, near Kinsale: written in the Annals of Innisfallen, *Rinn-róin,* the point of the seal.

Ringvilla (also Ringville), *Rinn-bhile* (villa), the point of the *bile* or ancient tree.

Rinneen, little point of land.

Rinville, in Galway: *Rinn-Mhil* (vil), the point of *Mil,* a Firbolg chieftain.

Risk, *see* Reask.

Roeillaun, *Ruadh-oilean* (Roo-illaun), red island.

Rooaun (also Rooghan, Rooghaun), reddish land (from *ruadh,* red).

Roosk, *Rusg,* a marsh. *See* Reask.

Roosca (also Rooskagh, Roosky), *Rusgach,* marshy, a marshy place.

Roscommon, *Ros-Comain,* F. M., Coman's wood, from St. *Coman,* who founded a monastery there in the eighth century.

Roscrea, written in the Book of Leinster, *Ros-cre, Cre's* wood.

Roshin, little *ros* or promontory.

Roskeen, *Ros-caein,* beautiful wood.

Ross, in the south generally means a wood; in the north, a peninsula.

Rossbegh (also Rossbehy), west of Killarney: the peninsula of birches (*beith*).

Rossbeg, small wood or promontory.

Ross Carbery, in Cork: the latter part from the barony of Carbery in which it is situated: it was anciently called *Ros-ailithir* (allihir), F. M., the wood of the pilgrims.

Ross Castle, at Killarney: from the little *ros* or peninsula on which it stands.

Rosses, in Donegal: i. e. peninsulas.

Rossinver, in Leitrim: *Ros-inbhir,* the peninsula of the river mouth; from a point of land running into the south part of Lough Melvin.

Rossmore, great wood or peninsula.

Rossorry, near Enniskillen: corrupted from *Ros-airthir* (arher) F. M., the eastern peninsula.

Roughan (also Ruan), *see* Rooaun.

Rousky, *see* Roosca and Rooskey.

Route. The northern part of Antrim was anciently called *Dalriada* (F. M.), i. e. *Riada's* portion or tribe, from Carbery Riada, son of Conary II. (*see* Corkaguiny), and the latter part (*Riada*) of this old name, is still preserved in the corrupted form of Route.

Rush, in Dublin: *Ros-eo* (Rush-oï), F. M., the peninsula of the yew trees.

Rusheen, small wood; a growth of underwood.

Russagh, *Ros-each,* F. M., the wood of the horses.

Rusky, *see* Roosca and Roosky.

Saggart, in Dublin: contracted from Tassagard, Irish *Teach-Sacra* (Tassacra), O'C. Cal., the house of St. *Sacra,* who flourished in the seventh century.

Saint Mullins, in Carlow: Irish name *Tigh-Moling* (Tee-Molling), O'C. Cal., the house of St. *Moling,* a native of Kerry, who erected a church there about the middle of the seventh century. *See* Timolin.

Salt, baronies of, in Kildare: *see* Leixlip.

Santry, in Dublin: *Sentreibh* (Shantrev; Mart. Taml.), old tribe.

Saul, near Downpatrick: *Sabhall* (Saul), a barn. *Dichu,* the prince of the surrounding district, was St. Patrick's first convert in Ireland. The chief made the saint a present of his barn, to be used temporarily as a church, and hence the place was called *Sabhall-Patrick,* St. Patrick's barn, now shortened to Saul.

Scalp, *Scealp* (Scalp), a cleft or chasm.

Scarawalsh, in Wexford: Irish name *Sgairbh-a'-Breathnaigh* (Scarriff-a-vranny), Walsh's scarriff or shallow ford (see Ballybrannagh), which, with an obvious alteration, has given name to the barony of Scarawalsh.

Scardan (also Scardaun), *Scardan,* a cataract.

Scarriff, *Scairbh* (Scarriv), a rugged shallow ford.

Scart, *Scairt* (Scart), a thicket or cluster.

Scartaglin, in Kerry: the thicket of the glen.

Scarteen, a little thicket or cluster.

Scartlea, in Cork: *Scairt-liath,* grey thicket.

Scarva, another form of Scarriff.

Seagoe, *Suidhe-Gobha* (Seegow), the seat of St. *Gobha* (gow) or Gobanus.

Seapatrick, Patrick's seat (*suidhe*)

See, *suidhe* (see), a seat or sitting place.

Seefin, *Suidhe-Finn* (Seefin), the seat of Finn Mac Coole.

Seein, in Tyrone: same as Seefin, with *f* aspirated and omitted (*Suidhe-Fhinn*).

Seirkieran, near Parsonstown. St. *Ciaran* or Kieran of Ossory, disciple of St. Finnian of Clonard, erected a monastery in the sixth century, at a place called *Saighir* (Sair), which was the name of a fountain, and after the saint's time it was called *Saighir-Chiarain* (Sairkeeran), now contracted to Seirkieran.

Seltan, a place of sallows.

Seskin, *Sescenn,* a marsh.

Sessia (also Sessiagh), *Seiseadh* (shesha), the sixth part.

Shallon, *Sealán,* a hangman's rope, a gallows.

Shan, *Sean* (shan), old.

Shanaclogh, *Seancloch,* old stone castle.

Shanacloon, old cloon or meadow.

Shanagarry, old *garry* (*garrdha*) or garden.

Shanagolden, in Limerick: *Seangualann* (Shanagoolan), old shoulder or hill.

Shanakill, old church.

Shanavally (also Shanbally), old *bally* or town.

Shanbogh (also Shanbo), old *both* or tent.

Shandon, old *dun* or fortress.

Shandrum, old *drum* or ridge.

Shangarry, *see* Shanagarry.

Shankill, old church.

Shanmullagh, old *mullach* or summit.

Shantallow, *Sean-talamh* (Shantalav), old land.

Shanvally, old *bally* or town (*b* aspirated).

Shean (also Sheean, Sheeaun), *Sidheán* (sheeaun), a fairy hill.

Shee, *sidh* (shee), a fairy, a fairy hill.

Sheeroe, red fairy hill.

Sheetrim, *Sidh-dhruim* (Sheedrim), fairy ridge.

Shelburne barony, in Wexford: from the tribe of *Siol-Brain* (O'Dugan), the seed of progeny of *Bran.*

Shelmaliere, in Wexford: the descendants of Maliere or *Maelughra* (Meelura).

Sheskin, *Sescenn,* a marsh. See Seskin.

Shillelagh, in Wicklow: *Siol-Elaigh* (Sheelealy: O'Dugan), the seed or descendants of *Elach.*

Shinrone, in King's County: *Suidhe-an-róin* (Sheenrone), F. M., the seat of the *ron,* i. e. literally a seal, but figuratively a hirsute or hairy man.

Shrone, *srón,* a nose, a pointed hill.

Shruel (also Shrule), *see* p 85.

Sion, *sidheán* (sheeaun), a fairy mount.

Skagh, *Sceach,* a white thorn bush.

Skahanagh (also Skehanagh), a place full of *sceachs* or white thorns.

Skeagh (also Skea), *see* Skagh.

Skeheen, a little *sceach* or bush.

Skelgagh, a place of *skelligs* or rocks.

Skellig rocks, off the coast of Kerry: *Sceilig* means a rock.

Skerries (also Skerry), *Sceir* (sker), a sea rock; *sceire* (skerry), sea rocks.

Skreen (also Skrine), *Scrín* (skreen), a shrine.

Sleaty, in Queen's County: *sleibhte* (Sleaty), F. M., i. e. mountains, the plural of *sliabh*: from the adjacent hills of *Slieve* Margy.

Slee, *Slighe* (slee), a road.

Slemish mountain, in Antrim, on which St. Patrick passed his youth herding swine, *Sliabh-Mis,* the mountain of *Mis,* a woman's name.

Sleveen, little *slieve* or mountain.

Slieve, *Sliabh* (sleeve), a mountain.

Slieve Anierin, in Leitrim: *Sliabh-an-iarainn,* the mountain of the iron; from its richness in iron ore.

Slievebane (also Slievebaun), white mountain.

Slievebeagh, a range of mountains on the borders of Monaghan, Fermanagh, and Tyrone: *Sliabh-Beatha* (Slieve Baha), F. M., the mountain of *Bith,* a legendary hero.

Slieve Bernagh, in the east of Clare: *Sliabh-bearnach,* gapped mountain. See Lisdoonvarna.

Slievebloom, *Sliabh-Bladhma* (Slieve-Blawma), F. M., the mountain of *Bladh* (Blaw), one of the Milesian heroes.

Slieveboy, yellow mountain.

Slieve Corragh, rugged mountain.

Slieve Donard, the highest of the Mourne mountains. *Domhanghart* (Donart), son of the king of Ulidia, and one of St. Patrick's disciples, built a little church on the very summit of this mountain; hence it was called *Sliabh-Domhanghart, Donart's* mountain, now anglicised Slieve Donard. Its ancient name was Slieve Slanga, from the bardic hero *Slainge,* the son of Parthalon, who was buried on its summit, where his carn is still to be seen.

Slieve Eelim, a mountain range east of Limerick: *Sliabh-Eibhlinne* (Slieve-Evlinne), Evlin's mountain.

Slieve Fuad, near Newtownhamilton in Armagh: Fuad's

mountain; from the Milesian hero Fuad, who was slain there.

Slieve League, in Donegal: *Sliabh-liag,* the mountain of the flag-stones.

Slieve Lougher, east of Castleisland in Kerry: *Sliabh-luachra,* rushy mountain.

Slieve Mish, near Tralee: *see* Slemish.

Slievenagriddle, near Downpatrick: the mountain of the griddle; the *griddle* is a *cromlech* on the hill.

Slievenamon, in Tipperary: *Sliabh-na-mban,* the mountain of the women. Full name *Sliabh-na-mban-Feimhinn* (Slievenamon-Fevin), the mountain of the women of *Feimheann,* the ancient territory surrounding it.

Slievenamuck, the mountain of the pigs.

Slievereagh, *Sliabh-riabhach,* grey mountain.

Slieveroe, red mountain.

Slievesnaght, the mountain of the snow (*sneacht*).

Sligo, named from the river: *Sligeach* (Sliggagh), F. M., shelly river (*slig,* a shell).

Sliguff, a corruption (*see* p 85.) from *Slighe-dhubh* (Slee-duv), a black road.

Slyne Head, in Galway: Irish name *Ceann-leama* (Can-leama), the head of the *lyme* or leap (*leim*), which has been corrupted to the present name by changing *m* to *n,* and prefixing *s.* See Stabannon.

Solloghod, in Tipperary: *Sulchoid* (sollohed), F. M., sallow wood.

Sonnagh, a mound or rampart.

Sragh (also Srah), *srath* (srah), a river holm.

Srahan (also Srahaun, Sraheen), little river holm.

Sroohill, *see* p 85.

Srough, *Sruth* (sruh), a stream.

Sroughmore, great *sruth* or stream.

Sruffaun, *Sruthán* (Sruhaun), a streamlet (p 85.).

Stabannon, corrupted from Tabannon, Bannon's house (*teach*), by prefixing *s.* See Slyne head.

Stakallen, in Meath: *Teach-Collain* (Tacollan), F. M., Collan's house.

Staholmog, in Meath: St. *Colmoc's* or *Mocholmoc's* house.

Stamullin, in Meath: *Maelan's* house.

Stang, a measure of land.

Stillorgan, in Dublin: *Tigh-Lorcain* (Teelorcan), *Lorcan's* or Laurence's house or church.

Stonecarthy, in Kilkenny: first syllable a corruption of *stang:* Carthy's *stang* or measure of land.

Stonybatter, in Dublin: stony road: *see* Batterstown and Bootterstown.

Stook, *Stuaic* (stook), a pointed pinnacle.

Stookan (also Stookeen), a little *stook* or pointed rock.

Stradbally, *Stradbhaile* (Sràdvally), F. M., street-town; a town of one street.

Stradone (also Stradowan), *Srath-doimhin* (Sradowan), deep *srath* or river holm.

Stradreagh, grey street.

Straduff, black river holm.

Straffan, in Kildare: *see* Sruffaun.

Straid (also Strade, Sraud), *Sráid* (Sraud), a street.

Strancally, near Youghal: *Sron-caillighe* (Srone-cally), the hag's nose or point.

Strangford Lough, in Down: a Danish name; *strong fiord* or bay, from the well-known tidal currents at its entrance. Irish name *Loch Cuan.*

Struell, *see* p 85.

Sylaun, a place of sallows.

Taghadoe, in Kildare: *Teach-Tuae* (Taghtoo), F. M., the house of St. Tua.

Taghboy, yellow house.

Taghmon, in Wexford: written in the Book of Leinster *Teach-Munna* (Taghmunna), the house of St. Munna or Fintan, who founded a monastery there, and died in A D 634.

Tallaght, in Dublin: *Taimhleacht* (Tavlaght), a plague monument. According to the bardic legend, 9000 of Parthalon's people died of the plague, and were buried in this place, which was therefore called the *Taimhleacht* or plague grave of Parthalon's people.

Tamlaght (also Tamlat), a plague grave; *see* Tallaght.

Tamnagh (also Tamny), *Tamhnach,* a green field.

Tanderagee, a corruption of *Tóin-re-gaeith* (Tonregee), *backside* to the wind. See Tonlegee.

Tara, *Teamhair* (Tawer), F. M., a residence on an elevated spot, commanding an extensive view. There are many places of this name in Ireland, besides the celebrated Tara in Meath.

The Tara Brooch, National Museum

Tarmon, *see* Termon.

Tat (also Tate, Tath), a measure of land.

Tattygare, short *tate* or land measure.

Taughboyne, in Donegal: *Tech-Baeithin* (Taghbweeheen), O'C. Cal., the house of St. *Baeithin;* he was a companion of St. Columkille, and governed the monastery of Iona after that saint's death. Died in A D 600.

Tavanagh (also Tavnagh), *Tamhnach*, a green field.

Tawlaght, a plague monument. *See* Tallaght.

Tawnagh (also Tawny), *Tamhnach*, a green field.

Tawnaghmore, great field.

Tecolm, in Queen's County: *Tigh-Choluim* (Teecolum). St. Columkille's house.

Teebane, *Tigh-bán* (Teebaun), white house.

Teemore, great house (*tigh*).

Teev (also Teeve), *Taebh*, the side, a hill side.

Teltown, on the blackwater in Meath. Lewy of the long hand, one of the Tuatha De Danann kings, established a fair or gathering of the people, to be held here yearly on the first of August, in which games, pastimes, and marriages were celebrated; and in honour of his foster mother *Taillte* (Telta), he called the place *Tailltenn* (Teltenn), now modernized to Teltown.

Temple, *Teampull*, a church.

Templeachally, in Tipperary: the church of the *cala* or marshy meadow.

Templebredon, in Tipperary: O'Bredon's church.

Templebreedy, St. Brigid's church.

Templecarn, in Donegal: the church of the carn or monument.

Temple-etney, in Tipperary: St. Eithne's church.

Templemichael, the church of the Archangel Michael.

Templemolaga, in Cork: the church of St. *Molaga*, a native of Fermoy, who died on the 20th of January, some short time before the year 664.

Templemore, great church; a cathedral.

Templemoyle, bald or dilapidated church (*mael*).

Templenacarriga, the church of the rock.

Templenoe (also Templenew), *Teampull-nua*, new church.

Templepatrick, St. Patrick's church.

Templeport, the church of the *port* or bank.

Templeshanbo, in Wexford. Ancient pagan name *Seanboth-Sine* (Shanboh-Sheena), *Sin's* or *Sheen's* old tent or hut. In Christian times, after a church had been erected there, the present name was formed by the addition of the word *Temple* to *Seanboth*: Templeshanbo, the church of *Seanboth*.

Templetogher, in Galway: the church of the causeway (*tóchar*), from a celebrated old *togher* across a bog.

Templetuohy, in Tipperary: the church of the *tuath* or territory, because it was the principal church of the district.

Tempo, in Fermanagh: shortened from the full Irish name *an t-Iompodh-deisiol* (an Timpo deshill), the turning from left to right. *Iompodh* (impo) means turning, *deisiol*, right handed, and the article *an* prefixed takes a *t* in this case, which became incorporated with the word. The place received its name, no doubt, from the ancient custom of turning sun-ways in worship.

Terenure, *Tir-an-iubhair*, the land of the yew.

Termon, *Tearmann*, church land.

Termonfeckin, St. *Fechin's* church land.

Terryglass, in Tipperary: called in Irish authorities *Tir-da-ghlas* (Tir-a-glas), which Adamnan in his Life of St. Columba translates *Ager-duorum-rivorum*, the land of the two streams.

Thurles, in Tipperary: *Durlios* (Durlas), strong *lis* or fort. In the annals it is commonly called Durlas-O'Fogarty, from the O'Fogartys, the ancient proprietors of the surrounding district. *See* Eliogarty.

Tiaquin, barony of, in Galway: shortened from *Tigh-Dachonna* (Tee-aconna), F. M., St. Dachonna's house.

Tibberaghny, in Kilkenny: *Tiobrad-Fachtna* (Tibbradaghna), F. M., St. Faghna's well.

Tibohine, in Roscommon: *Tech-Baeithin* (O'Cal. Cal.), St. *Baeithin's* house. The name is the same as Taughboyne, but this is a different *Baeithin*; he was of the race of *Enda*, son of Niall of the Nine Hostages, and was one of the ecclesiastics to whom the apostolic letter was written in the year 640, on the subject of the time for celebrating Easter.

Tieve, *Taebh* (teeve), a side, a hill-side.

Tievebrack, speckled hill-side.

Tiglin, in Wicklow: the house of the glen.

Tiknock (also Ticknock, Ticknick), *Tigh-cnuic* (Ticknick), the house of the hill.

Timahoe, in Queen's County: *Tech-Mochua* (Tee-Mohua), O'C. Cal., the house of St. *Mochua*, the original founder and patron, who flourished in the sixth century.

Timogue, in Queen's County: St. Mogue's house.

Timoleague, in Cork: *Teach-Molaga*, F. M., *Molaga's* house, from St. Molaga of Templemolaga.

Timolin, in Kildare: *Tigh-Moling* (Tee-Moling), St. Moling's house, from a church erected there by St. Moling of St. Mullins.

Tinamuck, *Tigh-na-muc*, the house of the pigs.

Tincurragh (also Tincurry), *Tigh-an-churraigh* (Tincurry), the house of the *currach* or marsh.

Tinnahinch (also Tinnehinch), *Tigh-na-hinnse* (Tee-na-hin-sha), the house of the island or river meadow.

Tinnakill (also Tinnakilly), the house of the church or wood.

Tinnascart (also Tinnascarty), the house of the cluster or thicket (*scairt*).

Tinnick (also Tinnock, Tinock), *see Tiknock*.

Tipper, a form of *Tobar*, a well.

Tipperary, *Tiobraid-Arann* (Tibrad-Auran), F. M., the well of *Ara*, the ancient territory in which it was situated. The well that gave this name to the town and thence to the county, was situated in the Main-street, but it is now closed up.

Tipperkevin, in Kildare: St. Kevin's well.

Tipperstown, in Dublin and Kildare: a half translation from *Baile-an-tobair* (Ballintubber), the town of the well.

Tiranascragh, in Galway: *Tir-an-eascrach*, the land of the *esker* or sand hill.

Tirawly, barony of, in Mayo: *Tir-Amha gaidh* (Awly), the land or district of *Amhalgaidh*, king of Connaught, brother of the monarch *Dathi*, and son of Ohy Moyvane, king of Ireland from A D 358 to 365.

Tirconnell, the ancient name of Donegal, *Tir-Conaill*, the land or district of Conall Gulban, son of Niall of the Nine Hostages.

Tireragh, barony of, in Sligo, *Tir-Fhiachrach* (Tir-eeragh), F. M., the district of *Fiachra*, son of *Dathi*, and grandson of Ohy Moyvane. *See* Tirawly.

Tirerrill, barony of, in Sligo, *Tir-Oiliolla* (oliila), Hy F., the district of Olioll, son of Ohy Moyvane (*see* Tirawly). *L* changed to *r: see* p **85.**

Tirkeeran, barony of, in Derry: *Tir-Chaerthainn* (Tirkeerin), the district of Kieran, the great grandson of *Colla Uais*, brother of *Colla Meann. See* Cremorne.

Tisaran, in King's County: from an old church which is called in the Calendars *Teach-Sarain* (Tasaran), the house of St. Saran, the founder, who was of the race of the *Dealbhna. See* Delvin.

Tisaxon, the house of the Saxons or Englishmen.

Tiscoffin, in Kilkenny: *see* p **86.**

Tober, *Tobar,* a well.

Toberaheena, the well of Friday (*aeine,* pron. eena); from the custom of visiting the well and performing devotions on Friday.

Toberbilly, the well of the ancient tree (*bile*).

Tobercurry, in Sligo: written by Mac Firbis, *Tober-an-choire,* the well of the caldron or pit.

Tobermore, great well.

Toberreendoney, in various counties: *Tobar-righ-an-domhnaigh* (Toberreendowny), the well of the king of Sunday (i. e. of God); these wells were so called because they were visited on Sunday.

Togher, *Tóchar,* a causeway.

Tomdeely, in Limerick: the tumulus (*tuaim*) of the river Deel.

Tomfinlough, in Clare: *Tuaim-Fionnlocha,* F. M., the tumulus of the bright lake (*fionn,* bright, clear); from an old church by a lake near Sixmile-bridge.

Tomgraney, in Clare: *Tuaim-greine* (Toomgraney), F. M., the tumulus of the lady *Grian,* about whom there are many traditions.

Tomies mountain, over the lower lake of Killarney, *Tumaidhe* (Toomy), tumuli or monumental mounds; from two sepulchral heaps on the top of the mountain.

Tomregan, in Cavan: *Tuaim-Drecon* (Toom-reckon: *D* aspirated–see p **85.**), F. M., Drecon's burial mound.

Tonagh, *Tamhnach* (Townagh), a field.

Tonbane (also Tonbaun), white *tóin* or *backside.*

Tonduff, black *backside* (*tóin*).

Tonlegee, *Tóin-le-gaeith,* backside to the wind.

Tonnagh, a mound or rampart.

Tonregee, *see* Tanderagee and Tonlegee.

Tonroe, red backside.

Tooman, *Tuaman,* a small tumulus.

Toome (also Toom), *Tuaim* (Toom), a tumulus or burial mound.

Toomore (also Toomour), *Tuaim-dha-bhodhar* (Toom-a-wour), F. M., the tumulus of the two deaf persons.

Toomyvara, in Tipperary, exactly represents the sound of the Irish *Tuaim-ui-Mheadhra,* the tumulus or tomb of O'Mara.

Toor, *Tuar,* a bleach green or drying place.

Toorard, high bleach green.

Tooreen, little bleach green.

Toormore, great bleach green.

Toortane (also Toortaun), *Tortan,* a small hillock.

Tor, a tower, a tall tower-like rock.

Torc mountain at Killarney, the mountain of the *torcs* or boars.

Tormore, great tower or tower-like rock.

Tory island off the coast of Donegal, *Torach* (Wars of GG.), towery, i. e. abounding in *tors* or tower-like rocks.

Touaghty, in Mayo: *Tuath-Aitheachta (Thoo-ahaghta),* Hy. F., *the tuath* or district of the *attacotti* or plebeians, i. e. the races vanquished and enslaved by the Milesians.

Tourin, little bleach green; *see* Tooreen.

Tralee, *Traigh-Li* (Tralee), F. M., the strand of the Lee, a little river which runs into the sea at the town, but which is now covered over.

Tramore, *Traigh-mor,* great strand.

Trean (also Trien), *Trian,* a third part.

Treanbaun, white third.

Treanboy, yellow third.

Treanlaur, middle third (*lár,* middle).

Treanmanagh, middle third (*meadhonach*).

Trevet, in Meath: *Trefoit* (Trefote), F. M., three *fods* or sods; so named, according to the *Leabhar-na-huidhre,* because when Art, the son of Conn of the Hundred Battles was buried there, three sods were dug over his grave in honour of the Trinity.

Trillick, *Tri-liag,* three *liags* or pillar stones.

Trim, in Meath full name *Ath-truim* (Ah-trim), the ford of the elder bushes.

Bridge and Castle, Trim

Tromaun, a place producing elder bushes (*trom*).

Trough, barony of, in Monaghan, *Triucha* (Truha), a cantred or district.

Trumman (also Trummery) *see* Tromaun.

Tuam, in Galway: *Tuaim-da-ghualann* (Tuam-a-woolan), the tumulus of the two shoulders, from the shape of the old sepulchral mound that gave name to the place.

Tubbrid, *see* Tober.

Tulla (also Tullach), *Tulach,* a little hill.

Tullaghan, a little *tulach* or hill.

Tullaghmelan, in Tipperary: Moylan's hill.

Tullahogue, in Tyrone: *Tulach-og,* F. M., the hill of the youths.

Tullahaught, in Kilkenny: *Tulach-ocht,* the hill of the eight (persons).

Tullamore, great hill.

Tullig, another form of *Tulach,* a hill.

Tullow, *Tulach,* a little hill.

Tullowphelim, a parish containing the town of Tullow in Carlow; contracted from Tullow-offelimy, the *tulach* or hill of the territory of the Hy Felimy, a tribe descended and named from Felimy, son of Enna Kinsella, king of Leinster in the fourth century.

Tully, *see* Tulla.

Tullyallen, *Tulaigh-áluinn* (Tullyaulin), beautiful hill.

Tullyard, high hill.

Tullybane (also Tullybaun), *Tulaigh-bán,* white hill.

Tullybeg, little *tulach* or hill.

Tullycorbet, the hill of the chariot (*carbad*).

Tullyglass, green hill.

Tullyhaw, barony of, in Cavan: so called from the Magaurans, its ancient proprietors, whose tribe name was *Tealach-Echach* (Tulla-eha: O'Dugan), the family of *Eochy* or Ohy.

Tullylease, in Cork: *Tulach-lias* (Tullaleese), the hill of the huts.

Tullymongan, at Cavan: *Tulach-Mongain,* F. M., Mongan's hill.

Tullymore, *see* Tullamore.

Tullynacross, the hill of the cross.

Tullynagardy, near Newtownards: *Tulaigh-na-gceard cha,* the hill of the forges.

Tullynaskeagh, the hill of the white thorns.

Tullynure, *Tulach-an-iubhair,* the hill of the yew.

Tullyroe, red hill.

Tullyrusk, in Antrim: the hill on which the old church stands was surrounded by marshy ground, hence the name, which Colgan writes *Tulach-ruisc,* the hill of the morass. *See* Rusk.

Tullytrasna, cross or transverse hill.

Tumna, in Roscommon: *Tuaim-mna,* F. M., the tomb of the woman (*bean,* gen. *mna*).

Tuosist, in Kerry: *Tuath-O'Siosta* (O'Sheesta), O'Siosta's territory.

Ture, the yew. The word *iubhar* (yure) has incorporated the *t* of the article, like Tempo.

Turlough, a lake that dries up in summer.

Twelve Pins, a remarkable group of mountains in Connemara; should have been called the Twelve *Bens,* i. e. peaks. Sometimes called 'The Twelve Pins of Bunnabola,' in which the word *beann* occurs twice; for Bunnabola is *Beanna-Beola* (Banna-Bola), the peaks of *Beola,* an old Firbolg chief, who is still remembered in tradition. *See* Mourne.

Tyfarnham, in Westmeath: *Farannan's* house (*tigh*); the same person that gave name to Multyfarnham.

Tyrone, in Tipperary: *Tigh-Eóin,* John's house.

Tyrella, in Down: *Tech-Riaghla* (Tee-Reela), O'C. Cal. the house of St. *Riaghal* (Reeal) or Regulus.

Tyrone. The descendants of *Eoghan* (Owen), son of Niall of the Nine Hostages, possessed the territory extending over the counties of Tyrone and Derry and the two baronies of Raphoe and Inishowen in Donegal; all this district was anciently called *Tir-Eoghain* (Tir-Owen: Wars of GG.), Owen's territory, which is now written Tyrone, and restricted to one county. *See* Inishowen.

Ulster, ancient Irish form *Uladh* (ulla), which with *ster* added (*see* Leinster), was pronounced *Ulla-ster,* and contracted to Ulster.

Ummera (also Ummery, Umry), *Iomaire* (Ummera), a ridge.

Ummeracam (also Umrycam), *Iomaire-cam,* crooked ridge.

Ummerafree, the ridge of the heath (*fraech*).

Unshinagh (also Inshinagh), *Uinseannach,* a place producing ash trees (*uinnse* and *fuinnse*).

Uragh, *Iubhrach* (yuragh), yew land.

Urbal, a tail; from shape or position.

Urbalreagh, in Antrim, Donegal, and Tyrone: grey tail.

Urbalshinny, in Donegal: the fox's tail (*sionnach*), from some peculiarity of shape, or perhaps from having been a resort of foxes.

Urcher, *Urchur,* a cast or throw. *See* Ardnurcher.

Uregare, in Limerick: *Iubhar-ghearr* (yure-yar), short yew tree.

Urney (also Urny), *Urnaidhe* (Urny), an oratory. *See* Nurney.

Urlar (also Urlaur), a floor, a level place.

Valentia Island, in Kerry: so called by the Spaniards. Ancient and present Irish name, *Dairbhre* (Darrery), a place producing oaks. *See* Kildorrery.

Vartry river, in Wicklow: a corruption of the old tribe name *Fir-tire* (Firteera), the men of the territory (*tir*).

Ventry, in Kerry: got its name from a beautiful white strand, called in Irish *Fionn-traigh* (Fintra), white strand.

Wateresk, upper channel (*eisc*). *See* Kilwatermoy.

Waterford, a Danish name; old form Vadrefiord, the latter part of which is the northern word *fiord,* a sea inlet. Old Irish name *Port-Lairge* or Portlargy *See* Strangford and Carlingford.

Watergrasshill, in Cork: a translation of the Irish name. *Cnocán-na-biolraighe* (Knockaun-na-billery), the little hill of the water-cresses.

Wexford, a Danish name; old form Weisford, which is said to mean west *fiord* or bay; old Irish name, *Carman.*

Wicklow, a Danish name; old forms of the name, Wkyynglo, Wygyngelo, Wykinlo. Old Irish name Kilmantan, the church of St. Mantan, one of St. Patrick's disciples. This saint, according to the Annals of Clonmacnoise and other authorities, had his front teeth knocked out by a blow of a stone, from one of the barbarians who opposed St. Patrick's landing in Wicklow; hence he was called *Mantan,* or the toothless.

Windgap (also Windygap), a translation of *Bearna-na-gaeithe* (Barnanageehy), the gap of the wind.

Witter, in Down: *Uachdar,* upper. *See* Wateresk and Eighter.

Wood of O, near Tullamore in King's County: the Irish

name is *Eóchaill*, yew-wood, the same as Youghal: modern name an attempted translation: Wood of O, i. e. the wood of the *eó* or yew.

Yellow Batter, and **Green Batter,** near Drogheda: batter here means a road. *See* Booterstown and Batterstown.

Yewer, near Killashandra in Cavan: an anglicised form of *Iubhar* (yure), the yew tree. *See* Newry.

Youghal, in Cork. A yew wood grew anciently on the hill slope now occupied by the town, and even yet some of the old yews remain; hence it was called *Eochaill* (Og-hill), F. M., i. e. yew wood. *See* Oghill and Aughall.

APPENDICES

Brief Chronology of Irish History

AD 200	Beginning of High Kingship at Tara, Meath
377-405	Niall of the Nine Hostages, High King
432	Saint Patrick comes as a Christian missionary
795	Vikings attack the Irish coast
852	Norse occupy Dublin and Waterford.
900-8	Cormac Mac Cullenan, King of Cashel
940-1014	Reign of High King, Brian Boru, killed at Battle of Clontarf
1119-56	Turlough Mór O Conor, High King
1134-71	Dermot MacMurrough, King of Leinster
1166-75	Rory O Conor, last native High King of Ireland
1170	Arrival of the Normans
1258	Gallowglasses (mercenary soldiers) come to Ulster from Scotland
1366	Statutes of Kilkenny enacted to prevent Anglo-Normans from integrating with Irish by using their language, laws or customs
1376-1417	Art MacMurrough, King of Leinster
1460	Irish parliamentary independence declared
1477-1513	Ireland ruled by Garret Mór Fitz-Gerald, Earl of Kildare
1513-34	Ireland ruled by Garret Óge Fitz-Gerald, Earl of Kildare
1536	Anglo-Irish parliament acknowledges Henry VIII of England as King of Ireland and head of the Church of Ireland. Suppression of the monasteries
1569-83	Revolt of the FitzGeralds, Earls of Desmond
1588	Spanish Armada wrecked off Irish coast
1592	Trinity College Dublin founded
1594	Beginning of Hugh O Neill, Earl of Tyrone's, nine-year war against the English
1598	Hugh O Neill, Earl of Tyrone, and Rory O Donnell, Earl of Tyrconnell, defeat the English at the Battle of the Yellow Ford
1602	Irish, reinforced by Spanish, defeated at Kinsale
1607	'Flight of the Earls' to Spain, led by O Neill and O Donnell
1608-10	British colony founded in Ulster
1641	Rising, which begins in Ulster, spreads
1649-50	Cromwellians devastate Ireland
1660	Restoration of Charles II
1689	Siege of Derry
1689	James II loses the English throne to his nephew and son-in-law, William of Orange
1690	Having rallied a Jacobite army in Ireland, James II, the deposed Stuart king, is defeated at the Battle of the Boyne by William of Orange
1691	11,000 'Wild Geese' soldiers sail for France
1692-1829	Exclusion of Catholics from parliament and all professions
1695	Penal Laws enforced
1778	Irish Volunteers organise
1782	Independent Dublin Parliament
1791	Society of United Irishmen founded
1798	Rising
1800	Act of Union. Ireland loses its independent parliament
1829	Catholic Emancipation inspired by Daniel O Connell
1842-8	Young Ireland movement
1845-7	The Great Famine. Population falls from eight millions to six-and-a-half millions
1867	Fenian Rising
1877-91	Charles Parnell
1916	Easter Rising
1918-21	Anglo-Irish war
1920	Six counties in Ulster vote themselves out
1922	Departure of British. Irish government takes over
1949	Repeal of External Relations Act. Ireland leaves Commonwealth and becomes a Republic
1955	Ireland joins the United Nations
1972	Ireland becomes a member of the European Economic Community

Irish Root Words—by P.W. Joyce
(The principal modern forms are given in italics.)

Abh (aw or ow), a river; *aw, ow.*

Abhainn (owen), a river; *owen, avon,* and in the end of words, with the *h* of the article, *hown, hone, howna, hivnia.*

Abhall (owl, ool, or avel), an apple, an apple tree; in some parts of the north it is used in the sense of 'orchard.' Modern forms *owl, ool, owle, aval,* etc.

Achadh (aha), a field; it is generally represented in modern names by *agha, agh,* or *augh,* but these also often stand for *ath,* a ford.

Aenach (enagh), anciently signified any assembly of the people, but it is now always applied to a cattle fair; *enagh, eeny, eena, eanig.*

Aileach (ellagh), a circular stone fort; *ellagh, elly.*

Aill (oil), a cliff; *ayle, aille,* etc. *See* Faill.

Aireagal (arrigal), a habitation, an oratory, a small church; *arrigle* and *errigal.*

Airne (arney), a sloe; *arneg.*

Ait (aut), a place, a site; commonly made *at*: frequently combines with *teach,* a house, to form the compound *ait-tighe* (aut-tee), in modern forms *atty* or *atti,* a house site.

Aiteann (attan), furze; forms the terminations *-attin, -attina.*

Aith (ah), a kiln of any kind; made *-haia, -hagh, -haha, -hay, -hey,* and *-hoy,* in the end of names.

Alt, a height, a cliff, a glen side.

An, the Irish definite article.

Ar (awr), slaughter; *are, aur,* and *air.*

Ard, high, a height.

Ath (ah), a ford; *ath, ah, augh, agh, a, aha, aw,* etc.

Bád (baud), a boat.

Badhun (bawn), a cow fortress, the *bawn* of a castle.

Baile (bally), a town, a townland; *bally, balli, vally* and in the eastern counties *bal.*

Bán (bawn), white or fair coloured; *bane, baun, bawn, vane, vaun.*

Barr (baur), the top, the highest point; *bar, baur.* The *Bar* of a townland (used in the north) is the high or hilly part.

Beag (beg), little.

Bealach (ballagh), a road or pass; *ballagh, vally.*

Bealltaine (beltany), the first day of May; celebrated as a festival by the pagan Irish.

Beann (ban, ben), a horn, a gable, a peak, or pointed hill.

Beannchar (banaher), horns, gables, peaks; *banagher, bangor.*

Bearn, bearna, bearnas (barn, barna, barnas), a gap, a gap in a mountain; *barna, barny, varna, varny, barnis, varnis,* and often in the north *barnet.*

Bearnach (barnagh), gapped.

Beith (beh), the birch tree; *beitheach* (behagh) a birchy place; *behy, beha, beagh, behagh, veha, vehy,* etc.

Bél, beul (bale), the mouth, an entrance, a ford; often joined to *ath* in the compound *bél-atha* (bellaha, bella), a ford-mouth or ford entrance.

Bile (billa), a large ancient tree; a tree held in veneration for any reason; *billa, billy, villa, ville, villy, bella, vella.*

Biorar (birrer), watercress; usually corrupted to biolar (biller); *viller, vilra,* etc.

Bo, a cow; *bo, boe,* and by eclipse, *moe* (mbo); see p 6.

Boireann (burren), a large rock a rocky district.

Both (boh), a tent or hut; *bo, boh, boha, bohy, voe.*

Bóthar (boher), a road; *boher* and *voher.* In some of the eastern counties it is corrupted to *batter.* Bohereen, a little road.

Braghad (braud), the throat; a gorge: *braid, broad, braud.*

Bran, a raven.

Breach (breagh), a wolf; occurs in the compound breach-mhagh (breaghvah), wolf-field.

Bri (*bree*), a hill; *bree, bray.*

Broc (*bruck*), a badger; *brock, brick,* and, by eclipse, *mrock; see p 85.*

Brocach (bruckagh), a badger warren; *brockagh, brocky.*

Brugh (bru), a palace, a distinguished residence; *bru, bruff.* Bruighean (breean) has the same meaning; but in modern times it is used to denote a fairy palace; *breen, bryan, breena, vreena.*

Buaile (boolia), a booley, a feeding or milking place for cows; *booley, boley, boola, voola, voula, vooly.*

Buidhe (bwee or boy), yellow; *boy, wee,* &c.

Buirghes (burris), a burgage or borough; *borris* and *burris.*

Bun, the end or bottom of anything; the mouth of a river.

Cabhan (cavan), a hollow; in some parts of Ulster it signifies a round hill; *cavan.*

Caech (kay), blind, purblind, one-eyed; *keagh, kee.*

Caenach (keenagh), moss; *keenagh.*

Caera (*kaira*), a sheep; *keeragh,* and, eclipsed with the article, *nageeragh.*

Caerthainn (kairhan), the quicken tree; *keeran, caran, kerane, keraun.*

Cairthe (carha), a pillar stone; *carra, carha,* and *car.*

Caiseal (cashel), a circular stone fort; *cashel, castle.*

Caisleán (cushlaun), a castle; *cashlaun, cashlane.*

Cala, a marshy meadow along a river or lake; a landing place for boats; *callow* and *cala.*

Capall, a horse; *capple, cappul,* and eclipsed with the article (*see* p 85.), *nagappul* and *nagapple.*

Carn, a monumental heap of stones; *carn, carna.*

Carr, a rock, rocky land.

Carraig (corrig), a rock; *carrig, carrick, carriga.*

Cartron, a quarter of land (Anglo-Norman).

Casan (cassaun), a path.

Cath (cah), a battle.

Cathair (caher), a circular stone fort, a city; *caher, cahir.*

Ceallurach (calluragh), an old burial ground; *calloragh.*

Cealtrach (caltragh), an old burial ground; *caltragh caldragh.*

Ceann (can), the head, front, or highest part of anything; *kan, can, kin, ken.*

Ceapach (cappa), a plot of ground laid down in tillage; *cappagh, cappa, cap, cappy.*

Ceard (card), an artificer; *nagard, nagarde,* 'of the artificers.'

Céardeha (cardha), a forge; *carte, cart, cartan, carton.*

Ceathramhadh (carhoo), a quarter, a quarter of land, *carrow, carhoo, carrive.*

Ceide (keady), a hillock, a hill level and smooth at top; *keady, keadew, keadagh, cady, caddagh.*

Ceis (kesh), a wicker basket, a wickerwork causeway; *kish, kesh.*

Cill (kill), a church; *kill, kil, kyle, keel, cal, kille, killa.*

Cinel (kinel), kindred, race, descendants; *kinel, kinal.*

Cladh (ely or claw), a ditch; *cly, claw, cla.*

Clann, children, a tribe; *clan, clann.*

Clar, a board, a plain; *clar, clare.*

Clais (clash), a trench; *clash.*

Cliath (clee), a hurdle.

Cloch, a stone, a stone castle; *clogh, clough, clo, clohy, cloy, naglogh.*

Clochan, a row of stepping stones across a river, sometimes a stone castle; *cloghan, cloghane, cloghaun.*

Cluain (cloon), a meadow, a fertile piece of land among bogs, marshes, or woods; *cloon, clon, clin, cloony.*

Cnap (knap), a knob, a round little hill; *knap, nap, crap, crup.*

Cnoc (knock), a hill; *knock, knick, nick, crock, cruck.*

Cobhlach (cowlagh), a fleet; *cowly, howly, coltig, holt.*

Coigeadh (coga), a fifth part, a province; *cooga, coogue.*

Coill, a wood; *kil, kyle, cuill, cullia.*

Coinieer (knickere), a rabbit warren; *coneykeare, conecar, conigar, conigare, kinnegar, nicker,* etc.

Coínín (cunneen), a rabbit; *coneen, nagoneen, nagoneeny.*

Coll, the hazel: *coll, col, cole, cull, cul, coyle, kyle, quill.*

Congbhail (congwal), a habitation, a church; *conwal, connell, cunnagavale.*

Cor, a round hill, etc.

Cora, a weir; *cor, corra, curra, cur.*

Corc, corca, race, progeny; *corka.*

Coreach, a marsh; *corcagh, corkey, cork.*

Corr, a crane or heron; *cor, gor, gore, nagor.*

Cos, a foot; *cuss, cush, cosh.*

Cot, a small boat; *cotty.*

Craebh (crave), a branch, a large brauchy tree; *creeva, crew, creevy, nagreeve.*

Craig (crag), a rock.

Crann, a tree; *crann, cran, crin, nagran.*

Crannog, an artificial island or lake dwelling; *crannoge, cronoge.*

Creabhar (crour), a wood-cock; *crour, nagrour.*

Creamh (crav), wild garlic.

Croch, a cross, a gallows, *crogh, crohy, crehy, creha.*

Crochaire (crohera), a hangman; *croghera, croghery, nagroghery.*

Cros, a cross; *cross, crush, crusha.*

Cruach, cruachán (cruagh, cruhaun), a rick, a round stacked up hill; *crogh, cruagh, croagh, croghan, croaghan*

Cruit (crit), a hump, a round little hill; *cruit, crotta, crutta, crit.*

Cu, a fierce dog, a hound: genitive *con; con, nagon, nagun.*

Cuas (coose), a cave, a cove; *coos, coose, cose, couse, goose, gose, nagoose.*

Cuil (cooil), a corner, an angle; *cool, cole.*

Cuillionn (cullion), holly; *cullion, cullen.*

Cúm (coom), a hollow, a dell or valley enclosed, except on one side, by mountains; *coom, coum, coombe.*

Currach, a marsh; *curragh, curry, curra.*

Da (daw), two; *da, daw, a.*

Daingean (dangan), a fortress: *dangan, dingin, dingle.*

Dair (dar), an oak; *dar, der, dara, darra, darraigh.*

Dairbhre (darrery), an oak forest, a place producing oaks; *darrery, dorrery, darraragh, derravara.*

Daire or doire (derry), an oak grove or wood; *derry, derri, der.*

Damh (dauv), an ox; *dav, dev, daw, duff, diff, aff, uff, iff,* and by eclipse, *nanav.*

Dearc, derc (derk), a cave; *derk, dirk, dark.*

Dearg (derg), red; *derg, derrig, durrig.*

Dearmhagh (darwah), oak-plain; *durrow, durra, derra.*

Disert, a desert, a hermitage; *disert, desert, dysart, dysert, ister, ester, isert, ishart, tristle.*

Domhnach (downagh), Sunday, a church; *donagh, donna, donny, don, dun.*

Draeighean, (dreean), blackthorn; *dreen, drain, drin.*

Droichead (drohed), a bridge; *droghed, drehid, drought drait.*

Druim (drum), the back, a ridge or long hill; *drum, drom, drim, drum.*

Dumha, (dooa), a burial mound; *dooey, dooa, doo, doe.*

Dún (doon), a fortified fort, a kingly residence; *dun, don, doon, down.*

Dur, strong.

Each (agh), a horse; *augh, agh, eigh,* etc.

Eaglais (aglish), a church; *aglish, eglish, heagles, eglir.*

Eanach (annagh), a marsh; *annagh, anna, anny.*

Eas (ass), a waterfall; *ass, ess, assy, assa.*

Eascu, eascan (asscu, asscan), an eel; *askin.*

Edar, between; *eder, ader, adder.*

Eidhneán (inaun), ivy; *eidneach* (inagh), an ivy-bearing place; *inane, inagh, eany, enagh.*

Eilit (ellit), a doe; *elty, ilty, elt, ilt.*

Eisc (esk), a water channel; *esk.*

Eiscir (esker), a ridge of high land, a sand hill; *esker, iskera, ascragh, eskeragh.*

En (ain), a bird; *naneane,* 'of the birds.'

Eó (o), a yew tree; *o, oe, yo.*

Eochaill (oghill) a yew wood; *oghill, aughal, youghal.*

Eudan (eden), the forehead, a hill brow; *eden, edn.*

Ey (Danish), an island; *ey, i, ay, eye.*

Fada, long; *fada, fad, ad, ada, adda.*

Faeileán, faeileóg (fweelaun, fweeloge), a sea gull *naweelaun, naweeloge* ('of the sea gulls'), *wheelion, eelan.*

Faill (foyle), a cliff; *foyle, foil, fall.* See Aill.

Faithche (faha), a green level space near a residence, for games, exercises, etc.; a level field; *faha, fahy, fa, foy, fy, fey, feigh.*

Fásach (faussagh), a wilderness; *fasagh, fassagh, fassa.*

Feadán (faddaun), a streamlet; *faddan, feddan, fiddan, fiddane, eddan.*

Feadóg (faddoge), a plover; *viddoge, vaddoge, faddock, feddock.*

Feannóg (fannoge), a scaldcrow; *finnoge, funnock, vannoge.*

Fear (far), a man; fir, feara, men; *fer, fir,* and by eclipse, *navar.*

Fearann (farran), land; *farran, farn, arran.*

Fearn, fearnóg (farn, farnoge), the alder tree; *farn, fern, farnagh, ferney, farnane, farnoge, navarn, navern, navarna.*

Fearsad (farsad), a sand bank formed in a river by the opposing currents of tide and stream; *farset, farsid, farsad, fast.*

Fert, ferta, a trench, a grave; *fert, farta, ferta, fartha, arta, navart.*

Fiach (feeagh), a raven; *ee, eha, eigh, naveagh*

Fiadh (feea), a deer; *eigh, eag, nareigh.*

Fidh (fih), a wood; *fee, fi, feigh, feth, fith, fid.*

Fionn, finn (fin), white, clear, transparent; *fin, finn, fune, foun.*

Fiord (Danish), a sea inlet; *ford.*

Fórnocht, a bare, naked, or exposed hill; *forenaght, fornaght, farnaght.*

Fraech (freagh), heath; *freagh, freugh, free, ree.*

Fuaran (fooran), a cold spring; *see* Uaran.

Fuinnse, fuinnseann, fuinnseóg (funsha, funshan, funshoge), the ash tree; *funcheon, funshin, funshinagh, funchoge.* The *f* is omitted in the north, giving rise to such forms as *unshin, unshinagh, inshinagh, unshog, hinchoge.*

Gabhal (goul, gole), a fork, a river fork; *goul, gole, gowel, goole, gola.*

Gabhar (gour), a goat; *gower, gour, gore.*

Gaertha (gairha), a thicket along a river; *gearha, geragh, geeragh, gairha, geary.*

Gall (Gaul), a foreigner, a *Gaul*; a standing stone; *gall, gal, gaul, guile, gill, gullia.*

Gallán (gallaun), a standing stone; *gallon, gullane.*

Gaeth (gwee), wind; *gee, geeha, geehy, geeth.*

Gamhan (gowan), a calf; *gowan, gown.*

Gamhnach (gownagh), a milch cow, a *stripper; gownagh, gawnagh.*

Garbh (garriv), rough, rugged; *garriff, garve, garra.*

Garrán (garraun), a shrubbery; *garran, garrane, garraun, garn.*

Gárrdha (gaura), a garden; *garra, garry.*

Gédh (gay), a goose; *gay.*

Glaise, glais, gals (glasha, glash, glas), a streamlet; *glasha, glash, glas, glush.*

Glas, green; *glass.*

Gleann (glan), a glen or valley; *glen, glin, glynn, glan, glanna.*

Gniomh (gneeve), a measure of land; *gneeve.*

Gobha, gen. gobhan (gow, gown), a smith; *gow, goe, go, gown, gowan, guivna.*

Gorm, green; *gorm.*

Gort, a tilled field; *gort, gurt, gart.*

Greuch (greagh), a marshy place; *greagh, greugh.*

Graig, a village; *graigue, grag, greg.*

Grian (greean), the sun; *green, gren, greany.*

Grianan (greenan), a summer house, a palace; *greenan, greenane, greenaun, grenan, grennan.*

Guala (goola), the shoulder, a hill; *goolan, golden.*

Imleach (imlagh), a marsh on the margin of a lake or river; *emlagh, emly, imilagh.*

Inbhear (inver), the mouth of a river; *inver, enner, ineer.*

Inis (inish), an island, a low meadow along a river; *inis, inish, ennis, inch.*

Iolar (iller), an eagle; *iller, uller, ilra, ulra, illard.*

Iomaire (ummera), a ridge or long hill; *ummera, ummery, umry, amery.*

Iubhar (yure), a yew tree; *ure.*

Ladhar (lyre, lear), a fork, a fork formed by glens or rivers; *lyre, lear.*

Laegh (lay), a calf; *loe, lea, leigh.*

Lag, lug; a hollow, a hollow in a mountain; *lag, lig, leg, lug.*

Lágh (law), a hill; *law, la.*

Lann, a house, a church; *lan, lann, land, lynn, lyn.*

Lárach (lauragh), a mare; *lara, laragh.*

Lathair, lathrach (lauher, lauragh), a site, a site of a building; *laragh, lauragh.*

Lax (Danish), a salmon; *lax, leix.*

Leaba, leabaidh (labba, labby), a bed, a grave; *labba, labby.*

Leac, lic, liag (lack, lick, leeg), a flagstone; *lack, leck, lick, leek, leege.*

Leaca, Leacán (lacka, lackan), the side of a hill; *lackan, lacken, lackaun, leckan, leckaun, lacka.*

Leacht (laght), a monumental heap of stones; *laght, lat, let, lett.*

Leamh, leamhan (lav, lavaun), the elm tree; *levan, levane, livaun, laune, lamph.*

Leamhchoill (lavwhill), an elm wood; *laughil, laghil, laghile, loghill, loughill, lamfield, longfield.*

Learg, leargaidh, leargan (larg, largy, largan), the side or slope of a hill; *largy, largan.*

Leath (lah), half; *lah, la, le.*

Leathard (lahard), half height, a gentle hill; *lahard, lard.*

Léim (lame), aleap; *leam, lem, lim.*

Leithinnsi (lehinshi), half island, a peninsula; *lehinch, lahinch, lynch.*

Leitir (letter), a wet side of a hill, plural leatracha (latraha); *letter, lattera, lettera, letteragh.*

Liagán (legaun), a pillar stone; *legan, legane, legaun, leegane, leagan.*

Liath (leea), grey; *lea.*

Liathmhuine (leewinny), grey shrubbery; *leaffony, leafin, liafin, lefinn, leighmoney.*

Lios (lis), a circular earthen fort; *lis, les, lish, lass, lassa.*

Loch, a lake; *lough, low.*

Loisgreán (luskraun), corn burnt in the ear: *luskraun, loskeraun, loskeran, lustraun, lustran, lustrin.*

Loisgthe (luska), burnt, burnt land; *lusky, losky, lusk.*

Lon, londubh (lon, londuv), a blackbird; *lun.*

Long, a ship; *long.*

Longphort (longfort), a fortress; *longford, lonart, lunkard.*

Lurga, lurgan, the shin, a long low hill; *lurraga, lurgan.*

Machaire (mahera), a plain; *maghera, maghery.*

Mac-tire (macteera), a wolf; *micteera, victeera.*

Madadh, madradh (madda, maddra), a dog; *maddy, maddoo, maddra, vaddy, vaddoo, vaddra.*

Madhm (maum), an elevated mountain pass; *maum, moym.*

Mael (mwail), bald, a hornless cow, a bald or bare hill; *moyle, meel, mweel.*

Maethail (mwayhil), soft spongy land; *mohill, mothel, mothell, mehill, moyle, weehill.*

Magh (maw), a plain; *moy, ma, may, moigh, moig, muff, mo.*

Más (mauce), the thigh, a long low hill; *mace, mas, maus, mass.*

Meall (mall), a lump, a round little hill; *maul.*

Míliuc (meeluck), low marshy ground, land near a lake or river; *meelick, mellick.*

Min (meen), smooth, fine, small; *meen.*

Moin (mone), a bog; *mone, mon, mona, vone.*

Mór (more), great, large; *more, mor.*

Móta, a moat, a high mound; *moat, mota, mote.*

Mothar (moher), in the north, a cluster of trees; in the south, the ruin of a fort, or of any building; *moher.*

Muc (muck), a pig; *muck, mucky.*

Muilean (mullen), a mill; *mullen, mullin, willin.*

Muine (money), a shrubbery; *money.*

Muintir (munter), family, people; *munter.*

Muirisc (murrisk), a sea-side marsh; *murrisk.*

Mullach (mullagh), a summit; *mullagh, mulla, mully, mul.*

Murbhach (murvah), a salt marsh along the sea; *murvagh, murvey, murragh, murreagh, murrow.*

Nás (nauce), an assembly place; *naas, nash.*

Nead (nad), a bird's nest; *nad, ned, nid, neth.*

Og (oge), young, little; *oge, og, ock.*

Oileán (oilaun), an island; *illan, illane, illaun.*

Omna, an oak; *omna, umna.*

Os, a fawn; *uss, ish.*

Piast (peeast), a beast, a worm, a serpent; *piast, peastia, beast.*

Pobul (pubble), people: *pubble, pobble, popple, pobul, phubble.*

Poll, a hole; *poll, poul, pull, pool, foyle, phuill, phull.*

Preachán (prehaun), a crow; *preaghaun.*

Puca (pooka), a *pooka* or spright; *pooka, puck, pook, phuca.*

Rath (raw), a circular fort; *rath, raw, rah, ray, ra, raha.*

Reidh (ray), a coarse mountain flat; *rea, re, rey.*

Reilig (rellig), a cemetery; *relick, relig.*

Riabhach (reeagh), grey; *reagh, rea.*

Riasc (reesk), a marsh; *riesk, reisk, risk, reask.*

Rince, rinceadh (rinka), dance; *rinky, rinka, rink.*

Rinn, a point of land; *rin, rine, reen, ring, ranna.*

Ros, generally means a wood in the south, and a peninsula in the north; *ross, rus, rush.*

Rusg, a marsh; *roosk, rusk, rusky.*

Saer (sair), a carpenter; *seer, teer.*

Sagart, a priest; *saggart, taggart, teggart.*

Saileach (saulagh), a sallow; *sillagh, sallagh, sill.*

Samhuin (sowen, savin), the first of November; *souna, sawna, hawan, haman, haven, hawna.*

Scairbh (scarriff), a shallow rugged ford; *skarriff, scarry, scarva, scarvy, scarragh.*

Scairt (scart), a thicket; *scart, scarty.*

Sceach (skagh), a whitethorn bush; *skeagh, skehy, skey, ske, skeha, skew.*

Scealp (skalp), a cleft; *scalp.*

Sceilig (skellig), a rock; *skellig.*

Sceir (sker), a sharp rock, plural sceire (skerry); *sker, skerry, skerries.*

Scrin, (screen), a shrine; *skreen, skryne, skreena.*

Seabhac (shouk), a hawk; *shoke, chock, touk, tuke.*

Sealán (shallan), a hangman's rope, a gallows; *shallon, shallan.*

Sealg (shallog), hunting; *shallog, shellig.*

Sean (shan), old; *shan, shanna.*

Seiseadh (shesha), a sixth part; *shesha, sheshia, sheshiv.*

Seisreach (shesheragh), a measure of land; *sheshera, shesheragh, sistra.*

Seiscenn (sheskin), a marsh, a quagmire; *sheskin, seskin, teskin.*

Sidh (shee), a fairy hill, a fairy; *shee.*

Sidheán (sheeaun), a fairy hill; *sheaun, sheehaun, sheean, shean, sion, shane.*

Siol (sheel), seed, descendants; *shil, shel.*

Sionnach (shinnagh), a fox; *shinny, shinnagh, tinny.*

Sliabh (sleeve), a mountain; *slieve, slie, sle, lieve, lie;* and by an eclipse of s, *tleva, tlieve, tlea.*

Slighe (slee), a road or pass; *slee.*

Sluagh (sloo), a host; *sloe, tloe, tloy, tlowig.*

Snamh (snauv), swimming, a swimming ford; *snauv, snave, sna, tna, tra.*

Sradbhaile (sradvally), street-town, a town with one street; *stradbally.*

Sraid (sraud), a street; *sraud, straid, strade, strad.*

Srón (srone), the nose, a nose-like hill; *sroad, shrone, stran.*

Sruth (sruh), a stream; *sruh, srue, srough, strew.*

Sruthair (sruher), *a stream; shrule, shruel, struell, srool, sroohill.*

Sruhán (sruhaun), a stream; *sroughan, sruffaun, straffan, truan, trone.*
Ster (Danish), a place.
Stuaic (stook), a pointed pinnacle, an out jutting point of rock; *stook.*
Suidhe (see), a sitting place, a seat; *see, se, sea, shi.*

Taebh (tave), the side, a hill-side; *teeve, teev.*
Taimhleacht (tavlaght), a plague-grave, a place where those who died of a plague were interred; *tallaght, tamlaght, tamlat, tawlaght, towlaght, toulett, howlaght, hawlagh, hamlat, hamlet.*
Tamhnach (tawnagh), a green field; *tawnagh, tawny, tonagh, tamnagh, tamny.*
Tarbh (tarriv), a bull; *tarriv, terriff, tarriff, tarf, tarry, herriff, harriff.*
Tate, tath, a measure of land; *tat, tate.*
Teach (tagh), a house; *tagh, ta, tee, ti, ty;* and by corruption, *sta, sti, sty.*
Teamhair (tawer), an elevated spot commanding an extensive view; *tara, touragh, tower, taur.*
Teampull (tampul), a church; *temple.*
Teine (tinna), fire; *tinny, tenny.*
Teotán (totaun), a burning or conflagration; *totaun.*
Tobar, tipra (gen. tioprad), a well; *tober, tubber, tipper, tubbrid, tibret.*

Tóchar (togher), a causeway over a bog or marsh; *togher.*
Tor, a tower, a tower-like rock; *tor.*
Torc (turk), a boar; *turk, torc, hirk, nadurk.*
Traigh (tra), a strand; *tra, traw, tray.*
Trian (treen), a third part; *treen, trean, trien.*
Triucha (truha), a cantred or district; *trough, true.*
Tromm, the elder or boor-tree; *trim, trom, trum.*
Tuaim (toom), a tumulus or burial mound; *toome, tom, toom, tum.*
Tuar (toor), a bleach green, any green field where things were put to bleach or dry; *toor, tore, tour.*
Tulach (tulla), a little hill; *tulla, tullow, tullagh, tully, tul.*
Turlach (toorlagh), a lake that dries up in summer; *turlough, turly.*

Ua, a grandson, a descendant; plural ui or uibh (ee, iv) descendants; *O* (in such names as O'Brien), *hy, i, ive.*
Uagh, uaimh (ooa, ooiv), a cave, gen. uamhann (ooan); forms the terminations *oe, oo, nahoe, nahoo, oova, ove, one, oon.*
Uaran (ooran), a cold spring; *oran.*
Ubhall (ool), an apple; *see* abhall.
Uisce (iska), water; *iska, isky, isk:*
Urchur (urker), a cast or throw; *urcher.*
Urnaidhe (urny), a prayer, a prayer-house or oratory, *urney,* and with the article incorporated, *nurny.*

Pronunciation Guide

There are a few basic rules to bear in mind when pronouncing Irish names. Letters in Irish have the same phonetic values as in English with the following exceptions:

a is pronounced like *o* in cot
á is pronounced like *aw* in paw
bh is pronounced like *v* (or *w)*
c is always hard, as in cattle
ch is pronounced like *ch* as in Bach
dh is pronounced like *y*
e is unpronounced before *a,* unless accented
é is pronounced like *ay* in play
fh is unpronounced
g is hard as in tiger
gh is pronounced like *y*
i is pronounced like *ee* in seek
mh is pronouned like *v* or *w*
ó is pronounded like *o* in go
s is pronounced *sh* before *e* or *i*
sh is pronounced like *h*
th is pronounced like *h*
ú is pronounced like *oo* in zoo